Seinology

Seinology

The Sociology of Seinfeld

Tim Delaney

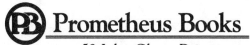

Prometheus Books

59 John Glenn Drive
Amherst, New York 14228-2197

Published 2006 by Prometheus Books

Inquiries should be addressed to
Prometheus Books
59 John Glenn Drive
Amherst, New York 14228–2197
VOICE: 716–691–0133, ext. 207
FAX: 716–564–2711
WWW.PROMETHEUSBOOKS.COM

10 09 08 07 06   5 4 3 2 1

Library of Congress Cataloging-in-Publication Data

Delaney, Tim.
    Seinology : the sociology of Seinfeld / Tim Delaney.
        p. cm.
    Includes bibliographical references and index.
    ISBN 1–59102–395–5 (pbk. : alk. paper)
    1. Seinfeld (Television program) I. Title.

PN1992.77.S4285D45 2006
791.45'72—dc22

                                                                            2005035124

Printed in the United States of America on acid-free paper

Dedicated to *Seinfeld* fans and proponents of sociology.

Contents

About the Author

Tim Delaney holds a PhD in sociology and teaches sociology and criminology at the State University of New York at Oswego. (As an interesting bit of trivial information, Jerry Seinfeld once attended this university, and people on campus speak very fondly of him.) Delaney has authored numerous books, book chapters, and articles. He serves as a "media expert" and is often quoted in newspapers and interviewed on radio and television. He is also a huge fan of *Seinfeld*.

Preface

Like millions of others, I am an admitted huge fan of *Seinfeld*. I love the television show and the comedy of Jerry Seinfeld. I watched every episode when they first aired, and I have seen every episode at least twenty times in syndication. The fact that I know nearly every detail of every episode does not take away from the entertainment value I still enjoy while watching the show. Somewhere along the way, it became apparent to me that the value of *Seinfeld* extended beyond its primary intention of providing comedic sketches for the amusement of a mass audience. *Seinfeld* seems to have great relevance to contemporary society. As a sociologist who focuses on the relevance of both classical and contemporary social theory to contemporary society, the relevance of *Seinfeld* to everyday life became increasingly important to me. I believe that much of the show's success is due to the keen sociological imagination demonstrated by Jerry Seinfeld and Larry David (cocreator of *Seinfeld*). Seinfeld and David have an uncanny ability for satirizing human behavior and interaction that most of us take for granted.

My students will attest to the fact that I often cite *Seinfeld* skits in class as a means of providing an example of a sociological concept. And the students get it! Despite the fact that the last original episode of *Seinfeld* aired May 14, 1998, a new generation of young adults are watching it for the first time in syndication. As *TV Guide* explains, "Even following its 1998 finale, *Seinfeld*'s life was far from over. The reruns still draw huge audiences in syndication, and they show no signs of slowing down."[1] In other words, the *Seinfeld* audience is still growing. In fact, *Seinfeld* continues to entertain more Americans than the majority of the lackluster shows of the present. Furthermore, the DVD sales of the first three seasons continue to be impressive. The future DVD release of the remaining seasons will only continue to add to its popularity. It should also be noted that *TV Guide* ranked *Seinfeld* number one on its list of the fifty greatest TV shows of all time.

Seinfeld is relevant to both popular culture and to sociology. The show was immortalized by the Smithsonian Institution when it entered the *Seinfeld* "Puffy Shirt" into the National Museum of American History in November 2004. During a stand-up performance in Syracuse (March 18, 2005), fans yelled for Seinfeld to do "the voice." Jerry hesitated at first and then relented with a "Helloooo" from the episode where he and his companions pretended the voice came out of the belly button of a woman that he was dating. Even Jerry Seinfeld wonders why that is so popular with fans. Festivus—the Festival for the Rest of Us—a secular alternative to the traditional religious holidays, has gained in popularity over the years as millions of Americans, myself included, celebrate Festivus every December 23 in honor of *Seinfeld*. The *New York Times* (2004) ran an extended article of the growing popularity of this "holiday." Kenny Kramer, the "real" Kramer (the character of Cosmo Kramer was based on his life), was honored with "Kramer Day" in New York City on March 19, 2005. This date coincided with Kenny Kramer's tenth anniversary of the first day he started doing his "*Seinfeld* Reality Tours," where he drove a bus around New York City pointing out spots where he, the real Kramer, likes to hang out, including the diner that is used as a "front" on the *Seinfeld* television show. It should be noted that in typical hilarious fashion, the show acknowledges the Kramer "Reality Tour" in the episode "The Muffin Tops" (#155) by doing a satire, "The Peterman Reality Bus Tour." In this episode, Cosmo Kramer proudly proclaims, "I'm a part of popular culture now!"

The harmonic convergence between *Seinfeld* and sociology leads us to *Seinology*, a sociological approach to the social significance of *Seinfeld*. *Seinology* represents a fresh approach to the study of sociology while providing fans of *Seinfeld* an opportunity to view this brilliant television show through the sociological imagination. I hope you join me as a fellow "Seinologist" and come to appreciate the sociological value of *Seinfeld*.

Chapter 1

Seinology

"I think I Can Sum Up the Show for You with One Word: Nothing."—George

There are many ways of looking at the world. Some people attempt to utilize a "common sense" approach to life while interacting with others in society. Others rely on faith (religious explanations) and tradition ("This is the way things have always been.") as their guiding force. Sociologists attempt to explain the social world through theory guided by systematic observation and data collection, known as research. Scientific research allows researchers an opportunity to go beyond the limits of common sense, faith, and tradition. Research offers a cause-and-effect account of phenomena; it provides an explanation of why something occurs. A number of significant social thinkers have emerged over the centuries who have provided their own unique interpretation of the world, including Aristotle, Kant, Marx, Spencer, and Einstein. At the end of the twentieth century, a new and fresh look at human behavior was presented to the masses by comedian Jerry Seinfeld. As we shall see, the observations articulated by Jerry in his television show have great relevance to the field of sociology—the academic discipline that provides the most significant revelations about human behavior.

What is Sociology?

Sociology is the systematic approach to thinking about, studying, and understanding society, social institutions, groups and organizations, and the interactions among people in the social world. The sociological perspective places great emphasis on the fact that humans are influenced by social forces. These social forces have a significant impact on the manner in which we interact with others. Because of its focus on social forces, sociology tends to be a macro-oriented (large-scale) discipline. Sociology promotes understanding and tolerance and instructs us to look beyond intuition, common sense, and limited individual past experiences.

Sociology is sometimes criticized as an academic field that describes the obvious, the "common sense" world that, assumingly, we all already know and understand. But what is common sense? Most people can think of numerous examples of common sense, such as not putting a fork into an electrical outlet, but isn't everything that is considered common sense really learned behavior? In other words, a child is not born with the knowledge not to stick a fork into an electrical outlet—that's why parents and guardians must keep an eye on young children all the time.

People violate the rules of common sense regularly, and this is due partly to the fact that nothing can be labeled common sense until it is learned. For example, in the *Seinfeld* episode "The Virgin" (#50), Jerry and George make a second pitch for their sitcom with executives from NBC. George commits a major faux pas when he kisses his girlfriend Susan, who is one of the executives. After the meeting Susan is fired because of the kiss. When she confronts George about how unprofessional his kiss was, George responded that he had no idea his behavior was so inappropriate. Susan, in amazement at his obvious lack of common sense, questions how anyone could not know that such behavior was unacceptable. In Susan's world, George's behavior violated expected behavior but George, new to this work world, was clueless. In George's mind, he was merely greeting his girlfriend with a kiss—a common sense thing to do when you are in a relationship with someone. Both Susan and George were acting upon common sense thinking, yet the end result was not what either expected.

Often ideas or beliefs derived from common sense turn out to be false and are contradicted by facts from sociological research.

Approaching life in a common sense manner can lead to many dis-
appointments and certainly has many shortcomings. In the episode
"The Seven" (#123), Kramer gives Elaine a chiropractic-type adjustment on her neck in exchange for the antique bicycle that she had
just purchased. Initially her neck and back feel great, better than ever
before. But after one night's restless sleep, Elaine wakes up in extreme
pain. She cannot even turn her neck. Consequently, Elaine wants her
bicycle back from Kramer, reasoning that he did not fulfill his end of
the bargain. When she confronts Kramer in Jerry's apartment,
Kramer (who was riding the bike in the apartment) asks her whether
or not she slept on a board? Kramer states, you should lie on a hard
surface. It's only common sense after an adjustment. Elaine
responds, as most people would, how was I supposed to know that?!

In its examination of social behavior, sociology goes beyond the
limits of a common sense approach to life. Sociology attempts to
generate facts concerning human behavior and ultimately hopes to
establish "laws."

Seinology

What is Seinology? Simply put, Seinology is the study of *Seinfeld*, the
brilliantly written comedic television show based loosely on the life
of Jerry Seinfeld. The suffix—*ology* means "the study of." *Sein* is the
abbreviated version of *Seinfeld*. Put together, *Seinology* is the sociological study of the television show *Seinfeld*. *Seinfeld* is filled with sociological relevance as the two subjects overlap a great deal.

When the television show *Seinfeld* first aired, it was criticized as a
show about *nothing*. This criticism was addressed in the episode "The
Pitch" (#43) when Jerry and George discuss their idea for a television
show to executives at NBC. During their meeting, Russell Dalrymple,
the head of the network, asks Jerry and George what the show would
be about.

> *George*: "I think I can sum up the show for you with one word:
>   Nothing!"
> *Russell*: "Nothing?"
> *George (smiling)*: "Nothing."
> *Russell (unimpressed)*: "What does that mean?"
> *George*: "The show is about nothing."

Jerry (a little worried, turns to George): "Well, it's not about
    nothing."
George (to Jerry): "No, it's about nothing."
Jerry: "Well, maybe in philosophy. But, even nothing is some-
    thing."

The truth is that *Seinfeld* is really a show about *everything*. It covered nearly all the topics discussed by sociologists. And sociologists
study everything from macro social systems to small group interactions. Thus, when George tries to explain to Russell Dalrymple that
the show could be about such mundane occurrences as what people
do on a daily basis; such activities would hold an interest for many
sociologists.

Sociology as a Science

Before the Industrial Revolution (circa, mid- to late-eighteenth century), most societies of the world were governed by faith and tradition.
In fact, many contemporary societies still rely on either religious explanations of life and abide by doctrines established by religious leaders
(see chapter 11 for a discussion on the role of religion in society), or by
tradition and follow the rules set forth by leaders who have inherited
their power (e.g., monarchies). Tradition suffered a major blow with
the success of the American and French Revolutions. People began to
rethink social life, and new ideas emerged, especially the concept that
individuals possess inalienable rights. People no longer accepted traditional customs and ways of doing things, resulting in many Western
monarchies giving way to democratic societies.
    With the emergence of new technology and innovation during
early industrialization, society began to turn to science for explanations regarding social life. Science incorporates nonbiased, systematic, rigorous testing of its principles or beliefs. Science attempts to
uncover causal explanations for why things occur. Empirical science
involves systematic data collection and statistical interpretation of
that data. Empiricism represents the "roots" of sociology, as sociology is firmly grounded on scientific principles. As a member of the
social sciences, sociology utilizes the research methods common to
the natural sciences, including observation, focus group studies, data
collection and analysis, and to a lesser extent, experimentation.

The Industrial Revolution is important to sociologists because it also represents the "origin" of sociology. The great social upheaval (numerous social problems common to urban life that were mostly nonexistent before industrialization) caused by the radical changes brought forth by industrialization provided the springboard for social reformers—people who wished to help the less fortunate. Many of these early reformers applied sociological principles and concerns shared by contemporary sociologists.

Theory and Methods

As a science, sociology is guided by theories that are supported by data generated from scientific methodology. Social theory and research methodology form the foundation of sociology.

Social Theory

The word *theory* is sometimes misleading because it seems to imply speculation or uncertainty. Some may even contrast theory with fact because facts are believed to be established truths, whereas theories are speculations about what might be true. For sociologists, theory is not mere speculation and may instead already be established as true. For scientists, theories must be empirically verifiable and they must provide an explanation or account for social phenomena. Sociological theory is grounded in the scientific tradition of belief that social patterns exist and therefore general abstract "laws" can be created through empirical study.

Among the early sociologists to clearly articulate upon the importance of social theory was Emile Durkheim (1858–1917). Durkheim studied suicide (because it is a relatively concrete and specific phenomenon) and applied empirical methods in an attempt to explain why people would choose to commit this act of self-destruction. Despite the fact that suicide would appear to be a very individualistic behavior, Durkheim found that a number of social factors influence and explain why some people (and some groups) are more likely to commit suicide than others.

In brief, Durkheim developed a theory that suicide is related to the degree that individuals are integrated (the strength of shared beliefs among group members) into society. Those who feel isolated from social groups (not well-integrated) may commit (egoistic) suicide because they are depressed; while those who are too strongly integrated may commit (altruistic) suicide because they believe in a cause (e.g., suicide bombers).

In the opening monologue of the "The Suicide" (#32), Jerry Seinfeld presents his own, less-than sympathetic, theory about suicide. He wonders why people who try to commit suicide, and for some reason don't die, stop trying. Their lives have not improved, and in fact, they have found out one more thing they are not good at. Jerry states, "That's why these people don't succeed in life to begin with. Because they give up too easy. . . . There's nothing more rewarding than reaching a goal you have set for yourself." In "The Suicide" episode, Jerry further ponders, why do people need "suicide machines" when all they have to do is jump off the top of a tall building?

Sociological Perspectives

In contemporary sociology there is a great proliferation of social theorists and a lack of a significant number of quality "grand theorists." As a result, modern sociology is dominated by "schools of thought." These "schools of thought" are also referred to as *perspectives*. At the introductory level of sociology emphasis is generally placed on the *functionalist, conflict*, and *symbolic-interactionist* perspectives.

The functionalist perspective has two primary components. First, all of society's social institutions (parts) are interrelated and are designed to maintain stability in society (the whole) in order to meet systems needs. Thus, like any organism, if society is to function smoothly, its various parts must work together in harmony. The second key element of functionalism centers on the belief that there exists a general consensus on values (among society's members). Thus, in order for any social system (society, organization, family, or personal relationship with others) to remain intact, there must be some commitment to general values, issues of morality, and goals. Talcott Parsons was instrumental in the development of functionalism in the 1950s. Functionalism represents a macrosociological approach (large-scale) to the study of society and human behavior.

The conflict perspective recognizes that society is comprised of many different parts but insists that these parts are in competition with each other over scarce resources. Conflict theories emphasize the role of power and the inequality found systematically throughout society. Conflict theorists argue that there is no true consensus and that instead, society's norms and values are those of the dominant group. Conflict theory is greatly influenced by the works of Karl Marx who argued that vested interest groups seek to fulfill the needs of specific groups. The power groups, because of their greater resources, are able to dictate the manner in which society is run and maintained. The people who lack power become disenchanted and seek change. The power group seeks to maintain its power (the status quo) which inevitably results in social conflict. Conflict theory arose as the primary alternative to functionalism as a macrosociological theoretical perspective.

Symbolic interactionism is essentially a social-psychological perspective and focuses primarily on the issue of *self, self-esteem,* and small group interactions. *Symbolic interactionism* is a term coined by Herbert Blumer and is a theoretical perspective most generally associated with George Herbert Mead. Symbolic interactionism, as a microsociological theory, is primarily concerned with the development of the self and the presentation of the self. Erving Goffman's work in *dramaturgy* is especially interesting. Goffman attempted to explain human interaction by comparing life to a staged drama. Individuals are referred to as *actors,* who give *performances* for *audiences* in *settings,* by using *props* in an attempt to convince others of their role (e.g., a waitress who acts concerned about her customers' happiness and the satisfaction of their dining experience). The role that people perform for others is conducted in the *front stage* setting and does not represent the actor's true self. One's true self is only revealed in private (*back stage*) where it would be shown that the concern of the waitress was simply motivated by a desire for a big tip. Goffman used "the waitress" as an example of his dramaturgical analysis by specifically addressing her front-stage and back-stage personas.

Seinfeld addressed this issue in the episode "The Soup" (#93). While George and Jerry were ordering their meal, the waitress harmlessly flirted with George. She playfully mentioned his "beautiful face." As the waitress walks away, George obviously feels good about himself and asks Jerry whether or not he thinks that she thinks he actually has a beautiful face, or whether she was just saying that. Jerry responded, "Well, they do work on tips." George, who suffers greatly from a lack of self-esteem, quickly allows Jerry's negative comment to compromise his delicate psyche and mutters, "Why should she like me? Who am I?"

Seinfeld seldom focuses on macrosociological issues; it does however, regularly address the concerns of symbolic interactionism, especially its focus on the development and maintenance of self-esteem. Many *Seinfeld* episodes expose George's low self-esteem and his constant attempt to boost his self-worth.

For example, in the episode "The Frogger" (#174), George and Jerry return to one of their favorite childhood hangouts, Mario's Pizza. George notices the Frogger game and is amazed to find that he still holds the high score. George reminisces about that magical day from his past when he had the perfect combination of Mountain Dew, mozzarella cheese, and the right amount of grease on the joy stick. George decides to purchase the Frogger from Mario (who is going out of business) because he believes it represents the high point of his life. Of course, in the end, while George is moving the Frogger machine, it is crushed by a truck when George attempts to wheel it across the street. Another blow to George's self-esteem!

In "The Airport" (#52), George is excited to purchase a *Time* magazine from an airport news rack because it is supposed to have a "blurb" (an article that mentions his name) about him. Because of his low self-esteem any mention of his name in print is very important to him. As he reaches for the last copy of *Time* another person attempts to grab it but George manages to secure it. The other person angrily demands that George give him the magazine but George does not relent. George tells the man that there is a blurb on him. The other man responds, "A blurb? You're a blurb. Look at the cover!" It turns out that this man is a killer and *his* picture is on the cover, along with an entire article on his crimes. Because this man is in handcuffs and guarded by law enforcement officers George is able to keep the article and feels pretty smug about himself. Once again, however, this is George Costanza, and he always seems to lose. Through a series of mishaps, George ends up on the same plane as the killer and is dragged into the bathroom by the killer and roughed up before the guards can rescue him.

George is so insecure that his personality is best summarized in the episode "The Pilot" (#64). Jerry and George have been working on a pilot called *Jerry* for NBC. The first episode is about to air and George is convinced that if the show is successful he will be punished for it. Thus, George's self-esteem is so low that he fears the worst even when he should feel the best.

Among the primary tenets of symbolic interactionism is the core belief that individuals, who are capable of communicating with each other through the use of symbols (e.g., language and gestures), are affected by language and that language helps to shape their perceptions of events. *Seinfeld* is filled with examples of the symbolic importance of language. For example, in the episode "The Nose Job" (#26), Jerry states in his closing monologue that the technical term for a nose job is *rhinoplasty*. Emphasizing the "rhino," Jerry wonders why, at that particular moment, do we need to insult the person who is about to have a nose job? Their self-esteem is obviously already compromised, so why the word *rhino*?

Social Research

Research is a process that involves systematically collecting information for the purpose of testing an existing theory or creating a new one. Although there are a wide variety of research methodology techniques available, sociologists have a commitment to use the scientific method in their study of society and social behavior. The scientific method refers to the systematic, organized series of steps taken by the researcher to ensure maximum objectivity, consistency, and reliability in researching a problem. Scientific research, based on empirical evidence, allows sociologists an opportunity to establish "social facts," which can be verified by other researchers.

The "ideal" research model generally involves eight steps:

1. Select a topic—any area of interest
2. Define the problem—including creating parameters for the study
3. Review the literature—find out what other people have done
4. Formulate hypotheses—specific statements to guide the research
5. Choose a research method(s)—which method provides the greatest insights
6. Collect the data—with special attention given to assure validity and reliability
7. Analyze the results—did your data support your hypotheses?
8. Publish/Share the results—this is important whether or not your research supports your theory

Social research may have either a *quantitative* (a reliance on statistics and an objective presentation through the use of data) component or a *qualitative* (a reliance on words and descriptions to analyze social behavior, resulting in a subjective analysis) component.

Research Methods

Typically, sociologists acknowledge six different research methodologies. The most commonly used is survey research. Survey research is any research that involves taking a sample of a population and then asking them a number of specific questions. The answers provided yield researchers with data. This data is then used to support (or not) a theory that the researcher is working on. There are three types of surveys: mail questionnaires, face-to-face interviews, and phone interviews. Nearly all of us have been confronted by some type of research firm or social researcher that wishes to gather information. Survey research is a favorite tool for quantitative researchers.

In the episode "The Pilot" (#63), Jerry reports in the opening monologue that according to most studies (social research) the number-one fear among people is public speaking. Death was number two. Without this research knowledge, most people might think (common sense) that the number-one fear of humans would be death. After all, if actually given a choice, wouldn't people choose to speak publicly instead of choosing death? Statistics reveal otherwise.

Focus group studies are a type of survey research. With focus group studies researchers randomly select a small number of people to be interviewed on a specific topic. Because focus group studies involve interviewing, it is considered as a variation of survey research. However, focus group research relies on the interaction within the group based on topics that are supplied by the researcher. Focus group studies are often underused in sociological research although they are very popular for marketing and political analysis.

In the episode "The Foundation" (#135), Jerry conducts a focus group study on his likability based on the manner in which his last relationship ended. Jerry had been telling everyone that his most recent breakup was mutual, but no one believed him and this made him less likable to potential new girlfriends. He asked his focus group (consisting of a waitress, a cook, and cashier, all from Monk's) a series of questions that dealt with a number of specific breakup scenarios (e.g., "What if I told you my fiancée left me for another man?") and whether or not that made him "more likable," "less likable," or "as likable."

Through his research, Jerry found out that being a widower

(George's story) "tested through the roof." Thus, based on Jerry's focus group research, the pick-up line that works best (in terms of your likability level) is to state that you are a recent widower. To attract very good-looking women, George used his own story (his fiancée Susan had recently died) but showed women a photo of Elaine's model friend who was gorgeous, compared to Susan who was more average looking.

Another common type of research is content analysis. Content analysis involves the systematic study of past written documents and/or oral forms of communication. Students conduct content analysis every time they review books and journal articles in order to write their research term papers. Content analysis is a safe and economically friendly form of research. However, the research is limited to the materials available to the researcher, and because the review is of the works of others (opposed to original research) it is an indirect form (using existing data sources) of social research.

Archival data is another example of an indirect research methodology. Nearly all businesses, including college campuses, have archives—an area where old and/or oversized documents and a variety of other possessions are kept. These are items that people want to save without prominently presenting them. In the episode "The Cartoon" (#169), Elaine has proudly displayed on her office door a cartoon from the *New Yorker* that she had submitted to the magazine. Mr. Peterman, Elaine's boss, walks by her office and reads the cartoon. Peterman laughs with enjoyment and begins to walk away when he suddenly and abruptly turns back to tell Elaine that he recognized the cartoon as a plagiarism of a *Ziggy* cartoon. Peterman summons Elaine, "Quick, Elaine, to my archives!" As a big fan of *Ziggy*, Peterman had a complete collection of *Ziggy* cartoons. After conducting his research, Peterman discovers that Elaine's cartoon was indeed originally a *Ziggy*.

The most commonly used research methodology among natural scientists is experimentation. At its most basic level, an experiment involves forming two groups with one serving as the control group and the other as an experimental, or treatment, group. The experimental group is given some sort of "treatment." Measurements are taken before the treatment and at the end of the treatment period. The measurement of both the control and treatment group allows researchers an opportunity to determine whether or not the treatment is effective.

Microsociologists will sometimes conduct their own types of experiments, called breaching experiments. Typically, researchers manipulate the social setting and measure the reactions of observers. In the *Seinfeld* episode "The Apartment" (#10), Jerry and George discuss the odd phenomena that when men wear a wedding band, women are more likely to hit on them. George wonders whether or not that is really true. Jerry responds, "That would make an interesting sociological experiment." Jerry tells George that Kramer has his father's wedding band and that he'd loan it to George. Jerry and George, who is wearing the wedding band, attend a party and sure enough, a number of attractive women hit on George. One woman is so attracted to George she tells him it's a shame that he's married. When George tries to inform her that he was simply conducting a sociological experiment (and frantically tries to take the ring off) and that he was not really married, the woman becomes disgusted with him (thinking that George was lying about not being married) and storms off. Ah, one of the many dangers confronting sociology researchers!

Two other forms of research methodologies involve observation. Unobtrusive observation involves the examination of past behavior based on clues found in the social environment. The researcher, much like a detective, examines physical traces—evidence that people leave behind them—as a means of collecting information (data) on a specific phenomenon or behavior.

Researchers may also participate in field observation, a method of research in which human behavior is directly observed by researchers as it occurs in real life situations. Field research is a critical element in generating new theories on behavior. Every one of us participates in field observation. We examine people and attempt to make some conclusion about them based on their behavior. For example, a single person out on a Saturday night looking to "hook up" will scan the social environment (e.g., a bar, party, or ball game) looking for someone with whom they feel they have a chance of "scoring."

Seinfeld was basically a show on Jerry's observations of human behavior. As Jerry stated in "The Serenity Now" (#159), "There's more important things than making shallow, fairly obvious observations about life." And that is why sociology goes beyond the obvious and utilizes a systematic approach to thinking about, studying, and understanding society, groups, and human behavior and interaction. *Seinfeld* represents a nonscientific approach to the understanding of human behavior. And yet, there are times when the advice offered by the four main characters is quite sound. On many other occasions it is quite bizarre. But either way, it is worth studying for the sociological observations one can make.

Applied Sociology

Much of contemporary sociology is applied, meaning that sociologists attempt to help solve social problems, design policy, and provide information relevant for decision making. In this regard, sociology is very focused on current, real life situations that occur in society; it's what makes sociology so relevant to everyone's lives. Many of the story lines in *Seinfeld* also provide reflections of real-life events and concerns.

In the episode "The Dealership" (#167), George is confronted with some of the classic challenges presented by vending machines. First and foremost, many vending machines appear to be temperamental. They don't always want to accept our money. Coins are sometimes rejected, seemingly for no real reason. And don't get started on those Canadian quarters (this reference only makes sense to those people living near the Canadian border). American washing machines warn against the evils and the harm that they can cause to the proper functioning of the machine.

Vending machines seem to attain great pleasure in rejecting currency. George displays his quick temper when the vending machine at the car dealership refuses to take his dollar. He tries shoving it in, turns it different directions, tries to straighten it out by rubbing it up against the corner of the machine (does this description remind anyone of his own behavior?), and still the machine refuses his money. Eventually, George attains coins for the machine. He selects a Twix candy bar. Unfortunately, the metal dials that turn to release the candy bar trap an edge of the Twix bar which impedes its descent to the bottom of the machine. Now George is really angry. He reacts as many people do. He yells. He screams. He tries to tip the machine so that the candy bar will fall to the bottom. But all to no avail. Now what do you do? George decides to get some more money from Jerry. He will have to buy two candy bars to get his first one. However, while he is gone, someone else comes along (a mechanic), notices the dangling candy bar and realizes he can get a "two for one" deal. When George returns to find "his" candy bar taken, he becomes angrier.

Often, it's the little things in life that drive us crazy. For example, in the episode "The Big Salad" (#88), Kramer drives a white Ford Bronco with his buddy Steve Gendason as the passenger. Gendason was accused of a crime, and Kramer is simply driving him home. This episode, of course, mirrors the famous O. J. Simpson "police chase" that captivated the nation and was shown live by every news network. "The Big Salad" episode cleverly incorporated actual footage of the O. J. Simpson chase with the Kramer and Gendason police chase.

In "The Postponement" (#112), Kramer attempts to sneak a cup of hot coffee into a movie theater and spills it on himself. He yells out in pain. After Jerry tips off the movie usher as to what happened, Kramer is thrown out of the theater. Kramer hires a lawyer to sue the coffee maker because the coffee was too hot. Jerry tells him it is supposed to be hot. Kramer responds, "Not *that* hot." This is reminiscent of the case where a woman sued McDonalds because the coffee was too hot. This woman drove off with the coffee in her lap and was somehow surprised when the coffee spilled and she got burned. Talk about a lack of common sense!

Another classic example of *Seinfeld* imitating life is displayed in the episode "The Understudy" (#110). Jerry is dating a woman named Gennice who is Bette Midler's understudy in the Broadway show *Rochelle, Rochelle*. The cast members of *Rochelle, Rochelle* are playing a softball game against Jerry's team, the "Improv." Bette Midler is her team's catcher. Bette and George have been "trash talking" throughout the game and on the game's last play George hits a ball to the outfield. He rounds the bases and heads toward home with Midler waiting for him with the ball. George decides to "take her out" of the game and knocks into her, causing her to drop the ball. He is safe at home and quite proud of himself. Midler, meanwhile, is suffering from the blow to her knee that George inflicted upon her. Midler's teammates immediately conclude that the understudy's boyfriend (Jerry) probably put his fat friend (George) up to the "knee-capping" that Midler endured. This episode parodies the real life knee-capping inflicted upon Nancy Kerrigan by associates of her rival, Tonya Harding, at the 1994 US national figure skating championships. Harding believed that her only obstacle toward attaining the championship was Kerrigan. Harding's ex-husband hired a hit man to attack Kerrigan, which was caught on amateur tape. In "The Understudy" George's knee-capping was also caught on amateur film, and Gennice professes her innocence to the public, just as Harding denied knowledge of the attack on Kerrigan. Gennice privately thanked Jerry and George, saying it was the nicest thing anyone ever did for her. The episode ends with Gennice performing in place of Bette Midler, but suffering a similar sad fate as Harding when her shoe string becomes unlaced at the beginning of the competition. She breaks down crying and pleads for a second chance: "Please let me start over."

Seinfeld and Its Sociological Relevance

Seinfeld was, and remains, a sociological phenomenon. Not only was the show hugely popular when it first aired, it remains very popular today as many young people are watching it for the first time. *Seinfeld* is not a show about *nothing*; it is a show about *everything*. Sociology is a discipline about everything found in the social world. The harmonic convergence between *Seinfeld* and sociology leads us to *Seinology*, a sociological approach to the social significances of *Seinfeld*.

So, if you're like George, who admitted in "The Butter Shave" (#157) that he appreciates the humor of comedian Kenny Bania because he tells funny stories about real-life events that happen to all of us (like a shopping cart that has one bad wheel) and uses words like "puke" because you don't have to think about why they are funny, you will enjoy the rest of this book. In addition, you may learn to appreciate the sociological perspective on everyday life.

Chapter 2

Cultural Norms and Etiquette

"Good Manners Are the Glue of Society."
—Kramer

As we learned in chapter 1, sociologists like to observe social behavior. The study of human interaction must take into account the fact that people are influenced by their culture. The different societies of the world establish their own guidelines for what constitutes proper behavior. Consequently, sociologists who attempt to establish universal social laws concerning human behavior must be careful to point out potential differences in mannerisms based on one's culture and/or subcultural membership.

Culture and Social Structure

Culture is like a "script" for acceptable behavior. Culture represents the totality of learned and socially transmitted customs, values, knowledge, beliefs, rules, and norms generated by a society. Groups and individuals are supposed to meet the expectations of their culture. Cultural expectations are reinforced in society as norms and laws. As a result, culture becomes the social determinant of behavior.

We learn culture through the socialization process and by observing others. Sharing a culture with others not only simplifies our daily interactions, it helps to define the group or society to which we belong. When large numbers of people share a culture and live in the same territory they constitute a society. As sociologist John Farley explains, "A society can be defined as a relatively self-contained and organized group of people interacting under some common political authority within a specific geographic area. Societies exist over an extended period of time, outliving the individual people of whom they are composed."[2]

All societies, small and large, industrial and agricultural, democratic and socialist, have culture and social structure. Social structure refers to the organization of society, such as the social positions that people hold, the different social groups within, and the various social institutions that comprise a society.

Social Norms

Social norms dictate behavior. As sociologist Richard Schaefer explains, "Norms are established standards of behavior maintained by a society. In order for a norm to become significant, it must be widely shared and understood."[3] For example, it is widely understood that students are to turn off their cell phones in class.

Sociologists generally acknowledge three different types of social norms: folkways, mores, and laws. Folkways represent the least formal norms. They are the conventional rules of everyday life that people follow almost automatically. It's generally no big deal if we violate folkways; that is to say, there are no severe punishments associated with violating these types of norms. When someone attends a wedding they are expected to bring a gift, dress formally (unless otherwise indicated), remain silent and attentive during the ceremony, and so on. Violations of these calls to etiquette may lead to raised eyebrows and looks of disgust, but they will not lead to imprisonment. Folkways, then, comprise basic etiquette and good manners, such as saying please when you ask for something or thank you as a form of acknowledgment and appreciation after you have received something from another person.

Mores are stronger norms that dictate specific ways in which people are supposed to act. Mores actually constitute demands, not just expectations of behavior. They have moral significance and include society's taboos (a norm so ingrained into society that the very thought of its violation is met with revulsion), such as adults being forbidden from having sex with children or engaging in cannibalism. Mores are established for the general well-being of society and, because of that, their violation may evoke strong emotional responses (anger and/or violence) by the citizenry. Violating society's mores may also lead to strong forms of punishment. In many cases, mores are so important that they are expressed in written form, called laws.

Laws are formal norms that have been written down by a political authority. Violating formal norms may lead to specific punishments that may include incarceration. The characters on *Seinfeld* often break the law, but those stories will be told in chapter 8. In this chapter, the focus is on informal norms (folkways) and the rules of behavior that are governed by cultural expectations and etiquette.

Seinfeld *and Proper Behavior and Etiquette*

Without question, one of the most dominant themes throughout the *Seinfeld* series was the issue of what constitutes proper behavior and etiquette. The four main characters (Jerry, Kramer, George, and Elaine) constantly discuss issues related to "proper behavior."

Saying "Thank You"

Among the most basic assumptions of proper behavior is the cultural norm of saying thank you to someone who has assisted you in some way or another. For example, in the episode "The Face Painter" (#109), Elaine and Jerry are having lunch at the diner when their friend Alec Berg (and as Jerry explained, Alec Berg has the perfect John Houseman name) offers them his season tickets for the Rangers-Devils play-off game at the Garden. It is only polite to express gratitude when someone offers you such a valued commodity. So, Jerry thanks Alec five times: Thanks. Thank you. Thanks a lot. Thanks again. Really, thank you. Alec acknowledges the thank yous and mentions that the same seats may be available for the next play-off game as well. The day after the hockey game Kramer asks Jerry if he called Alec to thank him for the tickets. Jerry said that he did not, and why should he? After all, he thanked him five times when he was first offered the tickets. Kramer informs Jerry that you have to call the next day to thank someone for things like tickets to sports events; it's only proper.

> *Jerry*: "I'm taking a stand against all this overthanking. I thanked him enough already."

Kramer: "Jerry, good manners are the glue of society. Don't you want to be a member of society?"

Jerry: "If I knew I had to give eight million thank yous, I would not have taken the tickets in the first place."

Kramer, disgusted with Jerry's attitude, replies that you know what will happen next, don't you? Alec won't give you those tickets for Friday night's game now because you did not call to give him his "day after" thank you.

Jerry sits defiantly on his couch, refusing to call Alec. He assumes that since Alec had already offered him the tickets that Alec would call him. Kramer pleads with him, "Get on the phone and give him his thank you. Jerry, this is the way society functions. Now don't you want to be a part of society? Because if you don't, you just get in your car and move to the East Side." Still in denial, Jerry states that there are still five hours left for Alec to call and offer the tickets. Kramer storms out of Jerry's apartment and says to him, "You stubborn, silly, stupid man."

Kramer returns to Jerry's apartment a few hours later and wonders whether or not Jerry has called Alec. Jerry tells Kramer that he has not called Alec. Finally, at the very last minute, Jerry changes his mind and calls Alec. At first he commends him on his great John Houseman name, and then thanks him for the tickets for the previous game. Alec responds, "You should have called me sooner. I gave away my seats. But a friend of mine has two extra tickets if you don't mind the nose-bleed seats." Jerry says that's okay because he just wants to be able to attend the game. As it turns out, there was one "little catch" attached to the seats. Kramer and Jerry had to agree to bare their chests and spell out D-E-V-I-L-S (each with a painted letter) with David Puddy and his friends in the cheap seats.

As illustrated in "The Face Painter," many people in society expect and demand thank yous whenever they are deemed necessary and appropriate. It seems you can never say thank you enough. But be warned, you must be certain to thank the right person. Giving someone credit (a thank you) for a deed performed by someone else may not go over very well with some members of society.

George Costanza, for one, is a person who expects his thank yous. In the episode "The Big Salad" (#88), George and his girlfriend Julie meet Elaine and Jerry on the street and ask if they would like to join them for lunch at the diner. Both decline, but Elaine asks them for a "big salad" from the diner. After making a fuss about a *big* salad, George agrees to drop it off to Elaine at Jerry's apartment. At the diner, George pays for lunch and the big salad, but the waitress hands the big salad to Julie. When arriving to Jerry's apartment, Julie hands the salad to Elaine and Elaine appropriately says thank you— to Julie. Well, George views this as a slight, a form of disrespect. After all, he is the one who purchased the big salad, so he expects, at the very least, to be thanked for that. In George's mind what made matters worse was the fact that Julie "took credit" for the purchase!

George finds it necessary to tell Elaine that he was the one who bought the big salad even though Julie was the one who handed it to her. Elaine, in turn, mentions something to Julie, who then realizes that George went out of his way to tell Elaine about the purchase. Julie, for some unknown reason, becomes upset by this and later questions George about it. George demands to know from Julie how she could claim responsibility for purchasing the big salad, and more importantly, for accepting a thank you under false premises.

Good Manners

There are nearly countless numbers of cultural expectations regarding what constitutes good manners. For example, everyone knows that cell phones are not to be brought into movie theaters. Talking on a cell phone would be rude. Talking during the movie is also rude. In the episode "The Movie" (#54), the question is raised whether talking during the coming attractions is rude. The concept of "saving seats" is also discussed. Is there a limit to how many seats you can save? And how long can you save a seat before you must relinquish them to other patrons? Elaine is asked to save three seats for George, Kramer, and Jerry. As the start of the movie looms closer and closer many people ask to use the seats that Elaine is saving. A movie patron suggests to Elaine that one person is not allowed to hold a total of four seats. This makes me wonder, is there a limit to how many seats someone can save? It is a reflection of good manners to save seats for friends, but when they are late, good manners would dictate that you have to "give up" your seats to others.

Theater etiquette is also discussed in the episode "The Stock Tip" (#5). Jerry and his date Vanessa are at a movie and the people behind them are rudely talking throughout the movie. Later, Vanessa asks Jerry why he did not do anything about the rude people. Jerry responded, "I gave them the one-half turn and the full turn with the eye-roll. Anything else risks a punch in the mouth." A punch in the mouth is certainly a sign of bad manners!

Many people believe that saying God bless you after someone sneezes is a sign of good manners. In "The Good Samaritan" (#37), George and Elaine are having dinner with a married couple, Michael and Robin. Robin sneezes. George hesitates, looks around the table, and says, "God bless you." Robin says, "Thank you." George, kidding around, mentions that he could see that Michael wasn't going to say it so he decided to. Well, this leads to a fight between Michael and Robin. When Robin sneezes again, George gestures to Michael to go ahead and say it.

George and Jerry discuss this "incident" later. Jerry asks George whether or not he allowed enough time for Michael to respond. After all, a spouse should be given the first right to say God bless you. George informs Jerry that he did give Michael enough time, but once it passes, it's open to others. Feeling the need to defend his actions, George also tells Jerry that he was raised to say God bless you. Jerry ponders the whole God-bless-you cultural norm. He offers an alternative to God bless you suggesting that people should instead say, "You are so good looking" after someone sneezes.

Different cultures, of course, have different cultural expectations of what constitutes proper behavior. The diversity of culture often tests the bounds of acceptable behavior. It is revealed in the episode "The Understudy" (#110), that George's father, Frank Costanza, has a problem with removing his shoes. He fears that he has bad foot odor. While Frank was a traveling salesman in Korea, his habit of refusing to take his shoes off while entering someone's home—the norm in that culture—was deemed poor manners and insulting to the host. Frank mentions that he doesn't like a culture that requires taking one's shoes off before entering a home.

When someone you know offers you food, it is polite to either graciously accept the offering, or to decline while providing some brief reason as an explanation. Something simple like, "I am too full to eat anything else, thanks anyway" will suffice. In the episode "The Pie" (#79), Jerry is at the diner with his girlfriend Audrey. After dinner, Jerry is enjoying his apple pie and offers some to Audrey. She declines without any explanation. In fact, she doesn't mutter a word, and simply refuses to try even a small taste. Afterward, Jerry discusses this incident with George and Elaine. They all agree that Audrey acted in a peculiar manner. Elaine even suggests that Jerry should break up with her because of it!

Telephone Etiquette

Seinfeld teaches us that there are many forms of telephone etiquette. The advent of cell-phone use (which occurred during the original run of *Seinfeld*) has led to many violations of telephone etiquette. In the episode "The Finale" (#179), Elaine calls her friend Jill to find out about her father's health. She makes this call on her cell phone while walking on the street with George and Jerry. They both chastise her for making a health inquiry call on a cell phone. Jerry informs her that such calls are like telling people you don't want to use your important time from home to call so instead I'll call from the cell phone while walking (or driving) about my normal routine. This violation was labeled the "cell-phone walk and talk." Elaine does make her follow-up call to Jill from home, but she blows Jill off to answer the call coming in on her second line—a sure violation of etiquette, as you are basically telling the first person the other call might be more important than her call! Jerry referred to this type of phone violation as the "call-waiting face-off." Elaine's third attempt to call Jill, about her father's health, is a rushed attempt while she is on her way to the plane. Jerry states that this is also impolite because you can't rush a health inquiry phone call. This violation was called the "on-the-way-to-the-plane call."

The advent of the cell phone has nearly completely replaced the need for public phones. This was not the case in 1991, as demonstrated in the episode "The Chinese Restaurant" (#16). George, Elaine, and Jerry are waiting to be seated at a Chinese restaurant. George's girlfriend is supposed to meet them, forming a party of four. (A classic line at the end of this episode is, "Seinfeld, Four.") None of the characters have a cell phone; in today's culture, it would be nearly impossible to find a group of three urbanites where at least one of them did not have a cell phone. Nevertheless, George is dependent on the restaurant's public phone. He impatiently waits his turn. One patron is talking for a long time, and George is pleading with him to get off the phone. But the caller simply ignores George. This irritates George even more. George even asks Jerry if he will back him up in case he gets in a fight with the caller. Jerry tells him to relax and informs him that the phone is free. However, before

George can walk over to the phone, a woman "cuts" ahead of him. George is really angry now, and he states in a loud voice, "You know, we're living in a society. We're supposed to act in a civilized way." When George finally gets his turn to use the phone, his girlfriend is not home and he has to leave a message. In a funny conclusion to the phone escapade, the restaurant host (for reasons unknown) yells out the name "Cartwright" for a phone call. George hears this and asks the host if he has received a call for Costanza. The host said that he did receive a call for "Costanza" but yelled out "Cartwright" (instead of Costanza). George looks at him in bewilderment.

Despite all the cell phones in use, it seems we still always leave messages instead of actually getting hold of anyone. And let's face it, we don't want to talk to everyone who tries to call us. We screen calls and return calls when we know the other person won't be home. Jerry explains all this in the episode "Male Unbonding" (#4). Jerry admits he has become a "screener." He doesn't want to talk to his old friend Joel—a childhood friend who had a ping pong table—any longer. Whenever Joel leaves a message, Jerry calls back when he knows that Joel won't be home. And just in case an unwanted caller slips through a nonscreen, Jerry creates a "list of excuses" to get out of doing things with people when they call. As Jerry explained, there are certain friends you will have for life. They call you. You don't call them back, and still they call.

Driving Etiquette

Everyone has most likely witnessed, or participated in, some form of road rage. A general disregard of others, manifested in the form of violating basic driving etiquette, seems to be a growing phenomenon in American culture. Jerry describes a few violations of driving etiquette in the episode "The Puerto Rican Day" (#176). Some of the forms of road rage include switching lanes aggressively, flipping people off, speeding up so that other people cannot pass or make their turn, and the "stare ahead" to avoid eye contact. Jerry expects that at the very least aggressive motorists should give the "I'm-sorry wave." The courtesy "go-ahead wave" is a nice example of driving etiquette.

On some occasions, people find themselves as passengers in a car, such as taxi cabs and car service companies. Issues of etiquette are a little unclear here. For example, is the driver obligated to start a conversation with the passenger, and if so, will the passenger find this attempt to start a conversation as welcome, or as an intrusion? What about the passenger? Are they obligated to talk to people that are doing their professional job? In the episode "The Lip Reader" (#70), Elaine, as an employee of Pendant Publishing, is allowed the use of a car service because her company has an account with one. Elaine tells her coworker that she hates using the service because its drivers want to talk all the time (this is not necessarily the norm with all car service companies). She hates this social requirement. But at 4:30 PM on a Friday, in New York City, Elaine fears she'll never get a cab, so she uses the service. She violates the norm of proper behavior by pretending to be "going deaf" in order to avoid communicating with the driver. But Elaine blows her cover when she overhears on the car service radio that Tom Hanks will be the next rider in the car. Elaine blurts out, "Tom Hanks? After me, you're picking up Tom Hanks?" The driver knew right away that Elaine was just pretending to be deaf so that she did not have to talk to him. As Elaine later explained to Jerry and Kramer, "He caught me hearing."

As a rule, the driving experience is over as soon as the driver parks the car. However, as demonstrated in "The Parking Space" (#39), there are rules of etiquette involved in parking a car. Not legal issues such as being within a certain distance from the curb; no, the issue discussed in this episode centers on the debate between "head first" parking versus "back in" parking. In other words, is there a proper parking etiquette that dictates you must back into a spot, or is driving head first acceptable? George and Mike (a friend of Kramer and Jerry's) fight over a parking space in front of Jerry's apartment building. George was taking his time backing into the space, while Mike attempted to go head first into the space. They both get halfway in and both refuse to give ground to the other. Before long, passers-by stop and discuss the merits of each style of parking. A pair of police officers eventually arrive on the scene to clear things up, but they end up arguing with each other as well. The issue of proper parking-rules etiquette is never solved during this episode.

Breaking Up Etiquette

Who hasn't been involved in a breakup? Most relationships end with one partner being dumped (more examples of relationship endings are provided in chapter 3). As Jerry explained in the episode "The Foundation" (#135), there is always a winner and a loser after every breakup. And, there is no such thing as a "mutual" breakup—someone *had* to initiate it. In fact, Jerry's girlfriend Delores (whose name rhymes with a female body part) did not believe Jerry when he told her that his broken engagement was a mutual parting of ways. Jerry conducted a focus group study (a common type of research methodology used in sociology; see chapter 1 for a discussion of its methods) to find out how people reacted to someone's explanation for a failed relationship. As it turned out, George's story as a widower "tested through the roof"!

There are many reasons why couples break up. It may be because one person grew tired of the other. Or maybe one person cheated on the other. There are occasions when breakups are relatively civil, and the personal feelings of the other are considered. However, many times a breakup results in hurt feelings, pain, and anguish. In cases of civility, people work within some preconceived ideas about what constitutes the "rules of breaking up."

Occasionally, the characters on *Seinfeld* discuss these rules. In the episode "The Frogger" (#174), Jerry wants to break up with his girl-friend but Elaine informs him that you can't break up with someone over the phone after you have had sex with them. Furthermore, in "The Baby Shower" (#15), Elaine tells Jerry that if you don't break up with someone face to face you're a coward.

In the episode "The Seven" (#123), Jerry meets a very attractive woman, named Christie, in an antiques and toy store. They agree on a date later in the week. But Jerry is very curious when Christie wears the same outfit as when they first met. George later suggested to Jerry that maybe she was at the end of her laundry cycle. Jerry wonders why she would move it up on the rotation. On their second date, Christie wears the same outfit again and Jerry is shocked. His curiosity leads him to believe that she has a closet full of the same outfits, like a superhero. In her apartment, Jerry finds a photo of her with another guy, and she has the same outfit on in the photo as well. Mysteriously, Christie asks Jerry to leave her apartment. Later that night she calls him and breaks up with him—on the phone! But Jerry is more intrigued by her clothing than her breaking up with him over the phone—a possible violation of the rules of breaking up. So, while she is breaking up with him on the phone, Jerry pleads with her to tell him why she always wears the same outfit. The audience is left to ponder this, as Christie never reveals the reason.

On many occasions people realize *during* the first date with someone that there will be no relationship in development. In fact, you can't wait for the date to end. Jerry discusses this topic in "The Baby Shower" (#15). Jerry ponders, what do you say to a person on a first date when you know you never want to see her again? "See you around. You'll be around. I'll be around. Around other people . . . not with me . . . take care now . . ." Polite people try to find a polite way to break up with someone.

Of course, there are situations where breakups are nasty, and people are harmed. Rules of etiquette on the manner in which one breaks up with another are not agreed upon. For example, are individuals required to be polite with someone when they break up, or are they allowed to be mean and point out the flaws of the other in an attempt to justify their decision? In the episode "The Andrea Doria" (#144), Elaine is dating Alan, a bad "breaker-upper." Just prior to dating Elaine, one of Alan's ex-girlfriends stabbed him. Elaine views this as a sign that he brings out the passion in his girlfriends. While on a date together, Elaine witnesses another ex-girlfriend of Alan's angrily confront him. As it turns out, Alan picks a feature that is a physical flaw of his girlfriends and uses that against her whenever he breaks up with them. Before long, Alan breaks up with Elaine and calls her "big head." At first Elaine is not offended. But then weird things happen to her. A cabbie can't see out his rearview mirror because her head is too big. A pigeon flies into Elaine in the park; a guy in the park tells her that the bird flew "right into [her] head, like he couldn't avoid it." She becomes increasingly self-conscious and eventually builds great hostility toward Alan, whom she eventually confronts. How many of you believe that Alan was justified in the manner that he broke up with Elaine?

In the episode "The Truth" (#19), George decides to break up with Patrice, an accountant. He tries to be gentle with her in his breakup, but she demands the truth. So he tells her the truth, saying such things as she is too pretentious. She becomes so distraught from hearing the truth that she has a breakdown and admits herself to a depression clinic. (A prime example of the old adage, the truth hurts.) Unfortunately for Jerry, George's breakup affects him, as she was doing Jerry's taxes for him. Jerry and George visit Patrice and ask about Jerry's tax papers. She informs them that during her breakdown she threw away all his tax documents and receipts. Since Jerry did not have copies, he is screwed!

Gift Giving

There are many social occasions that call for gift giving as a sign of proper etiquette. Gift giving reflects cultural norms, most of which are not written down in any formal manner but implied nonetheless. For example, when someone is invited to another's home for dinner, it is generally viewed as proper etiquette to bring something (such as a bottle of wine or dessert), or to at least ask if you could bring something.

In the episode "The Dinner Party" (#77), Elaine, George, Jerry, and Kramer are all invited to a dinner party. Elaine mentions to the other three that they will have to stop on the way to the party to pick up something for the hosts. George questions this requirement and wonders why he is required to bring something. George believes that simply showing up for the party is a sufficient sign of good etiquette. Elaine looks at George in a dumbfounded manner and reiterates that yes, they have to bring something. Furthermore, she insists that a bottle of wine is not enough for the four of them, and suggests stopping at the bakery to get a cake—chocolate babka. George suggests that they should bring Pepsi and Ring Dings instead. Elaine thinks George is crazy to make such a suggestion. George believes that people will be far happier with Pepsi and Ring Dings than wine and cake. Jerry, trying to remain silent throughout this discourse, says they are not bringing a jug of Pepsi to a dinner party (deeming this an unworthy gift for this specific occasion). After a series of mishaps, the four arrive at the party, tired, sick, and cold and hand the wine and a cinnamon babka to the hosts and turn around and leave—never actually attending the party.

In the episode "The Handicap Spot" (#162), Elaine, Jerry, Kramer, and George are invited to an engagement party for a friend—the Drake, as he is called. Elaine, once again the enforcer of the gift obligation rule, informs Jerry and George that they are all obligated to bring a gift. Once again, revealing his cheapness (or genuine disdain for gift giving), George complains. A present for the engagement, then the wedding, and then eventually for the baby. The gift-giving cycle never ends. The four characters agree to buy the Drake and his fiancée, Allison, a big-screen television. Shortly after, the Drake announces that he and Allison are breaking up and that Allison is keeping all the gifts. Understandably, George wants the gift back, or at least the money spent on the gift. Jerry mentions that maybe this was all a part of a giant scam. Pretend to get married just to get gifts.

People could do that from state to state, year after year. Even Elaine is concerned about this gift-giving situation and calls Allison. Allison informs Elaine that all the gifts were given to charity.

George constantly complains about the gift-giving obligation. In "The Reverse Peephole" (#168), the characters discuss an appropriate "apartment warming" gift for their friend, Joe Mayo. Predictably, George is upset about the endless line of gift-giving occasions. Birthdays, holidays, and so on. It never ends. George asks, can't we have at least one month off from giving gifts?

In the episode "The Strike" (#166), George attempts to save money in his gift-giving obligation to his coworkers at Christmas. Inspired by the "lousy" gift he received from Tim Whatley (a gift card that stated: "A donation in your name has been made to the 'Children's Alliance'"), George creates his own bogus charity, and hands out gift cards to his coworkers. The card reads, "A donation has been made in your name to 'The Human Fund.'" The catchphrase used by George's charity is "Money for people." Since George fictitiously created the Human Fund, he did not have to actually make the donations—thus saving a great deal of money. Eventually his plan backfires as his boss (Kruger), for tax purposes, makes a large donation to the Human Fund. When the company accountant informs Kruger that the Human Fund does not exist, Kruger demands an explanation from George as to why he handed out bogus gifts. George, in an attempt to cover his tracks, explains to Kruger that he does not celebrate Christmas. He celebrates Festivus instead and is, therefore, uncomfortable with the office policy of handing out Christmas gifts. (More on Festivus in chapter 11.)

Trying to pick out an appropriate gift is sometimes difficult. The gift should match the recipient's wants and desires, it needs to be appropriate for the type of relationship that the gift giver and recipient have with one another, and it must fit the budget of the gift giver. In the episode "The Deal" (#14), Jerry and Elaine have rekindled their love relationship and are dating each other once again. Elaine's birthday is drawing near, so Jerry discusses with George the appropriate gift to purchase. When they were just friends any sort of impersonal gift would be appropriate. However, now that they are boyfriend and girlfriend, a more intimate and personal gift is required. Jerry also tells George that George's gift can only be half as good as his gift to Elaine. Confused and lacking any real thought and sentiment, Jerry gives Elaine an unromantic card with $182.00 cash.

Elaine is visibly upset. Kramer walks in and states that a gift of cash is something that an uncle would give her. And in fact, Kramer's gift was what Elaine had really wanted, and his card had a quote from the poet Yeats. Elaine was impressed (even though the gift was inappropriate coming from Kramer). As an interesting note, George's gift to Elaine was $91 cash—because his gift had to be half as good as Jerry's.

Sometimes people like to give gifts to each other as a "peace offering" for some misunderstanding between them. In "The Cigar Store Indian" (#74), Jerry gives Elaine a cigar store Indian statue. Elaine's friends are initially impressed that Jerry would give Elaine a gift for no "real" reason. The gift loses it value when Jerry makes "Indian" jokes that are offensive to Winona, one of Elaine's friends, who happens to be Native American. (The Native American topic will be discussed in further detail in chapter 10.)

Tipping Etiquette

Many years ago, my brother Tom taught me the importance of tipping your bartender. If you want to be waited on a second time by a bartender in a busy bar you had better learn to tip, he advised me. I have never forgotten that valuable piece of advice. Bartenders *do* wait on known high tippers before waiting on stiffs who do not tip properly.

Sociologists, among others, teach the importance of cultural etiquette and the importance of realizing that some workers depend on their tips more than on their salaries as a means of paying bills. Many clueless patrons fail to tip properly.

Seinfeld taught its viewers the importance of tipping etiquette in the episode "The Airport" (#52); Elaine and Jerry discuss the proper tip for a baggage guy outside the airport. So, Jerry asks the guy. He replies that he usually gets $5 a bag. Jerry thinks $10 for 3 bags seems fair and pays the baggage handler. Elaine, complaining about tipping, refuses to tip the guy. Of course, now that the baggage guy is upset, he purposively sends Elaine's bag to the wrong destination. Jerry's bags arrive safely.

In one of my favorite episodes, "The Trip (Part 2)" (#42), George and Jerry discuss how much of a tip they are supposed to leave for the hotel maid. Jerry and George are in Los Angeles for Jerry's appearance on the "Tonight Show." When the maid, Lupe, comes into their room, George asks her not to tuck in the corners of the bedspread. Lupe, responding in broken English, attempts to demonstrate that she knows why George has made such a request by saying, "It's too tight." George agrees, yes, it is too tight. (Anyone who has ever slept in a hotel bed knows how tight the maids make the bed—they *are* too tight.) Feeling that he has developed a rapport with the maid, George wants to make sure they leave Lupe the proper tip amount.

Later in the episode, Jerry and George are riding in the back seat of a police car—they have information on the "Smog Strangler," reported by the police and media to be Kramer, when they are joined by a criminal suspect (Tobias) that the police have just arrested on a "possible 519." George and Jerry are uncomfortable sitting next to Tobias and they engage him with some small talk. First they talk about the weather and then George asks Tobias how much he tips a chamber maid.

> *Tobias*: "I don't know, five bucks a night."
> *Jerry*: "No, a dollar, two tops."
> *Tobias*: "A dollar a night?"
> *Jerry*: "Yeah, that's a good tip!"
> *Tobias*: "That stinks!"
> *Jerry*: "I read it in Ann Landers."
> *Tobias*: "Oh, Ann Landers sucks."

As it turns out, when the police make an arrest on Kramer as the suspected "Smog Strangler," Tobias escapes from the back of the police car. Tobias later becomes the number one suspect when Kramer is cleared. In the evening news a description of Tobias includes that he is 5'5", bald, and "reputably, a very generous tipper."

When Jerry and George return to New York, George mentions to Jerry that he was really disappointed in Lupe. George was upset because he lost a bet to Jerry on whether or not Lupe would remember not to tuck in George's bed sheets. Lupe did tuck in George's sheets (which meant Jerry won the bet), so it was George's obligation as the loser to leave the tip. When Jerry asked George how much of a tip he left, George yelled out in shame that he forgot to tip her.

In most cases, leaving a tip is a rather simple behavior. The most common tipping situations involve restaurants or food delivery. The tip money is included with the money to pay the bill. This makes it easy for the provider of the service to realize that a tip was left for them. However, there are times when leaving a tip is not acknowledged by the person intending to receive it. For example, in the episode "The Calzone" (#130), George leaves money in a tip jar, but the counter guy does not see George do it and actually thinks that George failed to tip him. George is aware of this. So, on his next visit to the restaurant to pick up calzones (for himself and New York Yankees owner George Steinbrenner) George wants to make sure that the guy sees him put the tip in the jar. But just as George does place the tip in the jar, the counter guy turns away. Having already established that George is rather cheap, he does not leave another tip, but instead makes a major violation of a cultural norm and reaches into the tip jar to "re-tip" the counter guy with his same money. The counter guy, of course, thinks that George is stealing from him and kicks him out of the store, banning him permanently.

To further complicate the tipping etiquette issue, there are many situations where people are unsure what type of tip, if any, is to be offered to various service people. It seems as though when people bring food to your house you are supposed to tip them. But what about when people bring other objects? Are we supposed to tip the UPS guy? What if it's a delivery of a gift, does that matter? Elaine seems to believe that if the object being delivered is heavy and makes the delivery person sweat, that a cold drink should at least be offered. In the episode "The Couch" (#91), delivery men carry a couch to Jerry's apartment. Kramer asks Jerry whether or not he offered them a drink. Jerry did not realize he was supposed to. Elaine points out to Jerry that they are men and they were sweating, which led Jerry to deduce from Elaine's thought process that any sweaty men who come into your house should be offered a drink.

In "The Robbery" (#3), Jerry is looking at an apartment that George is showing. Elaine joins them. She is impressed with the apartment. It has a fireplace. Jerry wonders how he is going to get the wood to burn in the fireplace up to his apartment. George replies that someone will deliver it. Jerry wonders whether or not he has to tip them? Elaine then notices that there is a garden in the outdoor patio. Jerry points out that he will need a gardener. Again he wonders, do I have to tip them? How much do I tip these guys?

Nobody seems to really know all the occasions that tipping is required. And, when tipping is required, what is the proper amount? It appears that only the restaurant business has a clear-cut education program designed to inform patrons of tipping expectations: 15 to 20 percent is the standard, the norm. Now, if only all these other service entities could just get as organized and inform us, the public, as to the proper tipping etiquette we would all know how to handle each situation. After all, Ann Landers and sociologists can't be around all the time to tell us what constitutes proper behavior!

Language and Culture

A critical aspect of culture is language. Language refers to words and their pronunciation, and the set of symbols by which people who share a common culture communicate. Language not only includes words and symbols but also gestures and other nonverbal forms of communication. Sharing a common language is a sign of cultural unity. Language is also used by subcultural groups who wish to distinguish themselves from others by using words that have meaning only to group members. For example, gang members use a variety of terms, expressions (e.g., what "set" are you with?), and symbols as a means of identifying in-group members and out-group members.

Language makes it possible for members of society to effectively transmit cultural expectations from one generation to the next. As sociologist Diana Kendall explains, "Verbal (spoken) language and nonverbal (written or gestured) language help us describe reality. One of our most important human attributes is the ability to use language to share our experiences, feelings, and knowledge with others."[4] Language allows us, then, to create visual images in our minds so that we can comprehend what others are expressing to us. It is especially useful in the development and conveying of abstract thought.

Linguistic relativity theorists (people who examine the structure of language) argue that language not only allows us to express our thoughts to others, it actually shapes our perception of reality. For example, when people say that a gasoline can is "empty" they come to think of it as "safe." Thus, someone may light a cigarette around an "empty" gas can believing that no harm may occur. However, gas fumes may still exist in the can and ignite when the cigarette is lit. Consequently, the word "empty" shaped the perception of the person who lit the cigarette who believed that it was safe to do so.

Seinfeld has introduced a number of words to popular culture. (In fact, in 1993, Jerry Seinfeld published a book titled *SeinLanguage*.) To the millions of *Seinfeld* fans, the very mention of certain terms, such as "Festivus," "man hands," "close talker," and "Schmoopy" conjure images of some of their favorite episodes.

SeinLanguage

Some of the words introduced by *Seinfeld* were used in connection with a previously discussed subject: gift giving. In the episode "The Label Maker" (#98), a number of terms are introduced:

- *Re-gifter*—someone who uses a gift they received as a gift for a third person.
- *Re-cycled gift*—the gift that the re-gifter used.
- *De-gifting*—when the gift giver asks for their gift back.
- *Gift grace period*—a period of time where a gift giver is allowed to ask for his gift back from the person he gave it to.

In "The Label Maker" episode Elaine had given Tim Whatley a label maker as a gift. Whatley (the re-gifter) is not impressed with the label maker (the re-cycled gift) and gives it to Jerry as a new gift. Jerry gives Tim Super Bowl tickets as a gift because he cannot use them. He then asks for the tickets back, attempting to de-gift. George suggests that there should be a gift grace period on such gifts in case the gift giver wants the gift back.

In the episodes "The Raincoats, 1 (#82)" and "The Raincoats, 2 (#83)," the term "close talker" is introduced. Elaine's boyfriend, Aaron, while talking with others, stands extremely close to the person he is talking with. As Jerry states, he is not maintaining proper "personal space." Jerry believes that people should always maintain a proper "conversational distance" from one another.

Jerry uses the term "the coup de toe" in "The Tape" (#25). The coup de toe refers to one of Jerry's stand up routines that George had suggested to him. George had described the fact that with some people the second toe is bigger than the big toe. Typically the big toe is the captain of the toes. However, whenever the second toe is larger, the big toe must watch out for "the coup de toe."

In several episodes of *Seinfeld*, the expression "It's in the vault" is used. The meaning of this phrase is to symbolically represent the fact that when someone asks you to keep certain information to yourself, and that you must not reveal that information to anyone, under any condition, you place that information in your own personal vault. This is not done literally of course; it simply means that you are telling someone that their secret is safe with you because you have locked it up in your memory vault.

The terms "shiksa" and "Shiksappeal" are used in the episode "The Serenity Now" (#159). A shiksa is a non-Jewish woman. Shiksappeal is a quality that non-Jewish females have that attracts Jewish men and teenage boys. Elaine has this quality and in "The Serenity Now" episode a number of Jewish males express a desire for her. Jerry explains that Jewish men love the idea of dating a woman who is not like their mothers. In "The Frogger" (#174) episode, Jerry breaks up with his girlfriend because she is a "sentence finisher." You know those people, the ones who find it necessary to finish your statement because they assume a certain conclusion to your line of thinking. The "low talker" remains as one of the all-time classics in *Seinfeld* folklore. Because Kramer's girlfriend spoke so softly (a low talker), Jerry inadvertently agrees to wear a puffy shirt on a *Today Show* appearance in the appropriately named "The Puffy Shirt" (#66) episode.

Seinfeld *Lives On*

While listening to the radio one morning in November 2004, I heard a DJ (on the Syracuse radio station KROQ, 106.5) mention that he relates all of his life references to *Seinfeld* episodes. I know how he feels! While researching this book, it was amazing how many times my daily conversations (and corresponding stories) with others were related to *Seinfeld* episodes. Equally amazing was the reality that so many people I interact with understand these references.

In fact, many people, including those found in the entertainment field, utilize *SeinLanguage* as a means of conveying their thoughts. For example, on ESPN, an announcer used the term "man hands" to describe good glove work in the outfield as a player made an outstanding catch of a batted ball. In another story on ESPN, an announcer used the term "Second Spitter" (a parody of the movie *JFK* and the use of the term "second shooter") while describing an incident involving Houston Astros pitcher Roger Clemens. Clemens was accused of spitting at an umpire during his son's little league game in summer 2004. He claimed that someone else spit at the umpire— thus the "second spitter" reference.

One announcer described a great tennis player (Andy Roddick) as a "master of his domain" (a term used in *Seinfeld* for someone who was able to control his sexual self-gratification). Yet again on ESPN, the term "close talkers" was used to describe an incident where an umpire and manager were yelling at each other face-to-face.

Regis and Kelly often reference *Seinfeld*. (Regis and Jerry are close friends in real life.) Regis mentioned on one of their shows that the owner of the real soup place referenced on *Seinfeld,* as being run by a "Soup Nazi," was starting a chain of soup shops. *Seinfeld* helped to make the soup store owner famous. On another episode of *Regis and Kelly* (Regis's birthday), Kelly's boob almost fell out of her top. Regis smiled with approval and Kelly stated, "I'm re-gifting this year!" In yet another episode, Kelly told a trivia contest winner of the show that if she did not like the gift, "[She] can always 're-gift' it if [she] want[s]!"

These are just a few examples of the impact of *Seinfeld* in contemporary society. *Seinfeld* has not changed American culture, but it has had an impact; for some this influence is relatively significant. *Seinfeld* is now firmly a part of American culture.

Chapter 3

Socialization and Personal Relationships

"Tub Is Love."—Jerry

Imagine having the same name as someone famous, like Jennifer Lopez or Jon Voight. Simple chores such as making hotel reservations ultimately lead to awkward conversations where one has to explain, "I am not *that* Jennifer Lopez." In the episode "The Masseuse" (#73), Elaine dates a man with an infamous name, Joel Rifkin. When this episode first aired in 1993, the news was filled with reports of a Joel Rifkin from Long Island who was a mass murderer. In this *Seinfeld* episode it was reported that he murdered eighteen prostitutes. (As an interesting note, I knew the "real" Joel Rifkin before he became a mass murderer because we attended the same undergraduate college.) Elaine becomes self-conscious dating someone named Joel Rifkin because of the reactions from others when they hear her mention his name. Her office mates tease her about being careful.

Initially, Joel is unaware of the controversy that surrounds his name, but that all changes at a New York Giants football game. Joel had left a ticket for Kramer at the will call window; but Kramer forgot his identification. As a result, the only way the will call attendant will give Kramer the ticket is if the original owner, Joel Rifkin, personally identifies him. The attendant calls the public address announcer, who in turn blares a message throughout Giants Stadium asking for "Joel Rifkin to report to the Stadium Office." The camera scans the audience, and everyone, including Giants player Lawrence Taylor, displays a look of grave concern over the mere hearing of Rifkin's name. Elaine's boyfriend stands up and asks aloud who would be calling him at Giants Stadium? Elaine proclaims that her date is not *that* Joel Rifkin, the murderer. Later, Joel and Elaine try to come up with different first names for Rifkin, but they cannot agree on any of them. Shortly afterward, they break up.

Dating someone with a "troubling" name is just one problem associated with sustaining a personal relationship. As we will see in this chapter, maintaining quality relationships is a difficult challenge.

The Socialization Process

In chapter 2 we learned about the importance of culture. It is culture that determines the ideals of proper behavior and etiquette. But how do individuals learn about society's cultural expectations? The simple answer is *socialization*. Most living animals rely on biological instincts in order to survive in their environment. Humans, on the other hand, are dependent upon social experience and interaction with others in order to learn how to best adapt to their cultural environment. Social interaction with others is a critical element of the "socialization process." It is through the socialization process that we learn about the norms, values, and beliefs of society.

As sociologist John Macionis explains, "Sociologists use the term 'socialization' to refer to the lifelong social experience by which individuals develop their human potential and learn culture."[5] Socialization is a life-long process where each of us learns, through interaction with others, the important things we must know in order to survive and properly function in society. In other words, life is filled with "lessons" that each of us must learn if we are to "survive" and flourish in society.

Clearly, socialization is an important element in human development. In fact, without significant social interaction with others, we would not quite be "human." Research on feral children (those raised in social isolation), for example, reveals the importance of socialization. If a young child is not properly nurtured (generally by a loving mother or caretaker), he or she risks never developing basic human skills, such as the use of language and bodily function control. The 1994 movie *Nell*, featuring Jodie Foster as a young woman hidden from birth by her mother in a backwoods cabin, provides a portrayal of what a real-case scenario of a child raised in isolation would be like.[6] Also see François Truffaut's *The Wild Child*.

Agents of Socialization

Sources of culture are known as agents of socialization. Agents of social-ization are the social influences (both people and institutions) in our lives that shape each of us. The initial agent of socialization in a child's life is, of course, the family (or guardian). The family is the most impor-tant influence on a young child and, therefore, serves a critical function in early development. Family, especially parents, defines the attitudes, values, and beliefs of a young child. This early period of influence is so important that sociologists refer to it as primary socialization.

Once a child enters school, she has entered the phase of develop-ment known as secondary socialization. While in school, the child is potentially exposed to a vast array of different ideas and beliefs from those who are taught at home. It is the responsibility of the school to teach youngsters the values and customs of the greater society. In addition, it is at this time when the child begins to form friendship attachments to peer group members. The child may come to value the opinions of peers over that of the family. Friends are very impor-tant to all of us, and especially so for children.

There are many other agents of socialization, including the media, religion, government, and employers. In short, every one of us interacts with others (agents of socialization) who have expecta-tions of our behavior.

Socialization and the Development of Self

Although we are all influenced by social forces, sociologists recognize that individuals have unique personalities. Each of us reacts uniquely to similar stimuli, and some people learn different life lessons during their interactions with the agents of socialization. Because of our life experiences we develop a *sense of self*.

The self is the identity that individuals develop; it's what distin-guishes humans from one another. Sociologists and psychologists have created a number of theories regarding the development of self. Among the more significant contributions to this area of study was that presented by George Herbert Mead. According to Mead, the self is something which has a development; it is not initially there at birth, but arises in the process of social experience and activity. The developmental process of the self is not biological, but rather it emerges from social forces and social experiences.[7]

The development of self is critical for the creation of conscious-ness and the ability of the child to take the role of the other and to visualize his or her own performances from the point of view of others. Mead believed that the development of self takes place through stages: imitation, play, game, and the generalized other.[8] Infants learn to imitate the behaviors of others. They mimic the encouraging sounds and gestures made by their parents. During the play stage children learn to role play; that is, they "play" being mom or dad. At the game stage of development the child has learned to take the role of multiple others at the same time (e.g., knowing the roles of all his baseball teammates). The game stage of development is particularly important because the individual has learned to abide by the rules of the game (society) and has the ability to exercise self-control. The final stage of development is the generalized other. At this point the individual has taken on the attitudes of the greater community, or society.

Mead is just one of many social thinkers to propose a theory of the development of self. Nearly all such theories agree on the impor-tance of social interaction with significant others. In chapter 10, the role of family will be explored, and in chapter 4 attention will be placed on the many different relationships people have with one another. In this chapter, the primary personal relationship to be explored is that of boyfriend/girlfriend.

Personal Relationships

Sociology teaches us that personal relationships are an essential aspect of human behavior. Meaningful contact with others helps to build a sense of community among fellows. It also helps to establish an individual's identity. An individual's self-esteem is also directly tied to relationships with significant others. Loving, nurturing, healthy, and positive experiences with significant others greatly assist the personal development of individuals. Positive bonding experiences lead to high levels of self-esteem. Conversely, negative personal relationships harm and damage the self-esteem and self-concept of an injured individual.

The subject area of personal relationships is a common theme in *Seinfeld*, and for good reason, as every one of us can relate to the trials and tribulations of dating. Some dates are successful and others are disastrous. Utilizing the *sociological imagination* (a means of gaining insights and understanding about the social world that other forms of reasoning fail to accomplish) we learn that many of the failures (and successes) experienced by individuals are felt to be unique, while in actuality they are experiences shared by numerous others. The use of the sociological imagination is beneficial for understanding a wide variety of events and behaviors that occur throughout our lives. This is certainly true when applied to the study of personal relationships.

The Relationship Quiz

An obstacle that many people have shared occurs during the early stages of a relationship. Namely, at what point during the dating process has a relationship formed? In other words, when do we "label" our dating a "relationship"? People who are happy with the early stages of dating often find themselves caught using labels, such as "boyfriend" or "girlfriend," when telling their friends about the person they are dating because they think that their relationship is serious enough to justify that label. But such a label may be presumptuous as the other person may not share the same sentiments. In addition, when exactly does a "dating relationship" evolve into a "committed relationship"?

The allocation and continuous use of labels represents an attempt to manipulate the situation. Symbolic interactionist theorists remind us that everyone attempts to negotiate their role identity. As Erving Goffman explains in his classic book *The Presentation of Self in Everyday Life* (1959), the "self label" is an identity that one presents to others in an attempt to manage their impression of self. Individuals will deliberately give off signs (e.g., clothing, facial expressions) to provide others with information about how others should "see" them.

Perhaps if there were some sort of a sociological relationship quiz available to couples a lot of the guess work related to the "where are we?" issue would be resolved. In the episode "The Virgin" (#50), Jerry introduces his relationship quiz. George has been dating Susan for a relatively short period of time. George admits to Jerry that he is interested in dating other women and seeks Jerry's advice. Primarily, George is wondering whether or not he is in a real relationship with Susan. Jerry gives George a "Relationship Quiz" to determine if Susan is George's girlfriend, or just a woman that he is dating. Jerry asks about the frequency of phone calls. Is the Saturday night date implied or asked? Does she have stuff in his medicine cabinet? And the ultimate question, does she keep tampons at his apartment? Based on George's responses, that they talk regularly on the phone, the Saturday night date is implied, and she keeps many items, including tampons, at his place (why would a bachelor have Tampax in his apartment otherwise?), Jerry proclaims, "You got a girlfriend!" Thus, based on George's responses to Jerry's quiz, George's involvement with Susan is labeled a relationship.

In a later episode, "The Mango" (#65), George and Jerry again discuss criteria to determine whether or not someone is in a relationship. George is dating a woman named Karen. Jerry quizzes George again, this time concentrating on the issue of cleanliness. Jerry asks George if he cleans up the apartment before she comes over for a date. George acknowledges that he does. Jerry continues his line of questioning: Do you clean the tub? On your knees? With Ajax? George admits that he does. Jerry responds, "Tub is love!" George repeats Jerry's words, "Tub *is* love." Thus, if you clean the tub because your girlfriend is coming over, you are in love. Jerry admits that this can be a good thing; after all, you have a nice girl and a clean apartment. Of course, most males stop cleaning around the house once they are in a relationship!

Starting a Relationship

Relationships begin with a first date. First dates come easily for some. Jerry once met a woman on an elevator. First dates are more difficult for other people. In fact, some people rely on fix-ups or blind dates.

In the opening monologue of "The Fix-up" (#33), Jerry addresses the issue of the fix-up and asks, "Why do we fix people up?" The answer is, we feel good about ourselves and, frankly, it's a power trip. Jerry suggests that God was the first to fix someone up. According to Jerry, God said to Adam, in regard to Eve, "She was going out with the snake, but I think that's over."

George expresses his worries to Jerry that he may never meet a woman again, especially one that he'll really like. George has become so frustrated with his life that he wishes he could just give up hope. "Hope is killing me. Hopelessness is best. When you don't have hope anymore you become attractive because you don't care."

Elaine's friend Cynthia is complaining to her that she can't find a guy. Cynthia believes that all the good guys are taken. The mediocre ones are so insecure about themselves that they complain that they are not good enough to date the woman willing to be with them. Cynthia adds that, eventually, "I just agree with them"—they are not good enough to be with her. Elaine comments to Cynthia that she is too young to be so bitter. Cynthia disagrees, "No, I'm bitter now, but not as bitter as I'll be in ten years."

This episode provides the typical portrayal of what goes on "behind the scenes" of a "fix-up." Jerry and Elaine get together the next day and discuss their respective evenings out. Eventually they conclude that maybe they should fix George and Cynthia up for a date. Both Jerry and Elaine believe that their "candidate" is the better of the two and therefore has more to offer in the potential, impending relationship.

Jerry informs George of his intent. Predictably, George wants details concerning Cynthia. What does she do? Ever married? Hair? Looks? And so on . . .

Meanwhile, Elaine is doing the same thing with Cynthia. Elaine attempts to present George's positive attributes. Cynthia asks most of the same questions as George. Elaine had to admit that George is currently unemployed because he tried to poison his last boss and that he was overweight and balding.

They both agree to the fix-up and George calls Cynthia on the phone. George meets with Jerry to share the details. He loves her voice. He has great hope for the date because he felt that the phone conversation went very well. He's ready to go! George and Cynthia have sex on the very first date. They agree not to mention anything to Elaine and Jerry. Of course, best friends tell friends everything, so George tells Jerry all the details and Cynthia tells Elaine the whole story. George and Cynthia swear their friends to secrecy.

Behind the scenes, Elaine and Jerry had agreed to share all the details that their respective friends shared with them. But now they have a commitment requirement to their friends. Initially both Elaine and Jerry play coy with one another.

They finally spill the beans to each other because they are fighting. Jerry takes George's side of the story. Jerry wants to know why Cynthia never called him back after the first and only date. Much to Jerry's surprise, Elaine informs Jerry that Cynthia missed her period. At that very moment, George walks into Jerry's apartment and overhears Elaine telling Jerry that Cynthia is pregnant. George is ecstatic and proclaims, "My boys can swim!" It is a proud moment for George, who now fantasizes of being a father. Later, George tells Cynthia that he will stick by her no matter what. Cynthia is happy to hear that George will stand by her and begins to fall for him. It turns out she is not pregnant. The show ends with the four of them going out to dinner together. But George eats like a pig and Cynthia is obviously disgusted by his lack of table manners.

The behind-the-scenes ploy utilized by Elaine and George in "The Fix-up" reflects the *dramaturgical* perspective (an attempt to explain human interaction by comparing life to a staged drama) found in sociology. This theoretical perspective resembles Shakespeare's famous quote, "Life is but a stage and we are all merely players." Dramaturgy, as articulated by Erving Goffman, states that all of us perform roles, like actors in a play.[9] All individuals perform many roles, such as student, sibling, employee, athlete, and friend. In an attempt to convey our role to others, we utilize various props and present ourselves in a deliberate manner. As already stated, Goffman, and other sociologists, believes that we have a front-stage persona and a back-stage persona. Elaine and Jerry present (performance) a front stage to George and Cynthia all the while talking behind their backs (back-stage persona).

The Relationship Barometer

There are certain tell-tale signs that indicate whether or not a relationship is going well. There are times when people outside the relationship have a better understanding about a troubled relationship than those actually involved. For example, in the episode "The Wallet" (#45), Jerry mentions that there is a sure sign "relationship barometer." When someone is asked about his relationship, he reaches for his body. The higher up the body that someone touches, the worse the relationship. Thus, if someone scratches their mouth area, the relationship is a little shaky. If they reach for their nose or eyes, the relationship is bad. And, if someone scratches the top of their head, well, their relationship is so rocky that it is either about to end, or they wish that it would end.

Another relationship barometer is one's position on the speed dial. Speed dial location tells the person you are dating just how much you think of them. The higher up the list, the stronger your relationship. Assumingly, the person you love the most would be number one.

In the episode "The Millennium" (#154), Jerry is dating a woman named Valerie. After two dates, he is number seven on the speed dial. George tells Jerry how good that is. After all, it's a pain to change a phone's preset numbers: you have to lift the little plastic cover, dial in the numbers, and so forth. After a so-so date, Jerry is dropped to number nine. Jerry blames it on his poor choice of restaurants.

Valerie's stepmother, Mrs. Hamilton, is threatened by Jerry's relationship with Valerie. Not because he is a bad influence on her or anything like that, but because she is worried over Jerry's potential acceleration up the speed dial. She does not want to be replaced by him. So, Mrs. Hamilton invites Jerry to her apartment under false pretense. She flirts with Jerry and offers him wine. She then lists Jerry as number three on her speed dial. When Valerie sees this she is really upset. In retaliation, Valerie takes her stepmom off the speed dial. Valerie will only place her back on the speed dial if she removes Jerry's number from her presets. Mrs. Hamilton agrees. But she "secretly" hides it under an emergency number listing; one that she assumes she will never have to use. However, Mrs. Hamilton is unsuspectingly poisoned (by Kramer of all people, but that's a different story!). Back in her apartment, Mrs. Hamilton feels progressively worse. So, Valerie calls "Poison Control" from the speed dial. When Jerry answers the phone Valerie is upset with her stepmother because she realizes that Jerry's number was hidden under "Poison Control." Jerry reacts happily because "Poison Control" on the speed dial is even higher than #1. Angrily, Valerie hangs up on him.

Seinfeld *Characters and Their Personal Relationships*

The four main characters of *Seinfeld* had numerous relationships over the nine-year run of the show. Jerry seemed to have a new girlfriend every episode. George, despite his many shortcomings, was once involved in a long-term relationship that led to an engagement. Even so, George still managed to date quite a few women. Elaine was involved with David Puddy off and on for years. But she, too, dated a lot of different men. Kramer's relationships were not as well documented as the other three and yet we learned of many of them.

A number of sociological insights are brought forth in the examination of the personal relationships of Jerry, Kramer, George, and Elaine. A sociological analysis reveals that, although we, the general public, may not have experienced the exact same situations as the four main characters of *Seinfeld*, we have all experienced many of the same general relationship obstacles and rewards.

Jerry's Relationships

Jerry dated many women. He never seemed to mind that his relationships were rather shallow and brief. He knew that when one relationship ended another one would begin shortly after. During the nine-year run of *Seinfeld*, Jerry dated over one hundred women, and nearly all of his relationships ended quickly.

The pilot episode, "Good News, Bad News" (#1), set the tone for the show. Namely, that it is a show about relationships as much as anything else. The pilot also made it clear that the characters on the show were going to have numerous challenges in their relationships. In the pilot, Jerry receives "mixed" messages from Laura, a political-science professor that he met at one of his comedy shows on the road. They had a great conversation and exchanged names and phone numbers. Laura calls Jerry to tell him that she will be coming to New York for a seminar, but that she would have some free time and would love to get together with him. She calls him a second time to ask if she can stay at his place.

George and Jerry discuss the implications of this. Does that mean she wants to sleep with him or just "crash" at his apartment? Many of us have been in this situation. What does it mean when someone asks to stay at your place overnight? Is sex implied, or is it just a sign of friendship? Not wanting to look like he is assuming anything, Jerry and George bring an extra bed into his apartment. Kramer wonders why Jerry would even give her the option of sleeping on an extra bed. Jerry informs Kramer that he respects Laura.

George tells Jerry that he has to look for "signs" of her intention. Jerry resents the fact that he now has to act like a detective, looking for clues and signals. Many readers can relate to this dilemma. Why are relationships so difficult? Why can't people simply tell others of their intentions? George assures Jerry that he'll know of her intentions based on the airport greeting. If the greeting is a handshake then you know you are just friends. A hug is good. A kiss is even better. George rides to the airport with Jerry to help him read the signs. While they discuss last minute strategies, Laura surprises Jerry by coming up from behind, covering his eyes, and saying, "Guess who?" George and Jerry look at each other dumbfounded. They had not planned an interpretation of "The surprise blind-fold greeting."

Back at Jerry's apartment, he is still looking for signs of her intentions. He asks Laura if she wants something to drink. She responds that wine would be nice. Jerry thinks this is a good sign. She then asks if it is okay to dim the lights, which he also sees as a good sign. Laura asks Jerry if after her seminar in the morning they could do touristy things. Thinking he is going to "get some," Jerry agrees to a five-hour boat ride around Manhattan. This is something, of course, that he would not commit to with just a friend. Jerry thinks all the signs are in his favor. The phone rings. Laura has left Jerry's phone number with friends just in case they needed to get a hold of her. The caller is Laura's fiancé. Jerry is understandably upset. Laura has an argument with her boyfriend; it seems he is jealous and concerned that she is staying at Jerry's apartment while she is in New York City, instead of a hotel. She gets off the phone and tells Jerry, "Never get engaged." Jerry is visibly upset as anyone in his position would be. At this rate, Jerry will never get engaged—although he will be engaged for a short period of time in a later episode ("The Invitations," #134).

When we date someone, it is nice if our friends approve (peer approval is something generally valued by most people) and get along with each other. After all, as the relationship develops, it begins to intrude into the other already established relationships with friends and family. In the episode "The Van Buren Boys" (#148), Jerry is dating an extremely attractive woman named Ellen. Their first date was on her birthday, which Jerry thinks is a little odd. When they leave the restaurant they run into a group of Ellen's friends. When Ellen excuses herself to check for phone messages, the girlfriends act like Jerry is doing some type of charity work taking her out. No one left Ellen any messages.

George and Jerry discuss the implications of this later in Jerry's apartment. Why wouldn't she be celebrating her birthday with her friends or family? George wonders if she is socially inept, or if maybe she is the loser of the group. Jerry is convinced she could not be the loser of the group. In his mind she is nearly perfect. So now, he searches for flaws. But she apparently has none. George and Kramer eventually meet Ellen and their reaction is that of shock—why would

Jerry date this woman? They keep their negative concerns to themselves. But when Jerry mentions that he wants to go away with Ellen on a little vacation, Kramer and George do an "intervention."

Jerry is shocked by their negative comments about Ellen. He believes that she is very attractive. Jerry even flies his parents up from Florida to meet Ellen. They love her. They think she is sweet, cute, and smart. Interestingly, *now* Jerry is turned off from Ellen and decides to call an old girlfriend.

In the episode "The Strike" (#166), Jerry is dating a "two-face" woman named Gwen. Jerry met Gwen at Tim Whatley's Happy Hanukkah party. At the party she looked hot. In different lighting she looked ugly. Every time they get together he's not sure which woman will show up. Jerry thinks she looks the best at the back booth of the coffee shop, so they eat there all time. Gwen is a little suspicious of this and thinks Jerry might be hiding something, like a wife or another girlfriend. When Jerry's friends meet her, she is the ugly version, and they suggest to Jerry that he break up with her.

Friends can interfere with relationships inadvertently. In the episode "The Bubble Boy" (#47), Jerry is dating a woman named Naomi, who has an obnoxious laugh. After a date, Jerry brings her home to his apartment and decides to check phone messages in front of her—a potentially dangerous thing to do, because you never know what your friend's messages are going to be. In this case, George has left a message about her laugh. Naomi is upset and storms off.

Jerry did have some "successful" relationships. Among the women he seemed to care for the most was Sheila (a.k.a. Schmoopy). Jerry dated Sheila in "The Soup Nazi" (#116) episode. They are all lovey-dovey and have the same pet nickname for each other, Schmoopy. (Note: Schmoopy is one of those unique words utilized in the *Seinfeld* language that have entered popular culture. Schmoopy refers to disgustingly romantic displays of affection.) Elaine and George, in particular, find their outward display of affection rather sickening. They want to say something to Jerry, but they don't know how to tell him that his relationship with Sheila is making them uncomfortable.

Jerry and Sheila are at the coffee shop. They are sitting on the same side of the booth, instead of across from each other. George and Susan walk into the diner. George can't help but say something to Jerry. Hoping to demonstrate how distasteful their public display of affection really is, George begins to use "baby talk" while conversing with Susan. Susan finds this side of George refreshing and continues with the emotional and physical display of affection. Before long, and in an effort to outdo each other, the two couples are making out like horny teenagers! The manager of the diner comes over and tells them to calm down. Inevitably, this relationship fails by the end of the episode.

Another gorgeous woman that Jerry dated and later dumped under unusual circumstances was Jenna. In the episode "The Pothole" (#150), after spending the night together (implied), Jenna and Jerry are in her bathroom brushing their teeth. As Jenna turns away momentarily to get a towel, Jerry accidentally drops her toothbrush into the toilet. Jerry, a cleanliness fanatic, reaches into the toilet bowl to retrieve the toothbrush and sets in down on the sink counter. He washes his hands and before he can say anything to Jenna, he looks up and she is brushing her teeth again, with the contaminated toothbrush. Looking adorable, Jenna gives Jerry a big smile. But Jerry is disgusted. When he leaves her apartment, Jerry refuses to kiss her goodbye. Jerry explains to her that he thinks he's coming down with a cold and doesn't want to give her his germs.

All Jerry can do is think about her brushing her teeth with a germ-infested toothbrush and the fact that it was his fault and he never told her about it. Without a proper explanation, Jerry buys her a new toothbrush and the mouthwash Plax, which he cut with bleach. And still he cannot kiss her. As Jerry later explained to Elaine, he felt that Jenna had a taint. Whenever anyone "discovers" a significant taint in the person they are dating's personality or character traits, he will generally lose interest in that person. For Jerry, the very idea that Jenna brushed her teeth with a dirty toothbrush was enough to lead him to break up with her.

Jerry had one relationship that led to an engagement. Somewhat distraught over George's impending wedding and Elaine's comment that she was tired of the single life, Jerry is feeling a little down. In a semi-daze, he walks into the street and almost into oncoming traffic. Out of nowhere, a woman arrives and saves him. She introduces herself to Jerry as Jeannie Steinman.

They hit it off right away. His daze is now caused by love. Later, Jerry informs Kramer that he thinks he's in love. He tells him all about her wonderful qualities. They share the same interests, they act alike, and they even have the same initials. Then it dawns on Jerry, he finally realized what he was looking for all these years: someone just like himself. Jerry states, "I've been waiting for me to come along and now that I have, I've swept myself off my feet." This freaks Kramer out.

Jerry and Jeannie's relationship gets stronger and stronger in a very short period of time. Jerry asks Jeannie to marry him and she says yes. They celebrate by drinking champagne at a restaurant-bar. Jerry is happily in love and proud of himself for keeping his pact with his best friend George (a reference to an earlier episode when Jerry and George agreed to grow up and act like responsible men). Before long, however, Jerry tires of dating someone so similar to himself. Jeannie is having the same doubts as Jerry and interestingly, they break up with each other simultaneously (the famed "mutual" breakup that Jerry had tested for believability during his focus group research study). And thus ends the most "promising" relationship that Jerry would ever have on the show.

George's Relationships

George had the most committed and long-lasting loving personal relationship of the four main characters. He dated Susan, off and on, for years and was only a tragic death away from marrying her.

George met Susan for the first time in the episode "The Pitch" (#43). Jerry and George are "pitching" their sitcom ideas to NBC executives, and Susan is one of them. After their pitch meeting, George tells Jerry that he wants to ask Susan out on a date. She later agrees. She is in favor of the sitcom idea, so now George and Jerry have an "inside" track toward getting it signed. Unfortunately for Susan, she will come to suffer through a series of misfortunes, including death, because of her relationship with George.

The bad luck begins the first time George brings Susan over to Jerry's apartment and Kramer throws up on her. Kramer was also responsible for later (in "The Bubble Boy," #47) burning down Susan's family cabin. Among the few items that survived the fire was a safety box of personal letters to Susan's father that revealed he had a gay lover whom he met at the cabin on a regular basis. This love affair put Susan's whole family in a state of shock.

George's relationship with Susan is interrupted by a breakup and Susan's experimentation with lesbianism. Eventually they reunite, form a committed relationship with one another, and became engaged. Unfortunately, George begins to regret all of this. He is used to talking endlessly about meaningless topics with Jerry but Susan has less patience. In "The Postponement" (#112), George gets extremely offended when Susan asks him if they can change the subject. They had been discussing the length of bathroom doors in public restrooms.

George discusses Susan's "rude" comment with Jerry. George and Jerry believe that a conversation should come to an end naturally, after all angles have been discussed. Certainly, not so rudely as, "Can we change the subject?" George wonders how he can even be in a relationship with someone that could make such a comment.

George is stressed about his impending marriage, but the comment was the last straw for him. Jerry suggests a postponement of the wedding, which is an idea George loves. When George proposes it to Susan she takes it very badly and begins to cry. Responding poorly to the sight of his girlfriend crying, George, like most men, caves in.

After his initial attempt to convince Susan for a wedding delay, George decides to try once again. This time, however, George cries and Susan relents and agrees to the postponement. With the postponement relieving some of George's stress, the relationship continues. As with all relationships, it is filled with tests of loyalty and commitment. George is still desperately trying to hold onto his "independence" in a variety of methods. For example, in the episode "The Secret Code" (#117), George refuses to give Susan his secret code for his bank card. Susan doesn't think there should be any secrets between couples.

George's independence takes a real hit in "The Pool Guy" (#118). Jerry suggests to Elaine, who has no girlfriends (because, as Kramer explained, she is a "man's woman") that she ask Susan to join her at a social event that Jerry passed on. Elaine thinks it's a great idea and leaves to go ask her. Kramer informs Jerry that there's going to be trouble because George's sanctuary will be compromised. Jerry is confused by this and Kramer elaborates. George's buffer zone away from his personal relationship with Susan is his world with his friends (Jerry, Kramer, and Elaine). But if Susan enters this world, well, the worlds will collide. This is referred to as the "world's theory." The world's theory is something we can all relate to, because we all need a world of our own away from the daily demands of those who expect so much from us.

The relationship between George and Susan ends very tragically in the episode "The Invitations" (#134). George, who has already been established as a cheap man, wants to start cutting costs on the wedding. Susan agrees to buy a cheap and discontinued set of wedding invitations. They stopped making the envelopes because the glue didn't stick well.

After visiting with Jerry, and complaining that he desperately wants out of the wedding, George returns to his apartment to find Susan unconscious on the couch. She is pronounced dead at the hospital. The doctor informs George that she died because of the toxic glue on the invitations.

Elaine's Relationships

Elaine's dating pattern is somewhere in between that of George's and Jerry's. She did have a long-term relationship with David Puddy (but not to the same extent as George and Susan), and she had a number of short-term relationships like Jerry (although not as many as Jerry). For the most part, Elaine's relationships are short-lived, and at one point, the men in her life had to prove that they were "sponge-worthy" (see discussion of "The Sponge" [#119] in chapter 6).

In one relationship, Elaine lost out to two cats. In "The Stock Tip" (#5), she is dating Robert, who has two cats. She is allergic to cats and wants him to get rid of them. She seeks out Jerry and George's support on this issue. George tries to help out by saying that he doesn't think it's "right" for a guy to have cats. Elaine sneezes all the time because of the cats and eventually gives Robert an ultimatum, the cats or me. He chooses his cats.

Most people date someone near their own age; typically it is because they have more in common with each other than when dating someone much younger or older. However, there are couples who date and marry who are decades apart in age. In the episode "The Alternate Side" (#28), Elaine is dating a sixty-six-year-old man named Owen. She explains, or attempts to justify, dating someone so much older than her by saying that Owen is vibrant and works out regularly. She asks Jerry if he could ever date a sixty-six-year-old woman. Jerry comments that she would have to be *very* vibrant! Before long, Elaine decides to break up with Owen. She asks Jerry if she has to do it face to face (more rules!). Jerry asks how many times she had sex with him. Elaine admits to eight times. Jerry believes that eight times constitutes a face-to-face breakup. If it had been six times, maybe she could slide by the face-to-face breakup obligation.

Just as Elaine was ready to break up with him, Owen has a stroke. He is temporarily invalid, and she wonders what obligation she has to him. Initially she cares for him and feeds him. But she quickly loses patience with him during his recovery period and breaks up with him before he completely recovers.

In the episode "The Wallet (1)" (#45), Elaine returns from Europe with her boyfriend, Dr. Reston. She does not want to see him any longer, as he is a rather domineering person. He refuses to accept her breakup, so she plots a plan: a plan that many people have utilized at some point in their lives. She pretends to have a new boyfriend. In "The Watch (2)" (#46), Kramer pretends to be Elaine's boyfriend. Reston insists on meeting Kramer and he manages to convince Kramer that Elaine would be much better off with him.

In the episode "The Maestro" (#113), Bob Cobb, a friend of Kramer's, is a conductor for the Police Benevolence Orchestra. His self-identity is so wrapped around this position that he insists on being called "the Maestro" all the time. Bob and Kramer go over to Jerry's apartment, and Jerry refuses to call him the maestro. He insists that the title of maestro is only appropriate in specific social situations, and certainly not in personal relationships. Elaine shows up and hits it off with Bob immediately. She shares a cab ride and decides to go out to dinner with him. Kramer informs Jerry that he hurt the maestro's feelings by introducing him to Elaine as Bob Cobb instead of the maestro.

On their date together Elaine mistakenly refers to the maestro as "Bob" when the waiter shows up to take their order. The maestro sends the waiter away and informs Elaine that he *always* wants to be called the maestro. She agrees to this peculiar request, and they hit it off. They even go away to Tuscany together on a vacation. The relationship will not last long, however.

Elaine traveled to Europe with yet another man, David Puddy. Puddy appears in many episodes of *Seinfeld*, usually as Elaine's boyfriend. Puddy is also Jerry's mechanic, and later a car salesman. Elaine and Puddy broke up and reunited numerous times. The breakups were generally the result of very trivial details. For example, in "The Butter Shave" (#157), Elaine and David are in Europe on an extended vacation. On their way to the airport for the flight home, Elaine breaks up with Puddy over his fascination with the different coins of the world, especially those with holes in them.

On the flight home together, Puddy flirts with a cute girl across the aisle from his seat. Elaine tries to make Puddy jealous by talking to the guy (known only as "Vegetable Lasagna"—a nickname given to him by Elaine because of his meal) in the window seat next to her (she has the middle seat). He is asleep. But now his trip will be interfered with by Elaine and Puddy's arguments. Elaine tells Puddy that they are back together and he agrees to it. They are happy, momentarily. She reads a magazine and he just stares blankly ahead. This bothers Elaine and she asks Puddy if he wants something to read. No, he replies. Elaine asks if he plans on just staring ahead and he says yes. This bothers her so much that she breaks up with him again. This episode provides a glimpse of Elaine and Puddy's continuous, off-again, on-again relationship.

In "The Junk Mail" (#161), Elaine breaks up with Puddy and meets a man named Jack at the diner. Jack has a certain charm that is hard for Elaine to resist. His smile seems to sparkle. She introduces him to Jerry and he thinks that Jack is familiar. Later that evening, while watching television, Jerry notices that Jack is "The Wiz" on commercials for an appliance store—nobody beats the Wiz! Elaine is horrified by this revelation and breaks up with Jack when he is rehired for new commercials as the Wiz. Elaine asks Puddy to get back together but he says no and mocks her with a comment about what if they were out one night and she saw the Maytag Repairman?

Kramer's Relationships

Cosmo Kramer certainly dated his share of women. In fact, he was so alluring to women that in "The Conversion" (#75), he is called the Kavorka—another word apparently created by *Seinfeld* that means the Devil. Possessed by the kavorka, Kramer has "the lure of the animal." Latvian priests perform a type of exorcism on him (see chapter 11 for a further discussion on this topic). Despite the unheavenly attraction that Kramer possesses, less attention was given to his relationships.

Kramer seems to be a far more passionate man than Jerry or George. When he falls, he falls hard. In the episode "The Library" (#22), Kramer meets a librarian at the New York Public Library. He "romanticizes" her personal life, telling Jerry that she is a lonely woman, maybe a virgin! The librarian also falls for Kramer. She skips out of work to be with him. At the same time, Mr. Bookman, the library cop who is after Jerry for his overdue book, almost catches her at Kramer's apartment. Later, Kramer and the librarian walk hand in hand throughout the library after closing time. Mr. Bookman catches them. The library is no place for romance! Kramer never sees her again.

In the episode "The Puffy Shirt" (#66), Kramer is dating a woman named Leslie. Jerry and Elaine go out to dinner with Kramer and Leslie, but they have a hard time understanding her because she is a "low talker." A low talker is someone who speaks so softly that you cannot hear what she is saying. Tired of constantly asking, "What's that?" and "Excuse me?" Elaine and Jerry decide to simply keep nodding in agreement to whatever she says. While Kramer is in the restroom, Leslie carries on a conversation with Elaine and Jerry. They have no idea what she is saying. The next day, Kramer thanks Jerry for agreeing to wear the "puffy shirt" that she designed, on his *Today Show* appearance for charity. Jerry will come to regret helping Kramer's girlfriend, as Bryant Gumbel, the host of the *Today Show*, mocks Jerry for wearing the shirt. When Jerry admits on the air that he thought the puffy shirt was a ridiculous-looking shirt, Leslie screams. Clearly, even low talkers, when properly motivated, will have their voices heard.

In a particularly hilarious situation, Kramer and his friend Mickey meet two women at the Gap. They agree to go to dinner with them. But no "couples" match up was determined. In other words, which woman was Kramer supposed to be with, and which one was Mickey to be paired up with? The two women can't decide either. Mickey and Kramer fight over who is with whom. Jerry tells them to get to the restaurant early, sit opposite of each other, and make the girls decide, thus saving them all the heartache. Kramer and Mickey agree that's a good idea, but when they get to the restaurant, the women have done the same thing, in order to force Kramer and Mickey to decide. They are clueless and fight over chairs and cause a big scene. Eventually Mickey ends up with Karen, and before long they get married. On her wedding day, Karen informs Kramer that she always wanted Mickey.

In the episode "The Soul Mate" (#136), Kramer believes he has found the woman that he is "meant" to be with—his soul mate. Her name is Pam, but there is a complication. Isn't there always? Pam is dating Jerry, so Kramer is keeping his feelings to himself out of respect for his friendship with Jerry. The very mention of her name makes Kramer excited. When Kramer finds out that Jerry is not "gaga" over Pam he informs Jerry of his desires for Pam. After describing all of her attributes, Jerry decides that he is also "gaga" over Pam. Eventually Pam tells Jerry that she has a crush on Kramer. Kramer states: "We are soul mates." But by the end of the episode, these "soul mates" are split forever, which is a typical ending to most loving personal relationships.

Ending Personal Relationships

One of the things that we all share is that, at some point, each of us has been involved in a relationship that ended. Some endings are more harmful and painful than others. After all, the greater the "high" (the love) the greater the fall (the breakup). When someone is truly in love with another and has his heart broken, the pain can last a lifetime. In other cases, both members of the relationship realize it's time to move on. In rare cases, former lovers remain as friends.

There's a cliché that states, When one door closes, another one opens. This is generally true with relationships as well. For as one relationship ends, one or two opportunities for a new relationship are established. In the episode "The Wait Out" (#133), Jerry and Elaine have the door of opportunity open for them when their friends David and Beth decide to file for divorce. Beth leaves Elaine a phone message that the marriage is over. Elaine has been "waiting out that marriage for years." And Jerry has always wanted to date Beth. Elaine tells Jerry they have to move quickly because there is no telling how many people have been waiting out their marriage. They attempt to devise some type of pretense to be with Beth and David. However, despite all their planning, Jerry and Elaine are not successful.

There are occasions when breakups occur and the "loser" (the term used in "The Wait Out") of the relationship wonders why the relationship ended. This is especially true if the breakup was not face-to-face. Or if the excuse given is "It's not you, it's me." The "losers" need "closure." In the episode "The Lip Reader" (#70), George intends to find out why his girlfriend Gwen broke up with him. Jerry is dating Laura, a deaf woman, who is an excellent lip reader. George, Jerry, and Kramer, who knows sign language, attend a party that Gwen will also be at. Whenever recent "exes" appear at the same party, trouble can occur. George assures the host that he will be a perfect gentleman, and insists that the host try and find out what happened between George and Gwen, and that he (George) will stay on the other side of the room. As Laura lip reads, she signs to Kramer, who interprets for George. Unfortunately, Gwen mistakes "sweep" together (as in sweep up the apartment after the party) for "sleep" together. George blows his top and blows his lip reading scheme all in one quick moment by running over to confront Gwen. Not quite the closure he was hoping for!

In the episode "Male Unbonding" (#4), George is exposed to the four worst words to hear while in a relationship: "We have to talk." Sure enough, George is dumped by his girlfriend. Worse yet, it happens over dinner and he still gets stuck with the bill. In the episode "The Susie" (#144), Jerry takes the we-have-to-talk concept one step further by stating, "No one *needs* to talk." Consequently, if you are in a relationship that you want to extend for as long as possible, you should avoid your partner when they say, "We need to talk." Once again, George is the intended victim. George has a big Yankees gala to attend and wants to make a "grand entrance" with his gorgeous girlfriend Allison. She is trying to break up with him before the event. She keeps calling, but George ignores her calls. All attempts to reach him fail. So, Allison confronts Kramer and convinces him to break up with George for her. When once-intimate couples break up, it is very difficult to remain "just friends." Elaine and Jerry dealt with this issue off and on throughout the *Seinfeld* series. In the second episode, "The Stakeout" (#2), Elaine and Jerry are *just* friends, after having a long romantic relationship. When couples like Elaine and Jerry decide to still be friends it's very difficult, at least initially, to hear about them dating someone else; or to see them with another person. The most effective way to attempt friendship after a breakup is clearly demonstrated by Elaine and Jerry throughout the years. There were occasions when they even became lovers again. But in the end, friends is what they remained.

Chapter 4

Groups and Organizations

"It is Important for Human Beings to Feel They Are a Part of a Group."—Jerry

Social interaction plays an important role in an individual's life. Everyone wants to feel that they are a part of a group or community. Individuals want to experience a sense of unity with their fellows. As Jerry states in his opening monologue of "The Bubble Boy" (#47), "It is important for human beings to feel they are a part of a group." By joining together in groups, individuals become a part of a whole. The group provides them with an identity because of their membership. Individual personalities allow for the maintenance of self-identity.

Sociologists have identified many types of groups. Among the most important distinctions is between two broad categories: primary and secondary. Primary groups are characterized by intimate face-to-face association and cooperation. Members of a primary group share a sense of "we-ness," involving the sort of sympathy and mutual identification for which "we" is a natural expression. Individuals share a sense of feeling toward the whole (the group). The "we" feeling helps to create a community. In *Seinfeld*, the four main characters are a primary group. They participate in a great number of activities together.

In fact, if one member of the group is not invited to participate in a group activity, he (or she) feels abandoned and left out. Primary group members want to know what the rest of the crew is doing, and if it is doing something, they want to be a part of it. For example, in the episode "The Parking Space" (#39), George has borrowed Jerry's car to go to a flea market. He takes Elaine with him, but they do not invite Kramer. When Kramer finds out later, he asks George and Elaine why they did not invite him. Kramer feels slighted by this snub and would later "side" with Mike over George regarding parking etiquette (discussed in chapter 2).

Secondary groups are characterized by members who interact with one another, but on an impersonal basis. Secondary group participation involves individual interactions with businesses, schools, and organizations. An example of a secondary relationship would be the interaction between a "regular" customer and a cashier at the local grocery store. Contact is made between these people on a fairly regular basis but it is not intimate. Conversation is generally limited to such mundane topics as the weather and the performance of the local sports team.

Social Groups

Sociology analyzes the behavior of individuals in social groups, organizations, and societies. Sociologists define a social group as a set of two or more people who interact regularly and in a manner that is defined by some common purpose, or meaning for existence, a set of norms, and a structure of statuses and roles found within the group.[10] There are two general requirements that must be met for a number of persons to qualify as a group: they must interact with one another in an organized fashion, and they must identify themselves as group members because of shared views, goals, traits, or circumstances. Thus, groups can be distinguished from aggregates (random clusters of people) and categories (a number of people who happen to share a particular attribute).

Primary Groups

A social group characterized by a great deal of intimacy (personal knowledge of one another's behaviors and past histories) would be a primary group. Primary groups play a key role in linking individuals to the larger society. As articulated by Charles Cooley, the fundamental properties of the primary group include:

1. Face-to-face association
2. Unspecified nature of associations
3. Relative permanence

4. A small number of persons involved
5. Relative intimacy of participants[11]

Most people, throughout their lifetime, will participate in a number of small primary groups. We are born into a family, form playgroups during childhood, and later form cliques of primary association. Many people will form their own family group. Throughout adulthood individuals form work groups and leisure groups. It is through these associations that individuals develop a sense of self.

Through thick and thin, members of the primary group are expected to be there for each other. For most people, the primary social groups in their lives are their immediate family and best friends. Family relationships will be discussed in chapter 10. The role of best friends will be discussed here.

Seinfeld, of course, centered on the life of Jerry Seinfeld, a comedian living in New York. George Costanza is his best friend dating back to elementary school. Before the television series began, Jerry had been dating Elaine for a number of years. When Jerry moved into his Manhattan apartment, he met his neighbor Kramer, and the two of them forged a friendship immediately.

The first meeting between Jerry and Kramer is explained in the episode "The Betrayal" (#164), sometimes known as "the backwards show"—because this episode starts at the end and works backward to the beginning. (All scenes were shown normally, but they were shown in reverse order with a caption indicating the time frame of the scene in relation to the previous scene.) Jerry is just moving into his apartment, and Kramer greets him in the hallway. Jerry enters his apartment and Kramer stands in the doorway, so as not to impose on Jerry, a man he just met. In an attempt to forge a friendship with his new neighbor, Jerry asked Kramer if he wanted to share the pizza that he had just ordered. Unlike the manner in which we grew to know and love Kramer, who helped himself to anything in Jerry's apartment, he is reluctant to impose on Jerry when they first meet. But Jerry assures him that as neighbors, they should share—"What's mine is yours." Kramer (looking around the apartment) responds, "Really?"

Kramer takes Jerry's invitation quite literally and over the years would help himself to nearly everything that Jerry owned—especially food! Sociologists such as Claude Levi-Strauss would explain that sharing food with someone is a great way to get to know strangers. However, like a stray animal, once you start feeding a stranger, he is not too likely to leave for any great length of time.

Kramer and Jerry become great friends. Joined by Elaine and George, these four characters share many life experiences while forging a solid primary group association.

An ultimate show of friendship and faith in another is demonstrated in the episode "The Keys" (#40). Trusting someone with spare keys is a sure sign of respect and primary group membership. One would never share one's spare keys with a marginal or secondary level friend. Jerry and Kramer are "key brothers." They have each other's spare keys in case of emergencies. Best friends realize that they are not supposed to violate the code of sharing spare keys. Among the most important aspects of the code is not taking advantage of the possession of someone else's keys by entering their homes unless it is an emergency. In "The Keys" episode, Jerry comes home to his apartment and needs to use the bathroom right away. But he finds Kramer in his tub taking a bubble bath. Later Jerry comes home from a date and finds Kramer and his date already in his apartment.

Kramer admits to Jerry that he broke the "covenant" of the keys. Jerry asks for his keys back. Upset with this request, Kramer asks for his keys back from Jerry. This scene is reminiscent of a breakup because there is clearly tension in the air. A friend's trust has been violated. Kramer informs George that he believes that he is living his life through Jerry and needs to get out from under him. This is not unusual among friends, as all relationships have moments that test the true level of commitment and loyalty. Kramer is actually going through a personal crisis and yearns for something else. He confides with George that he is moving to Los Angeles. Newman (Jerry's neighbor and enemy), trying to make Jerry feel guilty, tells Jerry that Kramer moved because of the key "incident."

Kramer does move to Los Angeles. A few days later, Jerry has a guest appearance on the *Tonight Show*. George joins Jerry (on NBC's tab) on the trip to help Jerry find Kramer, as Jerry feels bad about the key incident. A couple of episodes later, in "The Trip (2)" (#42), Kramer returns to New York and walks into Jerry's apartment. Jerry welcomes him back and in a sign of true, unspoken friendship, throws his spare keys to him. Kramer understands the importance of the symbolism of the keys and smiles at Jerry as he leaves for his own apartment. Kramer returns seconds later and throws his massive key collection toward Jerry. The friendship has resumed. Sociologists often speak of the importance of symbolism; sharing spare keys is a sure sign of a primary relationship.

Best friends enjoy spending a great deal of time with one another. And yet, as individuals we still want to maintain personal boundaries that separate us from our friends on a continuous basis. In the episode "The Apartment" (#10), an apartment in Jerry's building has become available directly above his own. Elaine wants to move in. Jerry is very excited about it at first, but then begins to worry about her being there *all* the time. As a rent-controlled apartment (just $400 a month) Elaine really wants it. Jerry pretends to be enthusiastic about her potential move in.

Alas, the building super was offered $5,000 (a type of bribe) by another prospective tenant, and Elaine will have to match this amount or she is out of consideration. Jerry realizes that she does not have that kind of money so he believes he is in the clear. Kramer suggests to Elaine, in front of Jerry, that she borrow the money from Jerry, because he has it. Elaine does not want to borrow money from a friend because that inevitably leads to problems. Kramer insists and eventually Elaine accepts Kramer's offer for her to take Jerry's money! Jerry remains silent because he did not want to tip off Elaine that he does not want her living so close to him. Jerry also yells at Kramer later for volunteering his money. Kramer eventually finds someone willing to spend $10,000 as a bribe to the super, as Elaine does not feel comfortable asking Jerry for that much.

From the department of "be careful what you wish for," Jerry was able to avoid having Elaine as his neighbor, but the person who did move into the apartment instead of her is a musician who plays loud music until late at night. And because of the bribe money, the super refuses to make the new tenant quiet down any sooner.

Friendships and primary group associations can be affected by many variables. Generally speaking, primary group members share a number of attributes with one another. These attributes might include racial and ethnic backgrounds, political beliefs, and socioeconomic status (SES). Money, in particular, can strain friendships. Group members who earn roughly the same amount of money usually have many of the same socioeconomic outlooks on life. If one member of the group suddenly "comes into money" this may cause a strain on the group dynamic.

Jerry's rapidly improving success as a comedian led to an increase in his SES. This issue comes to light in the episode "The Cadillac (1)"

(#124). Jerry comes home from a gig and Kramer is waiting for him inside his apartment. Jerry makes a comment that it was his highest paying job ever. Kramer, of course, wants to know how much money he made. Jerry, trying to remain modest, or perhaps realizing the consequences of his friends finding out how much money he makes might jeopardize the friendship of the group members, initially refuses to tell Kramer. Kramer insists on knowing. When Jerry shows him the check, Kramer is amazed by how much it is. Kramer now feels inferior to Jerry and tells him that his wealth changes the relationship.

Primary group members feel comfortable enough to tease one another, generally without hurting each other's feelings. In the "Wait Out" (#133), Jerry teases Kramer on the fact that he never wears blue jeans anymore; implying that he is either too old for them or that he cannot fit into them. Naturally, Kramer buys a pair of blue jeans, but they are too tight for him. They are so tight that he can hardly move in them. He asks for Jerry's help in taking off his pants—something that most people would not ask a stranger, or a marginal friend, to do. Even with Jerry's help, Kramer cannot get his new pants off.

Kramer has a commitment to help out his friend Mickey (they have a close relationship, but is hard to determine whether it is primary or not because we only see Mickey in a few episodes) with an audition. He is late getting there because he can hardly move with the tight jeans he is still wearing. The scene that Kramer is supposed to help Mickey with requires that Kramer sits down, but he literally cannot do it. Kramer blows the interview for Mickey, and Mickey snaps and attacks him on stage during the audition.

A sociological investigation of groups (and organizations) reveals that there is always a leader. Friendship group leadership is not as defined as organizational leadership. It is loosely organized. And yet, think of any group you are a part of, and sure enough, a leader either exists or will emerge in time of a crisis, or when a decision needs to be made. The leader of a group is one who can make decisions when other group members fail to. Debates over group activity can range from such mundane decisions as what bars to attend on a Saturday night, to decisions that lead to group vacations.

Throughout the series, the four main characters remain the best of friends. It is clear that whenever a decision needs to made, the group turns to Jerry. Jerry is the leader of the group. His ability to get the members to conform to a group decision is illustrated in the episode "The Finale (1)" (#179). Jerry receives a phone call from

James Kimbrough, the new president of NBC. He wants to sit down with Jerry to discuss his pilot, *Jerry*. Kimbrough informs Jerry that NBC is going to give him a thirteen-episode commitment. As a further gesture, NBC offers Jerry the use of their private jet for him to go anywhere he wants. Jerry offers George, Elaine, and Kramer to come along on one last fling before he and George move to Los Angeles to do the show. The four of them try to decide where to go on vacation but have a difficult time making a decision. After a lengthy discussion, the group agrees on Paris.

On their way to Paris, the plane takes a nose dive and it appears as though it will crash, leading to their deaths. They begin to admit their feelings to each other. George even admits that he "cheated on the contest" (see chapter 6). The pilot manages to regain control of the plane and they are all saved. The pilot lands in Latham, Massachusetts, so mechanics can check over the plane.

While waiting for the plane to be repaired, the four friends are in front of a store in Latham and notice (and film) a carjacking. They actually mock the victim because he is fat, and they merely stand by instead of offering to help him. They get arrested for violating the newly enacted "Good Samaritan" law (Sec. 223-7 of the Latham County Penal Code), which requires people to help or assist a victim of crime as long as they are reasonably able to do so. (See chapter 6 for a further description of this law and episode.)

In "The Finale (2)" (#180), the very last episode of *Seinfeld*, the four friends (known now as "The New York Four") are found guilty of violating the Good Samaritan law and are sentenced, by Judge Vandelay (Vandelay was a name once used by George as an alias), to one year in jail. During sentencing Judge Vandelay comments that he wonders about the circumstances that brought these four people together.

All of us can take stock of our own primary friendship groups and ask that same question. Equally important is an analysis of the circumstances that keeps the bonds between primary group members strong enough to endure years and years. Shared personal experiences appear to be a strong adhesive in all primary group relationships.

Secondary Groups

As described earlier, secondary groups refer to the relatively impersonal relationships that we have with others. In secondary groups there is little social intimacy or mutual understanding among the members. Membership in secondary groups is based on some common interest or activity that brings people together to interact. Members of a college class, for example, would constitute a secondary group. Most work colleagues have a secondary group relationship with each other.

Jerry, George, Elaine, and Kramer had many secondary relationships. Sometimes these "outside" friends joined the group of four, other times they remained on the periphery. For example, Kramer constantly mentions his friend Bob Sacamano, and yet we never meet him once in a single episode. Furthermore, while in Florida, Kramer once turns to Bob Sacamano's father for assistance in a scam that involved his running for condo board president.

The fact that these four characters had friendships separate from the primary group is consistent with real life. Each of us has friendships separate from our best friends. In many cases, these "outside" friends are just names that we hear, like Bob Sacamano. The acquaintances we associate with outside our primary group constitute our secondary group relationships.

In the episode "The Barber" (#72), Jerry is teased by Kramer because of his haircuts. They both go to the same barbershop, but they have different barbers. Jerry still has Enzo cut his hair. Kramer has Enzo's nephew, Gino, cut his hair. Jerry realizes that Enzo does not do a great job, but out of loyalty to Enzo, he feels it necessary to continue to see him. Elaine wants to enter Jerry in a charity bachelor auction that she is a part of, but she insists that he get his hair styled first. Kramer finally convinces Jerry to have Gino cut his hair. Consequently, Jerry goes to the barbershop on Enzo's day off. Unfortunately, Enzo happens to be there and generously offers to cut Jerry's hair—obviously, not what Jerry wanted to happen. Enzo does a lousy job. And when Jerry returns to his apartment, Kramer says there is no way Gino did that.

Primary group members are expected to remain loyal to one another. This high level of commitment is generally not found, nor expected, in secondary group relationships. And yet, Jerry's sense of loyalty is so strong that he feels the need to extend that obligation to Enzo, his barber. However, as demonstrated in "The Barber" primary relationships will supercede secondary ones. Kramer convinces Jerry to meet Gino outside the barbershop so that Gino can do Jerry's hair. Jerry and Gino agree to meet for the haircut, but then get caught "cheating" by Enzo. Enzo's reaction was that of a jealous spouse finding his partner in bed with another. When you think about it, there are many merchants (the regular butcher, mechanic, bar owner, exterminator, and so on) that provide services to regular customers who come to depend on such patrons and may view their shopping at a rival store as a type of cheating.

Typically, when we hear someone is "cheating" on another we inevitably think about sex. Committed partners are never supposed to cheat, especially married couples. The entire foundation of the relationship is centered on this basic moral, ethical, and social norm. When someone is cheated on by their significant other, it is nearly impossible to ever trust that loved one again. Members of primary groups are expected to never cheat with the significant others of their friendship group. This is one reason why cheating is done with strangers or people removed from the primary group. However, there are times when people who were far removed converge with the primary group.

In the episode "The Betrayal" (#164), many variations of the convergence between primary and secondary groups are revealed. First, Jerry tells George that Nina, an old friend of Jerry's, could "replace" Elaine if they ever needed to do so.

In another example of secondary and primary group convergence, Elaine's friend Sue Ellen is getting married in India. Elaine and Sue Ellen have a strained secondary relationship at best. Elaine has always been intimidated by Sue Ellen and is jealous of her. When Elaine receives the invitation just one week prior to the wedding, she feels as though she has been slighted. Adding another word to the lexicon of *Seinfeld*, Elaine refers to such a late invitation as an "unvitation"—an empty gesture, because who can make plans to go to India in just one week? Elaine decides to go, primarily in perceived spite of Sue Ellen. George, Nina, and Jerry join her on the trip.

A third convergence occurs once the four arrive in India. Sue Ellen is actually very pleased to see Elaine and asks her to be her maid of honor, a status generally reserved for the most primary friend of all. Elaine is flabbergasted and immediately accepts the honorable position.

In yet another convergence, Sue Ellen's husband-to-be, Pinter, is a man whom Elaine knew as Peter and had a relationship with years ago in New York City. As the wedding ceremony is about to begin, Elaine admits to George that she has slept with Pinter. George, without thinking, loudly repeats what Elaine just told him. Sue Ellen, and the rest of the invited guests, overhears George's comment and Sue Ellen screams at Elaine. The wedding is cancelled.

"The Betrayal" episode reveals some of the many dynamics that occur between secondary and primary relationships. Sociologists teach us that some secondary relationships can be transformed into primary relationships and vice versa. For example, an individual may continually go to the same restaurant on a regular basis because he wants to date the waitress who generally serves him. This secondary relationship, once based on superficial communication, will evolve to a primary relationship if she agrees to go out on a date with this regular customer. Conversely, if this newly formed couple break up with each other some time in the future, their relationship with one another will most likely deteriorate to a status far below the secondary level.

Ideally, everyone has a primary group of friends they can associate with, and a number of secondary level friendships that bring additional good cheer into their lives. It seems, however, that the older people get, the harder it is for them to make (or want to make) new primary friendships. In the episodes "The Boyfriend (1)" (#34) and "The Boyfriend (2)" (#35), former major league baseball player Keith Hernandez stars as himself. Jerry notices Keith stretching in the locker room of his fitness center and wonders if he should introduce himself. Meanwhile, Keith walks over to Jerry and introduces himself. Keith informs Jerry that he is a fan of his comedy. Jerry returns the compliment by telling Keith how much he likes him as a professional baseball player. They agree to get together some time soon. In other words, they "hit it off" right away.

Initially Jerry is acting like someone about to go on a first date. Three days have gone by since they met in the gym and still Keith has not called. Jerry is anxious and wonders why, when you give a guy your number, he doesn't call? Elaine attempts to console him. Finally Keith calls. He had been out of town, and they agree to get together. Jerry is so nervous he doesn't even know what shirt to wear. Elaine has to remind Jerry that he was only getting together with a guy as a friend. Jerry and Keith have dinner together and get to know each other. When Jerry is about to exit Keith's car at the end of their "date" he doesn't know whether to shake his hand or not. The significance of this is reflected when George asks Jerry later whether they shook hands or not. Jerry said yes, and George wanted to know what type of handshake he had (like asking if he was a good kisser). Jerry, proudly proclaims, "Single pump. Not too hard. Perfect."

Before long, Jerry feels that the friendship is moving too quickly.

Jerry employs a type of "best friends barometer" when Keith asks him for his help moving furniture into a new apartment. Jerry thinks this type of request is occurring too soon in a friendship, implying only *best* friends help each other move—not secondary ones. Jerry refers to such breach of friendship etiquette as "boundary jumping." He explains to Elaine later that helping a friend move is a big step in a male relationship: it's like going all the way. By the end of "The Boyfriend (2)" Jerry and Keith have "broken up" and, ironically, Kramer and Newman, who both had despised Keith Hernandez, befriend him and help him move.

Jerry's reluctance to build additional primary relationships was consistent throughout *Seinfeld*. And with good reason; after all, we can only spend so much time with our friends. The more friends we have, the less time we have for our primary group. Having many friends is always a good thing, but having them keep their distance for the majority of the time appears to also be a good thing, according to the logic of *Seinfeld*.

For example, in the episode "The Chicken Roaster" (#142), Jerry runs into an old college buddy, Seth. Jerry wants to reminisce but Seth tries to explain to Jerry that he has an important meeting to attend. Seth blows off the meeting and the two of them go to lunch. Before long, it becomes clear to Jerry that the ties that once bound him with Seth had disappeared now that their college days were long behind them. It's not just time that lessens the staying power of some primary groups; it is also the lack of constant shared activity and interaction that characterized most group associations.

In the episode "The Bizarro Jerry" (#137), Elaine nearly replaces her entire primary group (Jerry, George, and Kramer) with all new friends (just as Jerry acknowledged he was capable of doing in a later episode, "The Betrayal"). In this episode, Elaine is dating a boring, yet nice, guy named Kevin. She decides to break up with him but asks if they could remain friends. Kevin agrees. When Elaine explains to Jerry that she and Kevin are still friends even though they had broken up, Jerry wonders why anyone would want more friends.

Elaine is tired of her old friends and wonders whether it is time to replace her primary group association with the secondary group association she is forming with Kevin. Hysterically, from the *Seinfeld* perspective, each of Kevin's friends are similar (and yet the opposite) of her current friends. George is selfish, Kramer is wacky, and Jerry finds faults in everyone. Elaine meets Kevin's friends Gene and

Feldman. Gene is short and bald with glasses. Feldman is tall and a little goofy-looking. Elaine is thinking to herself this is like the bizarro world (as Jerry had earlier described Elaine's new emerging primary group, because they are the opposite of her current friends). These three men are caring and giving people, the opposite of Jerry, Kramer, and George. Kevin, Gene, and Feldman go to the library to *read*! Elaine is amazed by this. She informs Jerry of her growing desire to transform her secondary relationship with Kevin and his friends into a primary one.

Elaine visits Kevin in his apartment (the apartment layout is the reverse of Jerry's—what's to the left in Jerry's is to the right at Kevin's). Gene is already there. Elaine makes herself comfortable, notices a statue of Bizarro Superman on a stereo speaker. Feldman (who lives across the hall) comes over to visit as well. While the four are in Kevin's apartment there is a knock on the door. It's a Fed Ex guy named Vargus. Unlike Jerry and his postman neighbor Newman, Kevin and Vargus get along as good friends. Elaine thinks this social group is much more to her fitting. But alas, there is usually a reason people have the friends that they have—generally speaking, not too many others will put up with them. Elaine finds out the hard way that she actually *belongs* back with her original primary group. Elaine's behavior, acceptable within Jerry's circle, is not acceptable in Kevin's.

Elaine learns what the brilliant sociologist Herbert Spencer claimed long ago as part of his "survival of the fittest" doctrine (No, Darwin did not coin this term): that people must adapt to their changing environment in order to survive. Elaine could not adapt to this new group's norms and expectations. She was best "fit" for her old environment which included Jerry, Kramer, and George as her primary group and Newman as a member of her secondary group.

Dyad and Triad Groups

Beyond an analysis of the distinction between primary and secondary groups, sociologists are also concerned with distinguishing between dyad (two-person) groups and triad (three-person) groups. The terms *dyad* and *triad* were coined by German sociologist Georg Simmel. Simmel argued that the simple addition of one more person to a two-person group changes the group structure and dynamics radically. In a dyad, each member retains an equal level of individuality and power-making decisions (at least theoretically). The dyad is characterized by direct and immediate reciprocity, and each member is dependent upon the other for group decisions. Furthermore, if one member of a dyad withdraws or chooses to leave the group, it will dissolve.

The addition of a third person to the dyad causes radical and fundamental changes to the group structure (form). The addition of a third person provides the opportunity for the development of an external "super-individual" and the internal development of divisions. The triad group is less dependent on the immediate participation of the elements; it absorbs less of the total personality, and it can continue its existence if one member leaves. The third person may become the nonpartisan arbitrator or mediator to settle/mediate disputes among the original two (such as a marriage counselor who is trying to help a married couple keep their marriage intact).

The third person may also use her position for her own selfish interests. This is known as *tertius gaudens*, Latin for "the third who enjoys." In this sense, the third party can become the object of competition between the other two. One example involves two employees who are being considered for one promotion; they will try to make the boss (the third party) happy in order to get the promotion. And how many times has a friendship between two best friends been ruined because they both desire the personal attention of a third person?

The third person may deliberately seek to cause disputes between the other two in order to gain an advantage or superiority. This is known as "divide and conquer" (*divide et impera*) and is utilized in a variety of social settings. For example, a boss will find it advantageous if her two employees are fighting each other instead of joining forces to fight her. A person who has desires on one of the members of the group may find it necessary to cause a division between the original two members in order to gain superiority.

In *Seinfeld*, just as in real life, there were many occasions where the group dynamics of the dyad and triad were displayed. Examples of dyad relationships are so obvious and plentiful in number that it is unnecessary to mention any specific examples (just think of all the dating relationships and friendship relationships previously discussed). The transformation of a dyad to triad group is more interesting to illustrate. For example, in the episode "The Seven" (#123), Elaine and Kramer have a dispute over the ownership of a bicycle. Elaine originally purchased it. At Jerry's apartment she complains about a terrible pain in her neck. Kramer says he can help her out. She offers him the bike (in her mind, jokingly) if he can help. Kramer performs a chiropractic move on her, and instantly she feels better. Kramer claims ownership of the bike. Elaine is stunned that he actually expected the bike as "payment," but Kramer is insistent.

The next day, Elaine's neck is hurting worse than ever before. She demands the bike back. They ask Jerry for his advice. But he balks at the invitation to share his wisdom and suggests that they seek the advice of an impartial mediator. Kramer and Elaine go over to Newman's apartment, sit on his couch, and tell their story. Newman sits in his chair attempting to give an impression of great wisdom. He will ultimately make a decision based on the Wisdom of Solomon in the Bible. After hearing both Elaine and Kramer present their cases, Newman rules that the bike should be cut in half. Elaine is upset but agrees. Kramer tells Newman that he would rather have Elaine keep the bike than have it destroyed. Newman then rules the bicycle should go to Kramer because only the true owner would rather give it away than see it destroyed.

Many elements of a three-person group are illustrated in the episode "The Switch" (#97). Jerry is dating a woman named Sandi, but she has an annoying habit of never actually laughing. She acknowledges that Jerry's jokes and comments are funny, yet she never laughs out loud. This, of course, bothers Jerry.

Jerry goes over to Sandi's apartment and is greeted at the door by her roommate, Laura. Much to Jerry's delight, she laughs at all his jokes. Jerry is intrigued by Laura. Jerry tells George all about Laura and how he really loved her laugh because it had a feminine tone and not one of those big coarse "ha's." So now, Jerry would prefer to date Laura instead of Sandi. Unfortunately for Jerry, there is a big obstacle; Laura and Sandi are roommates. George begins to realize that Jerry is considering the unthinkable—the "roommate switch."

And yet, George and Jerry discuss a possible plan. They decide that Jerry should suggest to Sandi that they have a ménage a trois with her roommate. They assume that Sandi will be so upset with such a suggestion that she will break up with him. They also theorize Laura will provide Sandi with the requisite sympathy even as part of her cannot help but feel somewhat flattered by her inclusion in the unusual request. Sandi, they conclude, will want nothing to do with Jerry and will tell Laura that if you want to waste your time with that pervert, go ahead. Jerry thinks it's a perfect plan. So inspired, yet so simple.

Jerry does confront Sandi with his request for a threesome and she tells him she is into it! In fact, later on, Sandi calls Jerry and informs him that Laura is also into it. George thinks Jerry is the luckiest man alive. Jerry, however, is not into *that* variation of a triad. As he states, he's not an "orgy guy." Ahh, so many types of triads, and Jerry refuses to explore this group structure—if not for purely sociological research purposes.

Social Organizations

Western culture is dominated by social organizations. There are numerous organizations designed to cater to our every need: hospitals and clinics for our health needs; fitness centers and organized ball leagues for our recreational needs; professional clinics for our counseling needs, and so on. Although many students of sociology find the study of organizations boring, the fact of the matter remains very evident—that organizations nearly consume our daily life activities. Most people wake up to the sound of an alarm clock, a device created by an organization. Chances are the alarm clock is set to a radio station (an organization) that plays music (produced, manufactured, marketed, delivered, and sold by other organizations). After getting out of bed (made by another organization), most people go to the bathroom. The bathroom is filled with items made by organizations. The sewer lines that dispose of our waste are maintained by an organization. In a matter of a few waking minutes we have already been exposed to a large number of organizations, directly or indirectly. Trace your normal day and try to count all the different organizations that you come into contact with and the number may surprise you.

Despite the great diversity of organizations, they all share a number of characteristics. First, they all serve a specific purpose and are designed in such a way as to meet predetermined goals. All organizations are staffed by a number of people who (generally) have specialized job tasks to perform. This specialization leads to a division of labor. All organizations also have rules and regulations that its employees must abide by, and in many cases these rules extend to the customers who patronize the organization.

Considering the great number of organizations that exist in society it was inevitable for the characters of *Seinfeld* to have confronted them. Although the primary goal of most organizations is to make a profit, some are designed to be charitable. These types are collectively known as nonprofit organizations. The organizations discussed in this chapter are, for the most part, nonprofit. They need money to operate, of course, but their primary goal is to provide some type of service to others. (Note: *for*-profit organizations will be discussed in chapter 5.)

Foundations are a prime example of nonprofit organizations. They are usually named in honor of someone. In the episode "The Foundation" (#135), Susan Ross has been laid to rest in the cemetery after her untimely death caused by licking toxic wedding invitations. Her parents confront George days later informing him that they have decided to create a foundation to preserve Susan's memory—the Susan Ross Foundation. They want, and expect, George to play an integral part in the foundation by serving on the board of directors. George tries to get out of it by saying his schedule with the Yankees keeps him too busy. Mr. Ross assures George that the foundation will revolve around his schedule, even if it means meeting on evenings and weekends.

George, who had been trying to find a way out of his impending marriage to Susan anyway, certainly does not want to be involved in a foundation where he would be expected to actually do something to honor Susan. It is at this time, however, that George first finds out how wealthy Susan really was. Unfortunately for George, he did not receive a dime in Susan's will because he signed a prenuptial agreement. It had been Kramer who suggested to George he should ask Susan for a prenuptial, because he assumed that most women are upset by such requests and therefore she would break off the wedding. Instead, she signed it quickly because she knew that she was financially worth far more than George. (Note: the lawyers involved in creating a prenuptial represent another organization.)

Kramer reaches a boiling point when he is overwhelmed by an organizationally caused problem that nearly all of us can relate to—junk mail. The episode, appropriately titled "The Junk Mail" (#161), centers on the large volume of junk mail that Kramer is receiving, especially from the Pottery Barn. He gathers all the magazine advertisements from Pottery Barn (once he received three of them on the same day) and throws them back into a Pottery Barn store. Kramer later decides that he no longer wants any mail at all, not even from the post office. Initially he seals up his mailbox with bricks, but the postal delivery person simply leaves Kramer's mail in Jerry's box. Kramer goes to the post office and tells the clerk that he is canceling his mail service. Newman, fearing the governmental organizational repercussions about to be inflicted upon Kramer for making such an odd request, tries to intervene and convince Kramer not to try to stop the mail.

Later in the episode, as Kramer is walking on a sidewalk, he is confronted by Newman who is slowly driving by. Newman is trying to warn Kramer that he has upset the wrong people. Soon, postal security officials walk toward Kramer. Newman tries to convince Kramer to ride away with him, but Kramer refuses. Kramer is accosted by these federal officials and delivered to the postmaster general, Henry Atkins, for a discussion on the mail and Kramer's attempt to cancel his home delivery. Atkins intimidates Kramer to resume his mail service and he agrees to do so.

Although this story line overdramatizes the power of the post office, it does reflect the old adage that you can't fight city hall. Some organizations are so powerful, and "faceless" that it is impossible to confront them. When consumers have problems with the phone company or their credit card company, they seemingly never accomplish what they had hoped to accomplish.

Like Kramer, Jerry was also confronted by a "nonprofit" organization, the New York Public Library, in the episode "The Library" (#22). Jerry is accused of not returning a book, *The Tropic of Cancer*, since he checked it out in 1971, while in high school. Also like Kramer, Jerry has to deal with this organization's version of security, specifically, Mr. Bookman, a library investigator. Bookman arrives at Jerry's apartment to discuss the missing book. Bookman has an unpleasant attitude. He goes into a tirade about library etiquette. Ultimately, he is correct, of course. After all, if people steal books, then they are not available to the rest of the public. Jerry cannot prove he returned the book, and he later writes a check to cover the expenses. As it turns out, Jerry lent George the book in high school in 1971. The gym teacher stole it from George.

There is another organization deserving of mention: the Big Brother Program. Jerry and George are at the diner, and their friend Alec walks in with a boy named Joey. Alec heads the local chapter of the Big Brother Program. He asks Jerry and George whether or not they would be interested in doing some work for it. A sad-faced Joey also pleads his case laying a major guilt trip on George, who reluctantly agrees to volunteer. Jerry just keeps eating, and after Alec and Joey leave, he asks George what happened—as in, why did you just do that? George said he could not resist the "mug on that kid." Jerry, of course, did not have a problem saying no, even to a great organization such as the Big Brothers!

Chapter 5

The Workplace

"Why Would George Steal from the Yankees?"
—George

Nearly all adults are faced with the reality that they must work in order to support themselves and their families. If people are lucky, they have a job that they enjoy and that pays well. Unfortunately, many people work for organizations that make them unhappy, or cause them to feel unfulfilled. Among the many problems facing workers are overbearing or inept bosses, irritating coworkers, low pay, long hours, and lack of job security.

The growing power of international corporations (multinationals), automation, advances in agriculture, and globalization has led to massive job loss in the United States in the form of corporate downsizing, layoffs, and the relocation of many corporations to foreign markets. American corporations have set up offices in foreign countries where labor laws are lax, and the wages paid to workers are low. Thus, globalization involves a process in which the constraints of geography on social and cultural arrangements recede. This results in economic competition on a global scale. Consequently, it is more difficult than ever before for many Americans to find quality job opportunities in the United States.

The Employment Interview

Once somebody learns of a job opportunity they must secure an employment interview. It is critical to make a good impression with the potential new employer during the interview. One wrong comment or impression can sway the employer's decision on whether to hire the interviewee. George and Elaine found themselves in a number of job interviews throughout *Seinfeld*. On the other hand, Jerry was consistently employed as a stand-up comedian so he never had to look for work. Kramer, well, he seldom worked at all! Jerry and Kramer both had little experience with interviews.

In the episode "The Chaperone" (#87), Elaine interviews for a position as an editor with Doubleday Publishing. The position was formerly held by Jackie Onassis. Elaine's interview is with Mrs. Landis, who is a big fan of Jackie Onassis because she had grace. As the dialogue provided below reveals, an interviewee often realizes early on that the interview is not going well.

> *Landis*: "Not many people have grace."
> *Elaine*: "Well, you know, grace is a tough one. I like to think I have a little grace . . . not as much as Jackie."
> *Landis*: "You can't have 'a little grace.' You either have grace, or you . . . don't."
> *Elaine*: "Okay, fine, I have . . . no grace."
> *Landis*: "And you can't acquire grace."
> *Elaine*: "Well, I have no intention of 'getting' grace."
> *Landis*: "Grace isn't something you can pick up at the market."
> *Elaine* (fed up with the interview): "All right, all right. Look— I don't have grace, I don't want grace . . . I don't even say grace, okay?"
> *Landis* (equally fed up): "Thank you for coming in."
> *Elaine*: "Yeah, yeah, right."
> *Landis*: "We'll make our decision in a few days, and we'll let you know."
> *Elaine* (standing up to leave): "I have no chance, do I?"
> *Landis*: "No."

As Elaine prepares herself to leave (putting on her dark glasses and a hood because it had been raining), Justin Pitt, Landis's boss, enters the room and is clearly affected by Elaine's appearance. Pitt was a close friend of Jackie O's and when he sees Elaine, she reminds him of Jackie. Pitt simply states to Elaine: "Charmed!" Elaine meets with Mr. Pitt later for an informal job interview and, ironically, because he was so charmed by her, Pitt offers her a job as his personal assistant.

Elaine got lucky. She got a job because a higher-level boss found a certain quality in her. One never knows what may land, or cost, one a job during an interview. (Author's note: I once got a job because I wrote down bowling as one of my hobbies. The manager interviewing me headed up the bowling team and they needed a fifth player for the company team!)

In one of the best *Seinfeld* episodes, "The Opposite" (#86), George utilizes a rather unusual approach to a job interview, one might say the *opposite* approach that would normally be taken. Doing the opposite has now become more than a way of life; it is George's new religion. In "The Opposite," George has met a woman named Victoria—a woman that would be considered "out of his league"—by doing the opposite. George's unique way of presenting "the truth" impresses Victoria so much that she contacts her uncle, who works for the New York Yankees, to set up an interview for George. It has been George's lifelong dream to work with the Yankee organization.

At Yankee Stadium, George meets with Mr. Cushman (Victoria's uncle) to interview for the position of assistant to the traveling secretary. Cushman begins the interview in typical fashion by asking George to explain some of his previous job experiences. Cushman is amazed by the stories that George is telling him. George admits to being fired from a publishing job for having sex in his office with a cleaning woman and that he quit a job in real estate because his boss wouldn't let George use his private bathroom. Cushman tells him that he is the complete opposite of every applicant he has met. Just then, Mr. Steinbrenner walks by in the hallway. Cushman gets Steinbrenner's attention and asks him to meet George.

Steinbrenner, as manners would dictate, extends his hand to shake George's hand and offers a pleasant greeting, "Nice to meet you."

George, displaying either courage or stupidity, refuses to shake Steinbrenner's hand. "Well, I wish I could say the same, but I must say, with all due respect, I find it very hard to see the logic behind some of the moves you have made with this fine organization. In the past twenty years you have caused myself, and the city of New York, a good deal of distress, as we have watched you take our beloved Yankees and reduced them to a laughing stock, all for the glorification of your massive ego!" Steinbrenner immediately demands that Cushman hire George. And with that conversation, George's career with the New York Yankees begins.

Employers today have to be very careful not to violate laws that protect the handicapped. In the episode "The Butter Shave" (#157), George has an interview at Play Now, a sports equipment company. George is still recovering from a summer of physical rehabilitation and uses a cane to walk. During the interview, Mr. Thomassoulo is a little uncomfortable interviewing George because he thinks George is handicapped and he stumbles over his words, by saying things like, "differently, uh, advantaged." To make up for his perceived insensitivity, Mr. Thomassoulo informs George that he would have his own private, fully equipped bathroom. Thus, in essence, George got the job *because* he was perceived as handicapped.

Workplace Etiquette

Once one has survived the employment interview process, regardless of the ultimate factor that led to the hiring, one must now learn how to get along with coworkers, supervisors, and subordinates, and abide by company policies and procedures.

In some work environments, employers find it necessary to test their employees for illegal drug use. This is a highly controversial subject, as most people view this as an intrusion into their private lives. If job performance meets, or exceeds, the expectations, the personal behaviors of employees should be irrelevant to the employer. The few companies that do drug test usually make it part of their pre-employment interviewing process. On other occasions, employees may be asked to submit to a drug test after they have been hired.

Beyond the civil rights violation issue, drug testing has another huge potential problem: "false positives." That is, a person may really be "clean" (of drugs) but test results indicate that the person is taking drugs. This happened to Elaine when she was forced to take a drug test for her employer, J. Peterman, in "The Shower Head" (#126). In this episode, Elaine is sent to the doctor for a physical because she is scheduled to go to Kenya with Mr. Peterman. They are going to meet with the Masai Bushmen. The Masai have wonderfully durable sandals that Peterman intends on "knocking off" for his clothing catalog business.

The doctor asks Elaine for a urine sample as part of the physical requirement. Later, back in the office, Peterman informs Elaine that there is a problem. She has tested positive for opium. Elaine is perplexed by her urine sample results; she knows that she does not take drugs, so how could she fail a drug test? Elaine insists to her boss that there must be something wrong with the test and requests another one—a "pop urine test." Peterman agrees to have her retested.

Elaine takes the second drug test and still fails, again testing positive for opium. At Monk's coffee shop, Elaine, eating a muffin, tells a waitress her story. There is a man seated at the counter nearby who overhears Elaine's conversation with the waitress. The man points out to Elaine that she is eating a poppy seed muffin. Elaine replies that she eats them all the time. The man then points out to Elaine that opium is made from poppies. Despite her discovery, it is too late for Elaine to join Peterman on the company trip. She misses out on an opportunity of a lifetime because of a flawed company policy.

At many workplaces it is common for employees to celebrate birthdays, promotions, retirements, and other such occasions, with cake. At large offices, that can amount to a lot of cake! In the episode "The Frogger" (#174), Elaine has had enough of all the cake celebrations held in the afternoons. Her office has two hundred employees and it is always someone's special day. She explains to Jerry that workplace celebrations are a type of "forced socializing." Forced socialization is a common occurrence in the workplace. Management often expects its employees to attend various social functions, such as company picnics, participate in company-sponsored sports teams, "volunteer" for various committees and/or charity functions, and dine together in corporate cafeterias. Elaine believes that just because people work together, it does not mean that they have to be friends. Most employees agree with Elaine.

Elaine decides to take a stand and refuses to participate in any future office cake-related celebrations. Before long she realizes that she has become addicted to the regular afternoon sugar fix provided by the parties. But because of her very public anticake stand, she feels uncomfortable rejoining the celebrations. Elaine needs to ask Peterman about something. He is not in his office, but she walks in anyway. She snoops around his refrigerator and finds a cake inside a box. She helps herself to a piece of it and places it back in the fridge when she hears Peterman whistling down the hallway. When Peterman returns he brags to Elaine that he just spent $29,000 for a slice of cake from the wedding of King Edward VIII to Wallis Simpson, circa 1937. The next day, Elaine sneaks back into Peterman's office to even out the cake slice from which she snuck a piece. For some unknown reason, Elaine ends up eating the whole slice of cake and now realizes she must replace it, which she does with a slice of Entenmann's.

Elaine has clearly violated many rules of conduct in this episode. She has offended her coworkers, stolen from her boss, and will soon suffer great physical pain because she ate cake that was so old. Her downfall begins when Peterman invites to his office a Mr. Lubeck, a foremost appraiser in vintage pastry. Lubeck informs Peterman that the cake is valueless, that it is a fraud—it is an Entenmann's. Later, much to Elaine's chagrin, Peterman asks Elaine to come to his office where he reveals that he has security cameras in his office. He knows that Elaine stole the cake. She is rightfully worried about losing her job. Peterman asks Elaine if she has any idea what happens to a butter-based frosting after it has been sitting in a poorly ventilated English room for six decades. Elaine acknowledges that she did not think of the consequences. Peterman concludes that what she is about to go through will be punishment enough.

An odd issue of workplace etiquette confronts George in the episode "The Bottle Deposit (1)" (#131). George's boss (with the Yankees), Mr. Wilhelm, is giving George instructions on an assignment. Wilhelm, still talking, walks into the bathroom. George is puzzled, should he walk into the bathroom with Wilhelm, or stay out in the hallway and wait. George hesitates, and then enters the bathroom. Wilhelm is still "talking to" George the whole time, and when Wilhelm turns around and sees George, he assumes that George has heard the conversation. Normally, a worker would simply inform the boss that they were sorry and did not hear the instructions because they felt it polite to stay out in the hallway. But Wilhelm had been on George's case for not paying attention previously. Now, George has to try to figure out what exactly his project entails without tipping off Wilhelm. George never does find out what the project was, and instead, Wilhelm completes it for him. It is revealed later in the episode that Wilhelm had not been taking his medication and was completing tasks that he assigned to others (George at work and the gardener at home).

Coworkers

Sociologists have conducted research on the interactional patterns of coworkers since the days of Karl Marx and other early social thinkers. Marx believed that workers feel alienated at work, primarily because they can never reach their full human potential. Many workers today feel alienated at work. Toiling at a job that stifles creativity and freedom, many people find the workplace to be a source of stress. And stress comes from a variety of sources. Coworkers, especially annoying and incompetent ones, are often a source of great stress.

Most people have a number of coworkers. When colleagues get along with one another there is generally less stress in the workplace. The contemporary business world is experiencing a great deal of pressure from a number of political special interest groups and organizations demanding, among other things, that the work force should be a diverse one. As organizations continue to diversify, it is critical that management creates some sort of cultural diversity training program for its employees. After all, diversity implies differences among people. Diverse ideas almost always lead to conflict. Consequently, a real social problem confronting many organizations involves finding ways to assist coworkers to coexist in a productive work environment.

Seinfeld had no intentions of solving major diversity issues in the workplace, but it did address some of the many little nuisances found in the workplace that, if left unaddressed, could lead to open hostility. For example, in the episode "The Summer of George" (#156), Elaine has a new colleague, Sam, at J. Peterman's. Sam has a peculiar habit of not moving her arms while she walks. All of Elaine's male associates make fun of the way Sam walks. But, when Elaine joins in on the ribbing, the guys make a "meow" sound—as in a catfight between Elaine and Sam. As this episode reveals, males seem to have a little fantasy about catfights. Elaine and Sam have lunch together at Monks, and Sam asks why people are making fun of her. Elaine tells her that she needs to move her arms so that she's not lurching around like a caveman. Sam is offended, tells Elaine that she heard what a terrible shrew she was, and storms off.

The next day, Sam enters Elaine's office. Elaine attempts to apologize. Sam wants nothing to do with the apology and begins to swing her arms to the point that she angrily knocks everything off Elaine's desk. When Elaine complains to Mr. Peterman, he gives her a not so politically correct response, "Well, I see what is going on in here. I am smack dab in the middle of a good old fashioned catfight." Elaine tries to explain to her boss that what Sam did does not constitute a catfight; instead, it is an example of violent psychotic behavior. Elaine feels threatened in her workplace environment and turns to her boss for help, but is mocked for her "whistle blowing."

Interestingly, later in this same episode Elaine gets in a catfight with Raquel Welch. Jerry and Kramer think that is the coolest thing they ever heard. Younger viewers most likely do not realize that for men in their mid-forties and older, Raquel Welch represents the all-time fantasy girl.

In the episode "The Susie" (#144), Elaine and her coworker Peggy not only do not get along with each other, Peggy does not even know Elaine's name. Peggy refers to Elaine as Susie. Peggy even complains to "Susie" about Elaine.

> *Peggy*: "Did you get this memo from Elaine Benes?"
> *Elaine*: "Yeah. See that . . ."
> *Peggy*: "You know it's amazing Peterman hasn't fired that dolt. She practically ran the company into the ground."
> *Elaine*: "Well. Well, I thought she did a pretty good job."
> *Peggy*: "I heard she was a disaster, Suze."
> *Elaine* (upset with Peggy, she violates her personal space): "Look-it. It's not Suze. All right? It's Su-zie. My name is Su-zie!"

Well now, Peggy feels threatened by "Susie" and complains to Peterman. Peterman, in turn, demands to meet with Elaine, Susie, and Peggy for a meeting. Naturally, there is no Susie, and Elaine is the one who actually threatened Peggy, so Elaine does not know how to get away with this. Elaine manages to do some "double talk" and temporarily confuse Peterman and Peggy. Elaine eventually decides to "kill" Susie. Peterman arranges for memorial services for Susie. He offers up some words of remembrance, "I don't think I'll ever be able to forget Susie—ahh. And most of all, I will never forget that one night. Working late on the catalogue. Just the two of us. And we surrendered to temptation. And it was pretty good."

An interesting sociophilosophical debate arises from this episode. In the Marxist tradition (Marx wanted all people to have an opportunity to reach their "full human potential"), Did Susie reach her full potential? She was killed in the prime of her career which would suggest no, she did not reach her full potential. On the other hand, since she never actually "existed" she must have reached her full potential. Feel free to ponder this.

Often, coworkers create nicknames for each other. George, in an attempt to get along with his coworkers, tries to introduce a self-proclaimed nickname of "T-bone." In an attempt to accomplish this, George orders a T-bone steak for lunch during a working meeting. He overdramatizes his order by gesturing a T-bone. He even tells his coworkers that they should call him T-bone when all of a sudden he is interrupted by a coworker (Watkins) who shouts out that he would also like a T-bone steak. Watkins emphasizes that he loves them. Mr. Kruger (the boss) mentions that if Watkins loves T-bones so much that they should all call him T-bone.

Later, George argues with Watkins in the conference room for the "rights" to the nickname. While George is arguing, Mr. Kruger and George's coworkers observe his "monkey-like" movements while he is giving "it" to Watkins. Watkins finally relinquishes the nickname (mostly because he feels sorry for George, who is nearly crying). George excitedly attempts to proclaim his new nickname to his coworkers until Kruger interrupts him and states that his new nickname will be "Koko the Monkey." Everyone chants, "Koko, Koko, Koko . . ." George is very upset over this. He has not successfully bonded with his coworkers—he is alienated. He will not reach his full human potential!

The Mentoring Program

Sociologists are not only famous for their studies on the interactional patterns among coworkers; they also present expert analysis on the workplace organizational structure. The organization openly promotes a "company" way of doing things. However, as sociologists have routinely found, there exists an informal subculture within the organization as well. This informal structure possesses its own set of rules and expectations. It constitutes the things that people actually do on a day-to-day basis, in contrast to what the official company rules dictate. Consequently, a number of things that occur in the work environment are the result of the informal protocol established by employees.

New employees are often overwhelmed with the material they are expected to consume during an orientation. An employee's manual is often distributed to new employees so that they may become accustomed to the rules and expectations of the company. In an attempt to help new employees during an indoctrination period, many organizations provide new employees with a mentor. A mentor is a seasoned veteran of the company and someone who can show employees "the ropes" and answer any questions they may have in relation to their job role and position. Typically, the mentor will also teach the new employee about the informal aspects of the job as well.

A number of mentoring scenarios are introduced in the episode "The Fatigues" (#140). This episode begins with Jerry and his girl-friend Abby talking about financial investments while eating at a restaurant. Abby mentions to Jerry that her mentor suggested that she move into equities and that it was the best move she ever made. Jerry was taken aback that Abby had a mentor.

Later, Jerry and George discuss this mentor-protégé relationship. George is not quite clear what exactly the duties of the mentor are and what the obligations of the protégé are. Jerry explains to George that the mentor advises the protégé. George is disappointed to realize that the mentor does not receive financial compensation. He won-ders if the protégé would take on such responsibilities as running personal errands for the mentor.

Jerry later learns that Abby's mentor, Cynthia, is dating Kenny Bania, a fellow comedian whom Jerry does not respect. As Jerry rea-sons, if he cannot respect the mentor, he cannot respect the protégé. This causes an obvious strain in Jerry and Abby's relationship. Abby loses respect for Cynthia after she sees Kenny's act. She cannot respect a mentor who dates a "hack."

Meanwhile, George has been asked by his boss, Mr. Steinbrenner, to give a presentation on risk management, an area he knows nothing about and yet claimed knowledge of on his resume. Lying on a resume can often come back to haunt employees and can be used as grounds for automatic termination. George realizes the seri-ousness of his presentation and decides to check out a book on risk management. But the subject area is too difficult for him and he gives up in a state of stress and frustration. In a moment of deviant brilliance, George takes on Abby as a protégé and assigns her to write a full report on risk management. She is excited to have a new sense of direction and George is happy because his laziness would appear to be rewarded.

In this same episode, Elaine is the acting boss at J. Peterman. She is upset with the slow mail service from the company mailroom. She angrily demands to see the department head of the mailroom, Eddie Sherman. She has every intention of firing him for his incompetence (the mail is always days late). Company rules mandate that some sort of reprimand be sanctioned against Eddie. However, the informal structure comes into play in this soon-to-be developing mentor-protégé relationship. Responding to Elaine's summons to her office, Eddie walks in dressed in full military fatigues. He has a very raspy voice. He looks intimidating, especially to Elaine. Out of fear, Elaine decides to promote him to copywriter instead of firing him.

After just one day it is clear he cannot write copy. Violating normal company policies, Elaine decides to promote Eddie again. When Elaine informs her staff that Eddie is the new director of corporate development, she is besieged by resentment and disgust, especially by one employee who angrily yells at Elaine that she and her deranged protégé can run the catalog by themselves. Shortly afterward all of Elaine's employees quit because of the way she handled Eddie. Interestingly, a rival executive hears about Eddie's rapid promotion and steals him from J. Peterman by offering more money and a higher position.

Near the end of "The Fatigues" episode, Kenny pouts to Jerry that the mentor (Cynthia) saw his act and dumped him. Kenny feels like a failure. Jerry begins to point out to Kenny the many flaws in his comedic delivery and offers some advice. Kenny is very impressed and asks Jerry if he would be willing to serve as his mentor. Jerry agrees to take on Kenny as a protégé and teaches him various comedic techniques and helps him out with his material. Kenny's act rapidly improves. But now, Abby cannot respect Jerry because she perceives his protégé is a hack, and she breaks up with him.

A mix-up caused by George's protégé, Abby, results in George giving a presentation on Ovaltine (material that Jerry prepared for Kenny) to Yankee management. His presentation is so bad that Mr. Wilhelm (George's boss) decides to take George on as his own protégé. Kenny's presentation (a comedy act) on risk management goes over so well that he receives a number of corporate gigs, and Cynthia takes him back.

Various Occupations

The work history of the four main characters is quite diverse. Jerry was the most stable; George held a variety of jobs, his favorite being with the New York Yankees; Elaine held a number of positions, usually in publishing; and Kramer, well, that's a different story.

Jerry

Jerry's occupation was consistent, he is a comedian. However, throughout the *Seinfeld* series he flirted with the idea of creating his own television show for NBC, to be called *Jerry*. As a rule, Jerry's workplace varied from club to club and from city to city across the nation. The nature of Jerry's occupation dictates that a comedian, at least a successful one, will work at a large number of comedy clubs. This implies a great deal of travel. Travel can be quite stressful on people. Catching a plane or train, renting a car, eating restaurant or room service food, forced out of the regular routine of recreation and exercise, and separation from family, are all negative by-products that an employee who is forced to travel in order to be successful must endure.

Many people will point out that merely traveling *to* work can be stressful even when the commute is just "cross town." In the episode "The Movie" (#54), Jerry goes back and forth (via a taxi) between comedy clubs in New York City in order to juggle his attempt to both perform his comedy act and meet his friends for a movie. At one point, Jerry finds himself stuck with Pat Buckles—a fellow, but annoying, comedian—while riding in a cab from one club to the next. Jerry misses one gig, and shows up at a theater which is sold out, postponing his movie plans. He then tries to get to another club but is too late. Then he is too late to meet his friends at a different movie theater. Many people can relate to the difficulty of trying to balance personal and professional lives.

In the episode "The Pitch" (#43), Jerry is approached for the first time by NBC executives about the possibility for a television show. George, who was standing nearby when Stu Chermak and Jay Crespi of NBC approached Jerry, assumes that he is a part of Jerry's team and horns in on the planning. Jerry decides to accept him as a cowriter. They have to come up with an idea for a television series. After a number of bad ideas (Jerry as a gymnastics teacher, an owner of an antique store, and a circus manager), George concludes that the show should be about friends talking and basically doing nothing! (Note: This storyline reflected the criticism directed toward *Seinfeld* at the time, that it was a show about nothing.) George reasons that every show is about *something* and therefore the public is ready for a show about nothing.

And so Jerry and George make their pitch to NBC. After a number of episodes of negotiations and various problems, NBC shoots the pilot. The one episode airs but the studio pulls the plug when a new president takes over the company. At the end of the *Seinfeld* series NBC offers a thirteen-episode commitment to Jerry to do the show.

George

A television writer was just one of the occupations attempted/held by George throughout the *Seinfeld* series. At the beginning of the series, George is a real estate agent, who once showed an apartment (in the third episode, "The Robbery") to Jerry, but then decided that he wanted it for himself. In the early years of *Seinfeld*, George struggled so badly that he had to move back home with his parents. As Jerry explains in the opening monologue of "The Puffy Shirt" (#66), moving back in with your parents (as an adult) is never a good sign (e.g., of financial success). Just when things look the worst for George, he receives a rather unusual job offer—as a hand model—in a rather unusual manner. George is at the front of a restaurant waiting to meet his parents for dinner when he accidentally runs into a woman, causing her to drop her purse. As he bends down to pick up the spilled items the woman compliments him on his hands and offers him her business card. As it turns out, she is an agent for specialty models.

George is amazed by his good fortune. He later shows off his hands to Jerry and Elaine who don't understand the attraction. But then Kramer walks in and nods approvingly, and commenting that George's hands are smooth, creamy, delicate, and yet masculine. George leaves Jerry's apartment wearing his oven mitts to protect his hands. Eventually, George shows up for a modeling gig and within a few minutes has made a huge sum of money (the audience is not informed as to the total amount). Unfortunately, George has a freak accident and burns his hands with a clothes iron, ruining his potential career as a hand model.

Perhaps George's happiest moment occurs in the episode "The Opposite" when he is hired by the New York Yankee organization (as described earlier in this chapter).

A sure sign of professional status is having one's own secretary. Because of his job with the Yankees, George needs a secretary for the first time in his life. In the episode "The Secretary" (#95), George interviews for one. He describes to Jerry how excited he is about this prospect. In six months, George has gone from taking messages *for* his mother, to having someone who will be taking messages *from* his mother.

Jerry, of course, has never had a secretary either. So, he asks George whether or not he is going to hire a "spokesmodel" type secretary. George has contemplated whether to go the "tomato" route, but he realizes that he would never get any work done and would become frustrated. Therefore, he decides to hire a woman with total efficiency and ability.

George hires Ada, a very professional woman who is highly efficient. He feels confident now that there will be no sexual tension and therefore no temptation to fool around with her. From a sociological standpoint, George has good reason to be concerned about sexual tension in the workplace, as sexual harassment lawsuits are rather common today, and the courts do not look favorably upon the accused. But this is George after all, and he manages to get himself in trouble anyway. He is so turned on by Ada's efficiency that he has sex with her in his office. During the sexual excitement, George yells out that he is going to give her a raise. And she makes sure that he keeps his "promise." After convincing Mr. Steinbrenner to give Ada a raise, she makes more money than George. Supervisors are never happy when their secretaries make more money than they do.

Another story about George in the workplace deals with a social problem found in society—employee pilferage. In the episode "The Jimmy" (#105), it is revealed that someone is stealing from the Yankees—a pitching machine, a batting cage, the in-field tarp, and all of Steinbrenner's vitamins. All indicators point that it is an "inside" job. No one is above suspicion. Conditions such as these lead to a highly stressful work environment as everyone is looking suspiciously at each other and looking for any signs of guilt.

George happens to like hot, spicy food. For lunch one afternoon he eats hot Kom Pau and then goes back to work. George, like many people, happens to sweat a lot after eating spicy foods. George's supervisor, Mr. Wilhelm, is beginning to suspect George of the thefts. Wilhelm questions George about the missing equipment and George keeps denying any knowledge of it. But because of the hot chicken, George is sweating like a guilty person under interrogation. Wilhelm continues to drill George. In an attempt to explain himself, George replies to Wilhelm that, "It's the Kom Pau. George likes his chicken spicy."

Only George's new habit of talking in the "third person"—something he picked up from Jimmy (another storyline centered on a guy named Jimmy who constantly speaks in the third person) in this episode—saves him from being fired after being summoned to Yankee owner George Steinbrenner's office.

> *George* (entering Steinbrenner's office): "You, wanted to see me Mr. Steinbrenner?"
>
> *Steinbrenner*: "Yes George, come in, come in. You know George, I've been your biggest supporter around here and that's why I was so disappointed to hear that you have been pilfering the equipment."
>
> *George*: "George would never do anything like that."
>
> *Steinbrenner* (a little confused by George's comment): "No, why would I? I own it."
>
> *George*: "Right!"
>
> *Steinbrenner*: "So what are you saying?"
>
> *George*: "Why would George steal from the Yankees?"
>
> *Steinbrenner*: "He wouldn't."
>
> *George*: "Course not."
>
> *Steinbrenner*: "Exactly [mumbles to himself]. I don't know what the hell's going on here."
>
> *George*: "Sir?"
>
> *Steinbrenner*: "Nothing."

George walks away commenting that it was "about time for George's lunch." And Steinbrenner, totally distracted from the pilferage issue, agrees with George and states, "Yes it is. Well, let's see what I have today." George has saved his job by talking in the third person—normally a very irritating habit of some celebrities, athletes, and other people who think too highly of themselves.

Elaine

As previously mentioned, most of Elaine's work experience is in publishing, serving the role of editor. She worked at Pendant Publishing for Mr. Lippman. In the episode "The Statue" (#11), Elaine is assigned to edit a book written by a European snob named Rava. Rava shows great disregard for American social norms by engaging in such behaviors as smoking in public buildings and elevators. But that is not Elaine's biggest obstacle to working with her. Rava's boyfriend, Ray, is working as a maid (to pay his way through graduate school), who does an excellent job cleaning apartments. Ray cleans Jerry's apartment so well that Jerry is simply amazed. However, Jerry notices that a statue of his is missing. Jerry immediately suspects Ray. Jerry later notices the statue (or an exact duplicate) in Rava and Ray's apartment when he and Elaine go over there. Eventually, Elaine and Rava get into a heated argument over the stolen statue. Elaine becomes so upset that she throws Rava's manuscript in the trash. The audience is left to decide for itself whether or not Ray did actually steal the statue, but it certainly would appear that he did.

In "The Opposite" (#86), Elaine is indirectly responsible for the demise of Pendant Publishing. Ironically, Pendant was about to be saved as a result of globalization (generally Americans lose jobs domestically because of globalization). Globalization is a hot topic in many fields, including sociology. Globalization has been discussed by social thinkers for centuries. For example, French utopian scholar Claude-Henri Saint-Simon (1760–1825) envisioned a planned society and an international community united by industrialization. He believed all the societies of the world would some day unite, forming a worldwide community. Because he felt that the "common" people could not grasp such a concept of a worldwide community, Saint-Simon reasoned that the social elites (of the world) would be needed to oversee and lead society.[12]

Karl Marx (1818–1883) spoke of the "evils" of capitalism and feared the impending consequences of emerging globalization. Marx had pointed out, over a century ago, that the industrial nations, in their continuous pursuit to maximize profits, had already entered the labor markets of the economically poor nations. Cheap labor and raw materials will always be needed by industrial nations and as a result, "weaker" nations will always risk being victimized by greedy capitalists. Exploiting weaker nations is just one of the negative consequences of globalization. Downsizing (a process whereby companies reduce their workforce) and outsourcing (a process whereby employers hire many people outside the company to do work) together are responsible for shrinking the supply of good-paying jobs, especially for those lacking a college-level education. These higher-paying jobs (mostly in industry and manufacturing) are being replaced by lower-paying jobs domestically. Meanwhile, giant corporations continue to move their operations overseas and pay low wages to foreign workers, so that they can maximize their profits.

The new world order of global capitalism is under attack from many protest groups, but they seem to be suffering from the same nearsightedness as Marx and Engels. Namely, we are still at the early stages of globalization. Through proper cultural assimilation, all societies of the world should be capable of finding a way to benefit from this economic reality. One major problem remains, of course, as an obstacle to a peaceful world community: the lack of cultural assimilation among the very diverse nations of the world. Nonetheless, as witnessed by the relatively new formation of megasocieties such as the European Union (regionalism), this indicates that the trend of globalization is continuing.

At the start of "The Opposite," Elaine and Mr. Lippman are celebrating her promotion at Pendant. Elaine later retells Jerry of her good fortune. Jerry had thought that Pendant was in financial trouble. Elaine said that they were, but that they were being absorbed by Matsushimi, a big Japanese conglomerate. The only obstacle to the Pendant purchase was the signing of the final papers.

As the day of the signing finally arrives, Mr. Lippman excitedly reminds Elaine that without the merger, they'd be out on the street.

On the day of signing, Mr. Lippman has a bad cold. He leaves his handkerchief behind as he heads off for the meeting with the Matsushimi executives. Elaine realizes that Lippman will need his handkerchief and tries to yell to him but she can't because her mouth is filled with juji fruit. As Lippman walks down the hall he sneezes into his hands. Shortly afterward, the top Japanese businessman reaches out to shake hands with Lippman. Without realizing the consequences of his actions, Lippman refuses to shake hands and says that he is sorry but he can't shake hands because of germs. The Matsushimi executives feel dishonored. They think Lippman was inferring they had germs, but really he was trying to avoid giving them his germs. The deal is off. Cultural differences are just one obstacle that Pendant fails to overcome.

Elaine's position at Doubleday was that of Mr. Pitt's personal assistant. She is really a glorified "gopher," and takes care of such mundane details as shopping for Mr. Pitt's white socks. His peculiar habits extend to a ban on ballpoint pens in the workplace because they can make a mess. In the episode "The Gymnast" (#92), Elaine violates this mandate and winds up getting ink all over Mr. Pitt's clothing. She also gets ink above his mouth resembling a small mustache, like Hitler's. Mr. Pitt is running late for a meeting announcing his company's (Morgan Springs) merger with another (Poland Creek). As he gives a passionate speech he begins to take on the characteristics of Hitler. The company threatens to pull out of the merger because Elaine had earlier mocked the proposed new company's name of Moland Springs—Moland was the combined names of Morgan and Poland.

In the episode "The Chicken Roaster" (#142), Elaine gets in trouble with J. Peterman when she abuses an expense account. Peterman is missing, his whereabouts unknown. Before he disappeared, he places Elaine in charge of his company. As acting president, Elaine thinks that she has free reign to spend as she wishes. The accountant reminds Elaine that all expenses have to be business-related and that even the president answers to the Board. Sociological research has shown that many employees pad expense accounts —finding a way to justify these expenses is the real trick to "creative accounting" practices. But ultimately, everyone in the workplace, even the president of a company, has to answer to someone.

There comes a point in time in nearly everyone's life where she thinks about starting her own business. The idea of being one's own boss sounds great to most people. One must act quickly if one has a good idea, however, because someone else may "steal" it. Hard work and a great deal of luck are also needed. In the episode "The Muffin Tops" (#155), it is revealed that Elaine only likes to eat the tops of muffins. (Who doesn't? Admit it, how many times have you eaten just the top of a muffin. I do this regularly, especially at meetings and conferences.) Mr. Lippman, Elaine's former boss at Pendant, notices Elaine's eating habit and asks why she only eats the tops of the muffins. Elaine responds that the tops are the best part. She also mentions that's a million dollar idea right there—to just sell the tops.

As time goes by, Elaine happens upon a new muffin shop—called Top of the Muffin to You! She walks in and is surprised to see Lippman behind the counter. She is upset because she believes that Lippman stole her idea. Lippman, refusing to admit that he stole her idea, replies that "Ideas are in the air!" Later, Lippman is forced to turn to Elaine and ask for her advice because she is the "expert" on muffin tops. Elaine is hesitant to help Lippman, that is, until he offers her 30 percent of the profits. Elaine proclaims they have a deal. She explains to Lippman that his problem was that he was trying to make just the tops. You have to make the whole muffin and get rid of the "stumps." The storyline ends and *Seinfeld* never revisited the Top of the Muffin to You! However, for millions of *Seinfeld* fans, muffins have never quite looked the same!

Kramer

Kramer's work history is a slight enigma. He never seemed to hold on to a steady job for any length of time; but he did have a number of part-time jobs. He worked as a stand-in with his friend Mickey on various television shows. He was a part-time Santa Claus at a shopping store, and worked for a short period of time in a bakery.

Perhaps the most notable, or entertaining, work-related episodes that involve Kramer are found in "The Opposite" (#86) and "The Bizarro Jerry" (#137). In "The Opposite," Kramer has become a success in pop culture—he has published a book. Not just any book, but a coffee table book about coffee tables. Kramer excitedly shares his good news with Jerry. One of the things that excites Kramer the most is the impending book tour. What author does not want to tour such shows as *Regis and Kelly* (then cohosted by Kathy Lee) and the *Today Show* to promote their book?

A book tour, especially one that begins with *Regis*, and now Kelly Ripa, is a sure sign of a successful book. Unfortunately, Kramer is a bit of a dunce at times and his appearance on *Regis* is a disaster. Kramer comes on stage and greets Kathy Lee with a kiss. Kramer's coffee table book is equipped with its own fold-out wooden legs built into the book itself, in case someone does not have their own coffee table. Regis and Kathy Lee think it is a fabulous idea. Kramer, basking in the accolades, takes a sip of coffee and then (for some unknown reason) spits it out all over Kathy Lee's dress. His book promotion is a flop. Worse yet, Mr. Lippman of Pendant Publishing, the organization that signed Kramer, cancels the rest of the scheduled tour. Kramer is devastated. He had especially looked forward to his second stop, *Sonia Live*. Kramer begs Lippman not to cancel the booking because he has a thing for Sonia.

In "The Bizarro Jerry," Kramer accidentally gets a job. He is using a private bathroom in the Brand-Leland office building. When he walks out of the men's room, trying to act nonchalant, he overhears a man in a suit complaining about the copier. Kramer tries to help the man, but the copier is jammed. A second man briskly walks by and announces that Mr. Leland (the boss) wants everyone in the conference room right away. The first man looks at Kramer and tells him they better get going. Kramer decides to tag along.

For days, Kramer shows up at Brand-Leland and makes friends with his coworkers. He has after-work drinks with them and seems to be having the time of his life. He is definitely bonding. But stress catches up to him, since he is not used to a "real" job. Furthermore, he no longer has time for his friends, like Jerry. His "relationship" with Jerry is compromised (this involves some very funny scenes centered on a premise that Jerry is the neglected stay-at-home wife and Kramer is the workaholic husband). Kramer is bringing work home with him and begins to suffer severe stomach pains. He's drinking Pepto Bismol from the bottle. Jerry tells Kramer that he is probably getting an ulcer from the job. He also suggests that the job is killing Kramer, and that is killing their relationship.

Well, eventually the boss, Mr. Leland, calls Kramer into his office to confront Kramer on his poor quality of work. Kramer mentions that he is having "trouble at home" and that he is willing to work nights and weekends, whatever it takes. Anyone responsible for providing for a family is able to relate to Kramer's desperate pleas that the boss keep him on and give him another chance. However, in business, the most important thing is the bottom line, not the personal lives of people. Leland ridicules Kramer's work and informs Kramer that he can no longer keep on with the company. Kramer then points out that he doesn't really even work for the company!

And thus, Kramer's foray as a businessman ended, unsuccessfully. He was fired. Generally speaking, the last two words any employee wants to hear are "You're fired!" But ultimately, people are either fired, or they quit, retire, or die.

Terminating Employment

In organizational society there exists a certain reality: people are replaceable. In rare cases, the organization is dependent upon one or a few key individuals. Consequently, people do not control their employment destinies. If a company wishes to terminate an employee, there is generally little that the employees can do to stop it. Because of such economic realities as the shifting labor market and downsizing, a lot of people are constantly "on guard" that they may be terminated—talk about stress. Employees begin to look for clues that they are in disfavor with management/ownership.

One such clue of impending termination is demonstrated in the episode "The Library" (#22). Elaine has been at Pendant Publishing for three and a half years, and suddenly she is "out of the loop" on such basic company dealings as ordering lunch. Elaine asks her secretary, "Where's Karen?" The secretary tells her that she went to pick up lunch and must have forgotten her. Elaine wonders what is going on and questions her secretary on how anyone could forget to ask her, she has been ordering lunch every day there for three and a half years. Elaine clearly knows something is up. And it's a scary feeling when you begin to realize that your employer *is* out to get you fired.

Elaine is so paranoid she discusses this development with Jerry. He thinks that Elaine is making too much of it, but as Elaine realizes, what does Jerry know about the office work environment, he's never worked in an office.

Some workers feel that if they are going to be terminated, that they want to go down "in style." Many employees "on the way out" find great solace in telling the boss off. A classic example of this mentality is displayed by George in "The Revenge" (#12). In this episode, George enters Dan's (his boss) office and immediately starts into a rant that he is through working for such an idiot, a laughingstock, a joke to his employees.

Well, George sure feels good about himself afterward, but then it dawns on him: he is unemployed and without work prospects. He tries to pretend that the whole quitting incident never occurred and just shows up at work the following Monday. But George also learns that when you a burn a bridge you can never cross back. The lesson to disgruntled employees: be very careful about telling off the boss.

Chapter 6

Sex and Gender Issues

"Not That There Is Anything Wrong with That."—Jerry

Have you ever seen a man wearing a fur coat? What was your reaction to this behavior? Is it okay for men to wear fur, or is it somehow feminine? In the episode "The Reverse Peephole" (#168), Elaine is eating lunch at Monk's. Her boyfriend, David Puddy, walks in wearing a fur coat. She cracks up laughing (mockingly) at David. She feels that it is inappropriate for a man to wear fur—she is actually against anyone wearing fur (she is an animal-rights advocate), but especially a man. Puddy likes to wear a fur coat in the winter and this is the first winter that Elaine and Puddy have dated. When they later attend a party at Joe Mayo's (a friend of the four characters), she throws his coat out the window. Unfortunately, it turns out to be Joe Mayo's fur coat.

The next day, Newman finds the coat in a tree beneath Joe Mayo's apartment window. He climbs the tree and retrieves it. Newman is dating the wife of Silvio (the super in Jerry, Kramer, and Newman's building) and presents the fur coat to her as a gift of affection. Silvio suspects Newman and threatens to kick Newman out of the building. Jerry has to pretend that it's his jacket to alleviate Silvio's suspicions of Newman.

Meanwhile, Jerry is meeting Keri, a woman he met at Mayo's party, for a night out on the town. Keri wants to go dancing, an activity that most men consider to be feminine. Keri and Jerry meet

111

on the street. Jerry thinks that dancing is stupid. However, as previously established, Jerry is a shallow man, and as such, is willing to do almost anything to go on a date with an attractive woman—even if that means dancing. Jerry learns there is still another cost involved with dating this gorgeous woman. She asks him to hold a bunch of stuff for her: a compact, lipstick, a gigantic ring of keys, and a tin of Altoids. Jerry puts all this stuff in his pockets.

Jerry is especially upset with these encumbrances because he had recently gone "wallet free." He was so happy all he had to carry was some cash and an apartment key. However, he now has so much of Keri's stuff he needs a bag to hold it all. Jerry ponders, isn't holding a "bag" the same thing as carrying a purse? And, isn't it wrong for a man to carry a purse? Marketers tried (unsuccessfully) to promote a men's "carryall" bag, but it never did catch on. The men's carryall is like a fanny pack—it looks feminine and most men would never even consider wearing/carrying one.

Elaine promotes the idea of a carryall to Jerry after listening to him complain about carrying Keri's stuff. Jerry eventually decides to get one for their next date. Keri compliments him on his carryall. Jerry proudly proclaims that it's European, which somehow makes it all right. She asks for her lipstick and Jerry, stumbling through his carryall looking for the lipstick, complains to Keri that he can never find anything in there. Elaine and Keri have given their approval (gender appropriateness) to Jerry that it is okay and appropriate to use a carryall. Jerry's male friends will not act in such an "enlightened" manner as the women. George is dedicated to his wallet to the point where it has become too full of stuff to close. Jerry tells him to throw away some of the useless pieces of paper he has in it. Upset, George mockingly states that at least he is not carrying a purse.

Meanwhile, in his attempt to throw Silvio off Newman's track, Jerry agrees to a plan hatched by Kramer to wear the fur coat to the corner, purchase a newspaper and walk by Silvio who is shoveling snow on the sidewalk. Silvio asks Jerry for confirmation that the fur actually belongs to him and not Newman. Begrudgingly, Jerry claims ownership of the fur. To add "insult" to Jerry's manhood and in an attempt to substantiate his story, Kramer runs outside and yells to Jerry that he forgot his purse! Silvio is convinced that Jerry is a "fancy boy." Jerry is further humiliated when a purse snatcher runs by and steals his bag. Jerry yells out to a police officer for assistance that his European carryall has been stolen. The cop is confused and asks Jerry if he means a purse. As if ashamed, Jerry has to admit to the police officer that he had his purse stolen.

"The Reverse Peephole" episode such described provides a glimpse into the world of gender appropriateness. Gender-appropriate clothing and accessories represent just one small area of concern for sociologists who study sex and gender.

Sex and Gender

One of the largest subfields of sociology involves the study of gender, gender roles, sexual relationships, and sexual behavior. There is no other discipline that equals the level of expertise on the study of sex and gender than sociology.

In introductory sociology courses it is standard procedure to inform students of the meaning of specific terms such as sex, gender, and gender roles. One's sex refers to a biological distinction between male and female. Gender refers to the socially labeled characteristics that are expected of a person based on their sex. Thus, a male is expected to act masculine (as defined by society) and a female is expected to act feminine (also as defined by society).

Individuals are socialized to act a certain way, to abide by the rules, and behave appropriately. Gender expectations represent a significant variable when determining what constitutes proper behavior. Specific gender-based expectations of behavior are known as gender roles. For example, a sociological analysis of the workplace reveals that most nurses are women and most firefighters are males. Members of society generally expect firefighters and police officers to be male. These types of occupations are perceived as better suited for males. But what if a woman wants to be a firefighter or a police officer? Shouldn't she have the right to pursue such a profession?

Sociologists remind us that gender roles are tied to cultural mandates and are not a matter of biology. Thus, if a woman wants to pursue a profession traditionally held by a man, she should have the legal right to pursue it. Being born male or female should not dictate how a person behaves, and yet, this ideological belief exists in many cultures. Western societies, with their more liberal perspective, believe that women should have the right to pursue such occupations traditionally held by men. Other societies, driven by a conservative religious code, believe that a woman's role is to have babies and raise a family.

When people expect a man or a woman to behave in a certain manner simply because of their sex, they are guilty of a sexist ideology. Why should the man be expected to be the primary breadwinner of the family? Why should the woman be expected to quit her job to raise the children? These roles are traditional, but they are not linked to biological commands. The only true creed of nature and corresponding sex roles is that historically man and woman must procreate in order for the species to survive (today, science has found a way to create babies without male-female intercourse). Everyone understands this logic. But biological mandates do not extend beyond this simple fact.

Seinfeld introduced a number of sociological issues related to gender and sex appropriateness. This chapter reviews a few of the more memorable examples.

Gender Issues

Gender roles are taught. The teachers of gender roles include all the agents of socialization that individuals come into contact with. The primary agents of socialization are the family, especially the parents, and friends. Some parents are more concerned than others from a gender-appropriate position as to how their sons and daughters are raised. For example, most fathers would rather have their sons play football than dance ballet. Boys are often given trucks, toy guns, and sports equipment to play with starting at an early age, whereas girls are often given dolls and passive play toys. Boys are told, "Be tough" and "Big boys don't cry." And boys are mocked if they throw a ball inappropriately: "You throw like a girl!" Kramer once mocked George for "running like a girl" in the airport.

Parents provide their children with many direct and indirect messages as to what constitutes appropriate behavior for boys and for girls. By the time the child enters third or fourth grade, the peer group begins to have a stronger influence on children than their parents. Children are often brutal toward one another. Any sign of violating the norm is pointed out and ridiculed. Gender appropriateness is often a major issue for children.

The fact is we are continually bombarded by messages of gender appropriateness throughout our lifetime by such entities as the media, religion, the workplace, and adult friendships. All these messages lead people to develop a reflex reaction to issues related to gender stereotyping and gender advantages and disadvantages.

Gender Stereotypes

A stereotype is an overgeneralization about a group of people. Stereotypes persist in society for two reasons: many people repeat them so often that they seem to be true, and there is almost always some basis of truth behind the stereotype that is applicable to at least some of the members of that group. For example, it is a stereotype that men like sports more than women do. But there is some truth to this stereotype because, as a rule, men are more likely than women to like sports. Just as it is true that women generally enjoy dancing more than men do. Does this mean that there are not any men who like to dance or women who like sports? Of course not, it just seems to be true in general. Sociological research investigates stereotypes in order to determine their validity.

There are many examples of gender stereotype usages in *Seinfeld*. As far as we know, Jerry did not conduct any research on the validity of his claims, but he offers up many stereotypical views of the sexes.

For example, in the opening monologue of "The Stakeout" (#2), Jerry contrasts the check-writing habits of women and men at the checkout stand. Jerry believes that women are faster than men at writing out checks because women write more checks. Men, according to Jerry, have a different outlook on writing checks. It's as if writing checks makes them effeminate. Men tend to fumble over things like whom to write the check out to and producing a valid ID as proof of who they are. According to Jerry, men do not consider it masculine to write checks because a check is like a note from your mother that says you don't have any money but if you contact these people, surely they will vouch for you.

In the opening monologue of "The Male Unbonding" (#4), Jerry offers his stereotypical view of men and their desire to watch other men work. According to Jerry and his observations, men love watching other men use tools. All the men in the neighborhood are magnetically drawn to this activity. The sound of a drill is like a dog whistle that calls men from out of their homes. Interestingly, these men don't actually help the guy out; they just like to hang around the area where work is being done. Jerry expands on his theory of men and work to construction sites. He insists that the reason construction sites have those little holes is for men to peep through so they know what is going on. Otherwise, Jerry suggests, men will climb the fences to find out what is being built.

Jerry introduces a number of gender stereotypes in his monologues. For example, in "The Baby Shower" (#15), Jerry describes his observations about the television remote control. (Sociological studies have shown that men control the remote in more than 80 percent of households.) Jerry mentions that men like the television remote in their hands and that they like to channel surf more than women do. Jerry believes this is the case because women nest and men hunt. Women will want to see what the show is before they switch channels. Men like the thrill of the chase and therefore constantly switch from channel to channel.

Gender Advantages and Disadvantages

Ideally, people would be treated equally regardless of their sex. But this is not the case. There are times when men have an advantage because of their traditional power base in society. As a result, women are often victims of sexism. Of course, men may also be victimized because of changes made in the occupational structure to accommodate women. Furthermore, a number of women take advantage of their feminine prowess.

The episode "The Calzone" (#130) provides an excellent example of the advantageous position that attractive women have in American society. Jerry is dating a woman named Nicki who, because of her beauty, gets whatever she wants. For example, Jerry and Nicki meet up with Elaine and her date, Todd Gak. The movie they all wanted to see is sold out. Jerry turns to Nicki and suggests that she see what she can do about getting tickets. Nicki agrees and heads off to see the manager. Elaine is puzzled by Jerry's request; after all, what can she do if the movie is sold out? Jerry is confident in Nicki's feminine charm which she routinely uses to her advantage. Shortly thereafter, Nicki returns with two tickets for the sold out show.

The next day, Jerry rehashes the story with George. George is not surprised. He agrees with Jerry that beautiful women can get away with anything, including murder. Furthermore, George argues that beautiful women not only get whatever they want, they cannot be stopped. Jerry states that Nicki is like a "beautiful Godzilla."

In this same episode, Nicki later helps Jerry get out of a speeding ticket by charming a police officer. And she simply asks the officer if he really has to give him a ticket. The cop just looks at her like a deer caught in headlights. Jerry and Nicki drive off. Men and feminists alike are jealous of the fact that beautiful women get whatever they want just because of their looks.

George is so paranoid over the perceived power of beautiful women that he believes they have their own secret society. In the episode "The Bizarro Jerry" (#137), George discovers this hidden world. He cracks their code of entry by utilizing a combination of truth and lies. While talking to a gorgeous receptionist, Amanda, that he just met, George conveniently drops a photo of a model friend (Gillian, the "man hands" woman) of Elaine's and lies to Amanda that it is his deceased fiancée, Susan. Jerry had conducted a focus group study earlier (see chapter 1) and found that the best excuse someone could give to a potential dating partner was that the prior relationship ended because of a tragic death (rather than other options such as being dumped or being the one to dump the other). Amanda, who was impressed that George was engaged to such an attractive woman and therefore must have something going for himself, expresses her condolences.

Amanda introduces George to the fantasy world he dreamed existed. They arrive at a place that looks like a cheap bar on the outside, to an interior that is rich in design and filled with a roomful of gorgeous women. George retells the story of his dearly departed Susan, while showing the photo of Gillian to all the women at the club. He impresses all the women, and they warm to him quickly. The next day George informs Jerry that "the legends are true." Models and beautiful women are everywhere.

Full of confidence, George breaks off his relationship with Amanda, thinking that he no longer needs her. Jerry warns George about burning his bridge to Amanda, but George is not concerned. As regular viewers of *Seinfeld* know, George does not have the best of luck. He accidentally destroys the photo of Gillian with his hair dryer. When George returns to the "beautiful people" bar the next night, without Amanda and without the photo of Gillian to support his story, all the women blow him off. The bouncer escorts him out of the club. The very next day George reappears at the same location of the beautiful people bar with Jerry, who is anxious to enter the forbidden world occupied by only beautiful people, only to find that it has been converted to a meat-packing work site.

In the episode "The Pilot" (#63), Elaine is outraged at the new management of Monk's coffee shop. While having lunch with Jerry she notices that all the women have large breasts. Elaine asks Jerry if he thinks it's merely a coincidence. Jerry responds, "I have not seen four women like this together outside of a Russ Meyer film." (This is a reference to the Russ Meyer films of the 1970s that were characterized by women with large breasts, such as *Supervixens* and *Beyond the Valley of the Dolls*.) Elaine thinks that such hiring practices are discriminatory. That is, she believes that the new owner of Monk's discriminates against small-breasted women. Even Elaine acknowledges that beautiful women get away with things and she wants to draw the line at the hiring of waitresses. Interestingly, at this point in time, Jerry admits that good-looking men have the same advantages.

In fact, in 2004 researchers at the University of Waterloo in Canada found that people with the most attractive faces live longer. Attractiveness was operationalized as good facial symmetry, no visible scars or disfigurations of the face, a prominent chin and nose on a man and high cheek-bones on a woman. Jerry was right, good-looking people do have advantages.

Discrimination cases are generally taken very seriously; especially in a court of law. Elaine decides to apply for a job as a waitress at the coffee shop. She does not have any experience as a waitress, so she lies on her application form. She wears one of Jerry's over-sized shirts, untucked, so that she does not look attractive for the interview. When she is denied a job, she goes to the Equal Employment Opportunity Commission Office (EEOCO) to complain about discrimination. She informs the EEOCO that there is a diner with only large-busted women working there. She wants to file a complaint.

In "The Pilot (2)" (#64), Monk's coffee shop is filled with men who work with the EEOCO who are all enjoying the attributes of these waitresses. As it turns out, the new owner was not guilty of discrimination, as all the women that worked there are his daughters. Thus, Elaine should have done some research before making false accusations about an employer's hiring practices.

Same-Sex Relationships

A small percentage (estimates range from 1 percent to 10 percent) of the human population is gay. Historically, gay people have been victimized by outright discrimination and ridicule. They have been forced to hide their true identities. Over the past few decades, gay people have been coming out (as in coming out of "the closet" where their true selves were hidden). The gay population has become a very powerful lobbying political group. Many laws have been passed to stop discrimination against them. At present, the gay community is fighting for the right to have legal marriages so that they may enjoy all the same rights and privileges afforded by society to heterosexual married couples. Their attempts for equality in the marriage sector were given a major blow by the reelection of President George W. Bush in 2004. Many conservative states have countered the liberal movements of gay activists by passing legislation declaring that marriage can only occur between a man and a woman.

As we know, George Costanza started dating Susan when she was an executive at NBC and Jerry and George were trying to get their sitcom on the air. George and Susan broke up after the whole sitcom deal fell apart. While they were split up, Susan decided to give lesbianism a try. (This episode is "controversial" in that it reflects the belief by some people that homosexuality is a choice. Other people believe that homosexuality is determined biologically—there is no evidence to support this claim at the present time.)

In the episode "The Smelly Car" (#61), George and Kramer are at a movie rental store and George notices a lesbian couple holding hands. He is intrigued by this. George considers a lesbian sighting fascinating. The couple turns around and George recognizes one of the women—it's Susan. She introduces George to her girlfriend, Mona. Mona lets the two of them catch up and wanders off. Obviously, Susan realizes that George is a little uncomfortable or at least puzzled. George tries to act cool and tells Susan that he encourages experimentation. George is a little concerned when he finds out that Susan became a lesbian right after they broke up.

Meanwhile, Kramer has been flirting with Mona, a life-long lesbian. Mona is drawn to Kramer. She meets with him later, and they have sex. Susan finds out that Mona is cheating on her with Kramer —her nemesis from previous episodes. Susan pounds on Kramer's door to confront him and Mona. But they just ignore her until she leaves. Inside Jerry's apartment, Jerry and George hear the commotion in the hallway. They investigate and see Susan outside Kramer's door. She informs them that Kramer stole Mona away from her; another bad thing he is responsible for in Susan's life. George is baffled by Kramer's ability to pick up women and states, "Amazing. I drive them to lesbianism; he brings 'em back."

When Kramer burns down Susan's father's (Henry Ross) cabin, it leads to an interesting discovery in the episode "The Cheever Letters" (#48). Mr. Ross loved that cabin. His father built it in 1947, and his dying words to Henry were to cherish it. The cabin was like a sanctuary for Henry Ross. The only item saved from the fire that burned it down is a strong box that contained "love letters" from John Cheever to Henry. Not knowing of the content of the letters, Susan begins reading the first one aloud: "Dear Henry, last night with you was bliss. I fear my orgasm [Susan gasps and the whole room of relatives look at her very intently] has left me a cripple. I don't know how I shall ever get back to work. I love you madly, John. P.S. Loved the cabin." Susan's entire family is in shock, as Henry Ross had just been "outed"!

There are times when people are outed who are not even gay. This foul-up occurred in the episode "The Outing" (#57). Elaine, Jerry, and George are sitting in a booth together at the coffee shop. Elaine notices that the woman sitting behind George is eavesdropping on their conversation. So, Elaine decides to spice up the conversation for the benefit of the woman who is eavesdropping. She refers to Jerry and George as homosexuals and suggests that they come out of the closet and be openly gay. George plays along with Elaine. Jerry, on the other hand, is not comfortable pretending being gay just to amuse a couple of eavesdroppers. Jerry takes his disdain of George and Elaine's joking around to the level of comparing it to Nazi Germany. He says to George, "I can just see you in Berlin in 1939 goose-stepping past me. C'mon Jerry, go along, go along." The reference to Nazi Germany is relevant here because Hitler had also targeted gays, among the many groups other than Jews that he set out to exterminate.

Elaine is disappointed in Jerry for not playing. The eavesdropper walks away thinking Jerry and George are gay. Jerry then admits to Elaine that some people think he is gay because he single, thin, and neat—stereotypes of gay men. As a means of confirming his hetero-sexuality George jokes that those stereotypes leave him "in the clear."

Jerry is supposed to have met with a student reporter from New York University while he is at the coffee shop. They are playing "phone tag" and keep missing each other. And since they had never met before, Jerry and George have no idea that the woman who was eavesdropping on their "gay" conversation is in fact the reporter (Sharon). Jerry finally reaches Sharon and invites her to his apartment to conduct the interview. George is already in Jerry's apartment. When Sharon arrives, she recognizes Jerry and George from the coffee shop immediately. Jerry and George do not recognize her.

Sharon begins to misinterpret a number of "innocent" comments made by George and Jerry as confirmation that they are gay lovers. Sharon begins to ask questions aimed at probing Jerry's personal relationship with George. For example, Sharon asks Jerry if he does anything besides stand-up and when Jerry replies that he and George are doing a pilot for NBC, Sharon views this as further proof. Jerry is puzzled by a number of Sharon's comments.

Sharon: "And do your parents know?"

[One of the biggest challenges facing a gay person who has decided to "come out" is whether to inform parents, family, and friends.]

Jerry: "Know what?"
George: "My parents? They don't know *what's* going on."

[Suddenly it dawns on Jerry where he has seen Sharon before.]

Jerry: "Oh my God, you're the girl in the coffee shop that was eavesdropping on us. I knew you looked familiar!"

[Jerry, George, and Sharon all react nervously.]

Jerry: "There's been a big misunderstanding here! We did that whole thing for your benefit. We knew you were eavesdropping. That's why my friend said that. It was on purpose! We're not gay! Not that there's anything wrong with that."
George: "Of course not."
Jerry: "I mean that's fine if that's who you are."
George: "Absolutely."
Jerry: "I mean, I have many gay friends."
George: "My father is gay!"
Sharon: "Look, I know what I heard."
Jerry: "It was a joke."
George (again attempting to affirm his heterosexuality): "Look, you wanna have sex right now? Do you want sex with me right now? Let's go! C'mon, let's go baby! C'mon."

[Just as Sharon is about to leave, Kramer walks in.]

> *Kramer*: "Hey, C'mon! Let's go! I thought we were going to take a steam!"
> *George*: "No!"
> *Jerry*: "No steam!"
> *Kramer*: "Well I don't want to sit there naked all by myself."

Despite Jerry's denials, Sharon prints an article "outing" Jerry and George. The wire service picks up the NYU article and soon they are "outed" in the national media. George and Jerry have to deal with curious and anxious phone calls from their parents, friends, and strangers. Every time Jerry and George deny being gay they include a follow-up statement, "Not that there is anything wrong with that!"

Near the end of "The Outing" episode, Jerry and Sharon have "hooked up" and are making out on his couch. George, meanwhile, had been trying to break up with his girlfriend Allison since the beginning of the episode. She threatens to commit suicide if he does break up with her. George reasons that his "outing" might be a legitimate excuse to end the relationship without hurting her feelings. Consequently, George brings Allison over to Jerry's apartment so that he will play along with them being gay so that he can dump her. Jerry, who is making out with Sharon, of course, does not want to play along with George's deception.

George may have been willing to act gay in order to break up with Allison, but he demonstrates time after time that he is homophobic. In the episode "The Note" (#18), George and Elaine go to a physical therapist office to get a massage. They learned from Jerry that if you have a note from a doctor, the treatment is covered by insurance—thus, it's free.

George is assigned to a male masseuse, Raymond. The idea of a man rubbing and massaging him makes George very uncomfortable. He asks Elaine to switch because she has a woman masseuse. She refuses. George expresses his homophobic concerns to Elaine: "What if something happens? What if I like it?" Throughout the massage George is very nervous, he cannot concentrate or relax; all because he is afraid something sexual might happen. Primarily, he believes that if he enjoys this massage (even though it is from a professional masseuse) that is a sign he's gay.

After the massage, George has a shell-shocked look on his face.

He goes to Jerry's apartment to discuss the fact that he had a massage—from a *man*. George is especially concerned about an "incident" that occurred during the massage. He tells Jerry that he thinks "it" (his penis) moved. George thinks that's a sign of gayness, if a man makes "it" move. Jerry tells him that the real test is if it moves as a result of contact—it has to be touched. George asks if he is sure, and Jerry says that is what his gym teacher once told him.

George further explains his homophobia by exclaiming that he doesn't even like sitting next to a man on a plane because their knees may touch and he has to use a stall instead of a urinal in public restrooms.

In another example of George's homophobia, George refuses to sit in the middle seat between Jerry and Elaine in Jerry's car. This incident occurs in the episode "The Ex-Girlfriend" (#6). George is in the car with Jerry and they pick up Elaine, who asks George to slide over. George tells her to get in the back of the car. But, Elaine does not want to sit in the back seat because she will miss out on the conversation between Jerry and George. Elaine just wants George to slide over and be in the middle. She even suggests that the reason George will not sit next to Jerry is because he is homophobic. To solve this seating problem, George gets out of the car and insists on Elaine sliding into the middle seat.

A couple of other important concepts relevant to a sociological discussion on homosexuality are addressed in the episode "The Beard" (#103): "conversion" and "beard." A "beard" is someone who acts as a gay person's heterosexual partner. In "The Beard," Elaine goes on a date with a gay guy, Robert, who she finds gorgeous. He is trying to hide his true sexual identity from his boss, as he feels that "coming out" may be damaging to his career. Elaine plays the perfect "beard" for her date. She calls him "honey," they hold hands and kiss and overall, look like a heterosexual couple.

Elaine does such a good job being a beard and she has such a good time with Robert, that she discusses the idea of "conversion" with Jerry. She thinks that she can convince Robert to convert to heterosexuality simply by using her feminine charms. Jerry warns her that it is difficult to get someone to "change teams." As Jerry tries to explain to Elaine that someone does not change teams on a whim. (Note: This seems to imply that Jerry recognizes homosexuality as predetermined and not chosen.) Elaine's attempt at conversion almost works. Robert does switch teams. But his defection ends quickly, and he rejoins his original team. She reasons with Jerry that because she only has access to *that* equipment (a penis) for a short period of time, how could she be expected to compete with players who have access to that equipment all the time. Jerry tells Elaine that's why they lose so few players.

Sex

Few topics generate greater curiosity than sex. It ranks as one of the most pleasurable behaviors to participate in. Yet, there are many rules and norms attached to this behavior: Individuals must be of a "legal" age to have sex; it must always be consensual; it must not involve immediate family members; it cannot be done in public places; and most societies have laws limiting certain sexual activities (including the participants).

There are more complications related to sex than just some of the legal issues mentioned above. Finding someone to have sex with is a good start. Jerry only dates good-looking women and in the episode "The Wink" (#114), he concludes that only 5 percent of the population is attractive. Therefore, 95 percent of the population is undateable by Jerry's standards. Although Jerry's dating pool is determined solely by one criterion—attractiveness—his statistic may be quite accurate.

Let's do the math. Half of the population is undateable right at the start (unless, of course, you are bisexual). Within the gender pool of choice, the large majority are already involved in a relationship, thus eliminating them from consideration. Another large percentage of the population is not dateable because of age restrictions, mental incompetency, imprisonment, and so on. How many people are left? Not many. And, just because someone is single, does not mean they will accept an invitation for a date, let alone the ultimate goal of sex. It seems that less than 5 percent of the population is dateable for any given person.

Going Without Sex

A number of people go without sex—some by choice. Adults find it odd to purposely go without sex, especially those adults who want it. Children are encouraged and taught to wait to have sex until either they are "of age" or get married. Consequently, there are a number of young people of legal age who are virgins. They think it is best to "save themselves" until they are married, or at least, until they find a partner that they are in love with.

In the episode "The Virgin" (#50), Jerry is dating a woman, Marla, who is a virgin. Jerry finds it very uncomfortable to date a virgin. They start making out, "his troops are on the border," and then, it stops, because she is a virgin. He is sexually frustrated. Elaine further complicates issues by openly discussing with Marla and Jerry her diaphragm falling out of her purse at a party. And all the details just make Marla uncomfortable. Marla decides to leave Jerry's apartment. Elaine asks Jerry if he thinks she offended Marla. When Jerry tells Elaine that Marla is a virgin, Elaine worries that she may have said something that was "anti-virgin." She asks Jerry whether she should apologize to Marla and let her know that she is not anti-virgin.

There are times when adults choose not to have sex. In the episode "The Abstinence" (#143), George and his girlfriend, Louise, cannot have sex for six weeks because she has mononucleosis. Jerry asks George if he can go six weeks without sex. George informs Jerry that he is like a "sexual camel." Meaning, he can go without sex for long periods of time. George also learns that when his mind is not completely preoccupied on trying to find a way to have sex with a woman (as it would have been had George broken up with Louise as Jerry suggested), that he is capable of concentrating on a wide variety of subjects. In short, George becomes smart when he abstains from having sex.

Elaine also voluntarily decides to abstain from having sex with her boyfriend (Ben) in this same episode. Elaine is helping Ben study for his licensing exam to practice medicine. In an attempt to increase Ben's concentration of his studies, Elaine "cuts off" Ben from sex. His concentration level increases dramatically. However, Elaine becomes stupid. Jerry reassures Elaine that as soon as Ben passes the exam she can have sex again. Elaine does not want to wait and asks Jerry for a "quickie."

In the episode "The Contest" (#51), Jerry, George, and Kramer discuss masturbation and who can abstain the longest from pleasuring themselves. Elaine asks to join in on this unusual contest of abstinence. The guys all say "no" to her because the differences between men and women masturbating are like apples and oranges. Jerry tries to explain to Elaine that for men, masturbation is necessary; it is a part of their lifestyle. Kramer says it's like shaving. Elaine mentions that she shaves her legs. However, as Kramer explains, not every day!

The guys do allow Elaine to participate in the contest but she has to put up more money. George wants 2 to 1 odds and Kramer wants 10 to 1. But they agree that Elaine will put in $150 and the guys will put in $100 each.

Most people want sex on a regular basis. Someone like George can go long periods without sex, but even he has regular sex in many relationships, especially while dating Susan. Most couples enjoy sex on a regular basis. However, there are times when even loving couples must go without it. In the episode "The Raincoats (2)" (#83), Jerry has not been able to spend time with his girlfriend Rachel. Jerry's parents are visiting him and are crashing at his apartment and Rachel lives at home with her parents. Jerry and Rachel go to the movies to watch *Schindler's List*. They make out like two teenagers throughout the entire three-hour movie. Newman is sitting a few rows behind Jerry and Rachel and decides to squeal on Jerry to his parents knowing that they will be offended.

Public displays of affection are always in questionable taste. Making out in a theater while watching a movie like *Schindler's List* represents a violation of cultural mores.

In the episode "The Hamptons" (#85), the whole gang has been invited to the beach home of Carol and Michael so that they can meet their new baby. (Viewers of *Seinfeld* will remember Carol's obnoxious voice: "Jeh-Ree, you gotta see the Bay-Bee! You gotta see the Bay-Bee!") Rachel is going to meet Jerry later in the evening. George's new girlfriend, Jane, is joining him for the weekend.

George and Jane have not had sex yet, but George is very excited that they are going to be spending the weekend together. The way George looks at it, "It's like she signed a letter of intent." As the two of them head to the Hamptons, George is thinking to himself how lucky he is about to become. At this very moment he cannot reach over and grab Jane's breasts, but as he anticipates the evening's events he realizes that at this same time tomorrow he will be able to touch them all he wants.

George has every reason to believe that his abstinence from Jane is about to end. They arrive at the beach house and everyone is excited about the weekend. George drives off to get some tomatoes for his mother. Jane decides to go topless and gives Kramer, Jerry, and Elaine a full view. George is upset when he later finds out that they all got a peek before he did. He also wonders why she would walk around topless in front of his friends. Kramer reasoned that she was most likely trying to create a "buzz" or good word of mouth.

Still, George has every reason to be happy; soon he will see and touch Jane's breasts. Or so he thinks. After swimming in the pool, he undresses in his room. Rachel walks into his room by mistake and sees George naked. Rachel screams out that she is sorry to burst into his room, she thought it was the baby's room. She looks down at George's groin area and emphasizes, "I'm *really* sorry!" She exits the room and George realizes he has just been "short-changed" in Rachel's impression of him. For you see, George was suffering from "shrinkage," a strange phenomenon known to all men. Namely, that the penis shrinks after it's been in cold water (like a pool). George tries to yell out to Rachel to explain himself.

George dresses and confronts Jerry in his room as to whether Rachel walked in on him on purpose or not. George informs Jerry that Rachel saw him naked, which he wouldn't normally mind, except this time he had just got back from swimming in the pool and the water was cold. Jerry immediately thinks of shrinkage; and George admits that there was significant shrinkage. George is worried that Rachel has the wrong impression of him. He soon realizes a worse fate, that Rachel may say something to Jane. Jerry is under the naive impression that Rachel won't say anything because women are not like men. George explains to Jerry that they are much worse. They can talk about everything. George asks Jerry to say something to Rachel about the shrinkage factor. He does not want bad word of mouth.

Jerry tries to reassure George that all women know about shrinkage. George wonders why they would. They decide to ask Elaine if she knows about the shrinkage problem. Elaine initially thinks they are talking about laundry. When George and Jerry explain to her that it shrinks like a frightened turtle in cold water she is shocked and wonders why it happens. George tells her that it just does, that men cannot control it. Elaine mockingly asks George and Jerry how men can possibly walk around with those "things."

As it turns out, Rachel does inform Jane about George's perceived shortcomings and before George has any time to explain himself (or see her naked) she takes off in the middle of the night. Once again, George is without sex.

Having Sex

Despite some of the obstacles to having sex described above, the four main characters do have a lot of sex. An interesting thing about the

Seinfeld series: although there was a near parade of attractive women and plenty of implied sex, the producers rarely relied on titillating displays. In fact, Rachel's display at the beach house ("The Hamptons"), where the audience sees her from behind wearing a bikini bottom, was one of the very few times "skin" was shown.

People don't just have sex. They have a number of fantasies that go along with it. One of men's favorite sexual fantasies is having a gorgeous woman frolic in the nude. In the episode "The Apology" (#165), Jerry has a girlfriend (Melissa) who he just had sex with for the first time. The next morning he is cooking breakfast and yells to Melissa that the waffles are ready. Melissa shows up in the kitchen stark naked and without any shame or embarrassment. Jerry looks at her in glad delight.

Much to Jerry's surprise however, naked is not *always* good. Jerry distinguishes between good naked and bad naked. Bad naked, for example, occurs when the person coughs. This is because there are thousands of unseen muscles that suddenly spring into action. Pinching skin while fixing a bicycle and straining to open a pickle jar are other examples of bad naked. Jerry explains that good naked is an attractive woman brushing her hair. Jerry goes naked in his apartment to see how Melissa reacts. She informs him that naked is not good on men, because they are generally too hairy and overweight.

Another sexual fantasy involves receiving a sexy message. In the episode "The Tape" (#25), a mysterious woman leaves a sexy message on Jerry's answering machine that he had set up while he performed on stage. Jerry plays back the tape for Jerry and Kramer and they all fantasize about who the woman is and wonder why she left an anonymous message. The message is so "dirty" that the guys play it back over and over again. As it turns out, it was Elaine just messing with Jerry. But the three amigos look at Elaine quite differently now.

Somewhere along the way, usually in high school, males learn of a legend—a legend that centers on a woman so gifted in her ability to perform sexual stunts that men dare not dream of her—this woman is the gymnast. Jerry meets a former Olympian silver medal winner gymnast (Katya) from Romania.

Jerry ends up having sex with Katya, but he is not that impressed. He discusses it with Elaine. Elaine makes fun of Jerry and his fantasy and asks what he expected. Jerry admitted he wasn't quite sure. But he pictured being ridden like a pommel horse. There is an interesting twist to the ending of this storyline as Katya explains to Jerry that in her country a legend exists of a man so virile and so potent, that a woman would not dare spend a night with such a man. This man is known as a "comedian." It seems that Katya was as disappointed with Jerry's sexual prowess as he was of her. As Katya stated, "You may tell jokes, Mr. Jerry Seinfeld, but you are no Comedian."

One of George's fantasies was to combine his two loves: food and sex. In the episode "The Blood" (#160), George fulfills this fantasy with his girlfriend Tara and salted cured meats. Tara had burned vanilla incenses while she and George had sex. All he could think of was food. The next night they are together he tells her that he would like to add food to their lovemaking. He brings strawberries, chocolate sauce, and pastrami on rye with mustard to bed.

George tells Jerry about his evening. Tara was not happy with the sandwich. George thinks it is only natural to want to combine his two favorite passions. Jerry doesn't think there is anything natural about trying to combine sex and food. Jerry tells George that sex is supposed to be between a man and a woman. Not a man and a sandwich as George would prefer. Jerry thinks that George should spend time trying to please his woman instead of pleasing two of his own needs first.

The next night George shows that his selfishness has no bounds, as he attempts the trifecta: food, sex, and television! While having sex with Tara, he is eating and listening to the TV while wearing headphones. Tara has had enough and breaks up with him. At the end of "The Blood" episode, George meets Elaine's friend Vivian, who has an equal passion to the same trifecta pleasures as George. They wind up having sex on Vivian's floor while eating fresh baked pastrami and watching television.

In "The Mango" (#65) episode, another very interesting sociological issue is introduced—faking an orgasm. Among the issues involved in "faking it" is why someone would fake it and how people react when they find out their partner is doing so. In this episode, Elaine admits to Jerry that she faked with him. Jerry is stunned that he didn't know the difference.

When she admits that she faked all the time (because she couldn't get orgasms back then) Jerry is upset. He refers to such orgasms as "orgasms under false pretenses." Furthermore, faking an orgasm, in Jerry's mind, is like committing "sexual perjury."

Jerry is so upset with this whole fake orgasm issue that he wonders if all his ex-girlfriends faked with him. He begins to call them all, and he is happy to learn that they did not fake. He is upset with Elaine because he now feels inadequate because he could not bring her to orgasm. He hounds Elaine relentlessly demanding one more chance in bed with her. She finally agrees, mostly just to get him to stop asking. Well, poor Jerry suffers from a problem older men do from time to time: he could not perform. Now he really feels inadequate. He blames his poor performance on George for talking about his problems performing with Karin.

Chapter 7

Social Deviance

"You Double-dipped the Chip!"—Timmy

There are a number of behaviors that are not criminal but perhaps should be. For example, "picking your nose" in public, I believe, should be illegal. I have noticed people in their cars picking their noses and it always amazes me. Do they think they have a "cloak of invisibility" in their cars? In the episode appropriately named "The Pick" (#53), Jerry's model girlfriend, Tia, is in a taxicab that pulls aside Jerry in his car. Jerry is legitimately itching the outside of his nose, but from Tia's perspective it looks as though Jerry is actually picking his nose. She is so disgusted with Jerry that she breaks up with him.

Defining Deviance

In simple terms, deviant behavior includes any act that violates a social norm. Such behaviors do not conform to the expectations and guidelines of a group or society. The sociological study of deviant behavior reveals that a number of circumstances influences how some behaviors come to be defined as deviant, while others are defined as acceptable. After all, no behavior is inherently deviant; it must be labeled as deviant in order to be deviant.

Unfortunately, the study of deviance is not so simple. One problem with the classification of behaviors is that definitions of deviance vary from culture to culture. For example, eating dog is considered deviant in American society, but not in Korean society.

Conservative American society has determined that it is inappropriate for women to go topless at the beach. This explains the astonishment demonstrated by Jerry, Elaine, and Kramer with George's girlfriend Jane when she goes topless in the episode "The Hamptons" (#85). In many other societies it would have been normal for Jane to go topless at the beach. Then again, if Jane went topless in nearly any Middle Eastern society, where women are expected to wear clothing from head to toe, even to the point where it is impossible to see the female form, she would likely be stoned to death.

Other problems related to defining certain acts as deviant is the fact that definitions change over time and by situation. For example, in 1872, Susan B. Anthony was arrested and convicted for casting a ballot in the presidential election. She was arrested because women did not have the right to vote in 1872. Today, of course, women not only have the right to vote, they are encouraged to. In 1919 the manufacture, sale, and transportation of intoxicating liquors were banned in the United States as a result of the ratification of Amendment XVIII. A number of political activist groups deemed alcohol consumption as evil and, as a result, a behavior that was acceptable suddenly became unacceptable. Realizing the flaw in logic on this matter, Amendment XVIII was repealed in 1933 with the passage of Amendment XXI. Now, because of a new definition, the manufacturing, distribution, and sale of alcohol are legal again.

Some behaviors will be labeled deviant in one situation, or context, but not in another. For example, it would seem that killing someone might be inherently deviant; but this is not always the case. Killing an innocent person is considered deviant (and constitutes a violation of a law). Killing a person who breaks into your house and threatens you with bodily harm is not deviant—it is a matter of self-defense. A police officer, who abides by legal guidelines, may kill a perpetrator without being labeled a deviant. A soldier at war must certainly kill the enemy, or risk being killed himself (or herself), and therefore, this behavior is not labeled deviant. Torturing a prisoner of war, however, is considered deviant.

Perhaps the most important aspect in this labeling of behaviors centers on who makes the judgments. The people in power positions dictate which behaviors will be labeled deviant and/or criminal. Sociologists often cite the role that power plays in defining certain drugs as legal and others as illegal. The two deadliest and most dangerous drugs in society are both legal. Tobacco and alcohol kill more than a half million Americans a year. Marijuana has never been linked to a single death, and yet, quite illogically, is illegal. The simple reason for the legality of the drugs tobacco and alcohol is that they are represented by politically powerful special interest groups and corporate conglomerates. Tobacco and alcohol are also perceived differently, as they enjoy a long-standing tradition of cultural acceptance.

Regardless of definitions and certain circumstances that fuel great controversy, there is a general agreement about many behaviors that simply do not seem right. Deviant behavior is distinguished from criminal behavior in that deviance refers to violations of the less serious norms of society (e.g., folkways), whereas criminal behavior refers to violations of the law. Criminal behavior will be addressed in chapter 8.

The focus of this chapter is to provide a glimpse of the deviant behaviors of the main characters of *Seinfeld* and to provide a brief explanation why they are deemed so. Discussion begins with a sampling of general deviant behaviors, then a quick look at some of the obsessions that the characters possess, and concludes with an examination of borderline illegal deviant acts.

Deviant Behaviors

Throughout my fairly extensive world travels, I have noticed that nearly everyone understands the meaning behind "flipping the bird." On one visit to Russia, a member of my group enticed another to flip the bird to someone (merely as a sociological experiment) in order to determine if he knew the meaning of this rather odd gesture. He did know the meaning of this and took great offense.

During the opening monologue of the episode "The Robbery" (#3), Jerry discusses this rather curious behavior of flashing the middle finger at someone and how we, as the recipient of "the bird," are supposed to be offended. A woman thought Jerry had cut her off in traffic. Jerry ponders this deviant behavior (it is deviant, no matter how common it is) and questions why he is supposed to feel bad just because someone flashed a middle finger. As Jerry reasons, flashing the middle finger seems very arbitrary and ridiculous. Jerry suggested that he would be far more offended if someone gave him "the toe." After all, it is very easy to flip someone off with a finger, but a toe, well, that's far more impressive. To "give someone the toe" involves taking off a shoe and sock, while still driving, mind you, and then lifting the foot in the air—all that, just to flip someone off. Consequently, it would be far more insulting to "get the toe" than to "get the finger."

In "The Pledge Drive" (#89), Elaine's boss, Mr. Pitt, uses a knife and fork to eat his Snickers bar. Elaine tells George and Jerry about this and they find it quite peculiar. As George thinks about this odd behavior he theorizes that Mr. Pitt, as a high society type, probably just doesn't want to get chocolate on his fingers. During a working lunch with his Yankees-organization coworkers, George decides to eat his candy bar with a knife and fork. Initially, Mr. Morgan, George's boss, mocks George for his strange way of eating a candy bar. In a condescending manner, George replies, "I am eating my dessert. How do you eat it, with your hands?"

A bit of sociological analysis is needed here. The definition of deviance also varies based on who is committing the questionable act. If a wealthy person behaves oddly, they are likely to be labeled eccentric. However, when a lower SES (socioeconomic status) person acts oddly, they are likely to labeled "crazy" or "weird." Thus, when Mr. Pitt, a wealthy bourgeoisie eats a candy bar with a knife and fork, he is "cultured" because he does not use his hands to eat his food. A person like George Costanza (middle class, semi-slacker) eating a candy bar with a knife and fork is generally immediately laughed at.

As "The Pledge Drive" episode continues, Noreen, a friend of Elaine's, notices Mr. Morgan (looking quite proud of himself) at an outdoor café, eating a candy bar with a knife and fork. Noreen meets Elaine for lunch. When dessert arrives, Noreen begins to eat her cookie with a knife and fork. Elaine asks Noreen why she is using a knife and fork. Noreen tells Elaine that she has seen a lot of people eat a cookie that way. By the end of this hilarious episode, Jerry and Elaine are again back at the coffee shop and notice a person at a table next to them use a knife and fork for an Almond Joy candy bar. Jerry tells Elaine that he saw someone on the street eating M & M's with a spoon. Elaine surveys the entire coffee shop and discovers that everyone is using utensils to eat desserts that don't require them.

Revisiting this type of behavior as a form of a sociological breaching experiment could be quite interesting. Have a group of people eat candy bars with a knife and fork or a spoon and observe the looks from passers-by.

Another sociological note should be made here. Despite the fact that nearly everyone has "given the finger" to someone else, this behavior is still labeled as deviant. However, other behaviors that catch on in society, such as women getting tattoos, may become so routine that they are no longer labeled as deviant.

As far as I know, it is not against the law to urinate in your pants. Logic would dictate that you would not want to do this in public because anyone who notices this leakage problem will most assuredly point it out to others in a mocking manner. It should also be clear that one should not pee on someone else's furniture—especially on purpose. In the episode "The Couch" (#91), Poppie, a restaurant owner, is very upset with Jerry and Elaine. Elaine had started an argument on abortion rights with Poppie the night before in his restaurant. Elaine, and most of the restaurant patrons, walked out in protest of Poppie's "anti-choice" stand.

A couple of days later, Poppie goes to Jerry's apartment to collect money that Jerry and Elaine owe him. When Jerry goes to his bedroom to get the money, Poppie sits down on Jerry's brand new couch. A few seconds later, Jerry returns with the money, Poppie gets off the couch to accept it, and leaves Jerry's apartment. Jerry turns around and notices a huge stain on his couch; obviously, Poppie had urinated on Jerry's couch. Jerry, of course, has to get rid of the couch and he suspects that Poppie did it on purpose. Poppie not only committed a deviant act, but a disgusting one as well.

Seinfeld provided many examples of "disgusting" deviant behaviors. For example, in the episode "The Smelly Car" (#61), the body odor of the restaurant valet driver was so offensive that his stench stuck to Jerry's car long after the valet returned it to Jerry. The odor was so powerful that it was able to attach itself to Jerry's clothing and Elaine's hair. The next morning, Jerry took his car down to the garage. He assumed that by this time the odor molecules had time to "de-smellify." Instead, the stench was so bad Jerry fears that it has actually gained strength throughout the night.

Jerry decides to take his car to the car wash. They want $250 to custom clean it. Jerry goes back to the restaurant seeking reimbursement for this cost. Jerry makes the restaurateur sit inside his car so that he believes Jerry on just how bad the inside of the car really smells. The restaurateur agrees to pay for half of the cleaning. Despite this expenditure, the car still smells. Jerry decides to sell the car, but the dealer refuses because the smell is so bad. At the end of "The Smelly Car" episode, Jerry drives his car to a rough-looking part of the city, parks the car, gets out of it, shows the keys to a street tough, throws the keys back in the car, and walks away. The street tough happily hops in Jerry's car but is quickly overwhelmed by the stench.

A number of disgusting behaviors are associated with food. First of all, the very foods that people eat, and find as "normal" cuisine, vary by geographic region and from society to society. For example, in Colorado there is a delicacy known as Rocky Mountain Oysters. Sounds interesting, doesn't it? In reality, Rocky Mountain Oysters are bull testicles. The French are found of escargot; other people scrape snails of the sidewalk in disgust of their very presence. In some societies people eat monkey brains. Some people eat meat regularly and some people eat only vegetables. In short, there are a number of foods that some people consider deviant to consume that others find acceptable. It is all a matter of social definition, and these definitions vary among groups of people and diverse cultures.

The "proper" manner in which to eat is also under consideration when discussing deviance. As previously discussed, most people find it deviant to eat a Snickers Bar with a knife and fork. However, one might eat rice from a bowl with a fork, chopsticks, or with their fingers. While living in Los Angeles in the 1980s, I was invited to a dinner by some coworkers who had just moved to the United States from Bangladesh. It was considered the norm to eat rice with your hands. In an American restaurant it would be considered deviant to eat rice with your hands or to pick up a steak and eat that with your hands.

There are also expectations of proper food consumption, especially in the public sphere. For example, in the *Seinfeld* episode "The Implants" (#59), George violates the "double-dip" rule. George is at a wake in Detroit with his girlfriend Betsy. As George helps himself to the buffet, Betsy's brother Timmy catches him "double-dipping the chip."

Timmy: "What are you doing?"
George: "What?"
Timmy: "Did you just double-dip that chip?"
George: "Excuse me?"
Timmy: "You double-dipped the chip."
George: "'Double-dipped?' What are you talking about?"
Timmy: "You dipped the chip. You took a bite. And you dipped again."
George: "So?"

Timmy: "That's like putting your whole mouth right in the dip! From now on, when you take a chip, just take one dip and end it!"

George: "Well, I'm sorry, Timmy, but I don't dip that way."

Timmy: "Oh, you don't, huh?"

George: "No. You dip the way you want to dip; I'll dip the way I want to dip."

Timmy: "Gimme the chip! Gimme the chip!"

A small fight ensues between George and Timmy because of George's double-dipping. Timmy is disgusted. He realizes that George could be spreading all kinds of germs to others. It is often interesting to sociologically analyze public (or family) functions where a buffet of food is available. How many people double-dip the chip?

Fighting a member of the family who just lost a loved one is also an example of deviant behavior. Of course, this is George we are talking about and he is known for his lack of common sense. Remember, in the episode "The Gymnast" (#92), George takes a partially eaten éclair out of the trash and eats it. He is caught doing this by his girlfriend's mother, Mrs. Enright, in her kitchen. Mrs. Enright is understandably disturbed by what she sees.

In the episode "The Doodle" (#106), discarded food becomes a topic of concern. At a restaurant Jerry and Shelly are on a double date with George and Paula. Jerry picks up a pecan and starts to chew it. George purposely drops his napkin, motions for Jerry to bend down so that he can whisper something to him. He informs Jerry that Shelly had those nuts in her mouth and had spit them out without Jerry noticing. Jerry is disgusted that he ate discarded food and yells at Shelly for sucking on the nuts and then putting them on her plate. Shelly is upset with Jerry. First of all, she did not put them on her plate thinking Jerry would eat them and second, she is offended that Jerry found her so repulsive that he would not want something from her mouth. It is easy to see Shelly's point, after all, when they kiss, they will have their tongues in each other mouths.

Upset, Shelly heads for the ladies room. Paula joins her. Jerry is appalled that he ate discarded food. George reminds Jerry that he once ate discarded food. Not feeling any relief from George's comment, Jerry points out to George that he did it intentionally. Interestingly, near the end of this episode, George is on a date with Paula and he discards a pit from a peach. Paula takes the pit and puts it in her mouth. George stares at Paula in disbelief, and then, ironically, he is disgusted with her for putting discarded food in her mouth.

There are a number of other behaviors that are deviant but not criminal. We all go to the dentist on a regular basis. Proper dental care is essential for overall healthcare and maintenance. Most patients appreciate a highly sterile, professional dental office where the staff and dentists are well-trained, competent, and, perhaps, a little personable. With this ideal dentist office in mind, Jerry goes to see his dentist, Tim Whatley, in the episode "The Jimmy" (#105). When Jerry arrives for his appointment he is told, of course, to sit in the waiting room. He reaches for a magazine and finds a *Penthouse*. He is shocked to see this type of magazine in a dental office. He notices another patient looking at the centerfold of a different *Penthouse*. Whatley has recently adopted an "adults only" policy so he is not worried about kids looking at porno in the waiting room.

A magazine such as *Penthouse* seems to be out of place in a professional setting. And yet, if Dr. Whatley found enough patients who found it acceptable, it would not be deviant in that setting.

In the episode "The Contest" (#51), George is caught masturbating. Now, masturbation is not deviant, but being caught by your mother, as George was, introduces elements of deviance. George was "using" a *Glamour* magazine—although, again not itself deviant, but certainly not a "normal" choice of literature to stimulate oneself—while he was in his parents' home. She "catches" him and faints! As she falls toward the floor, George does not know whether to reach to stop her from falling or pull up his pants. He chooses to pull up his pants and his mother hits the floor hard enough to be hospitalized. As George later explains to Jerry and Elaine, he couldn't very well run over to catch her from falling while he had his pants down and his penis out. Elaine and Jerry laugh at him for using a *Glamour* magazine.

It was because of this incident that George vows never to do "it" again. Eventually the contest ensues with George, Jerry, Kramer, and Elaine betting on who can hold out the longest. A number of classic expressions are used in this episode to refer to one's ability to control oneself from doing "it." Among them are "Master of my own domain," "Lord of the Manor," "King of the County," and "The Queen of the Castle."

Deviant Obsessions

Some deviant behaviors turn into obsessions. An obsession is a persistent preoccupation with an idea or feeling. Many people have obsessions, and some people have an obsessive-compulsive personality that drives them to repeat certain behaviors over and over. Obsessive compulsive behaviors include such things as overeating (e.g., eating a whole bag of cookies just because they are in the house), repeatedly washing your hands for no real reason, checking to make sure the door is locked twenty times before going to sleep at night, as well as the ritualistic behaviors that many athletes and actors go through before they perform, and so on. In most cases, obsessive behaviors are considered deviant, or at the very least not "normal."

As with many us, the four main characters of *Seinfeld* have a number of obsessions. Jerry, for example, seems to have an obsession with beautiful women. He is also a clean freak. Now there is certainly nothing wrong with wanting to live in a clean, sterile environment (the opposite would be deviant), but not to the extreme that Jerry often demonstrates. For example, in the episode "The Pothole" Jerry throws away any item small enough to fit in his toilet because Jenna told him that she put something of his in the toilet.

George is certainly the most neurotic character on *Seinfeld*. His emotional problems could fill a social-psychology journal. Among George's quirky obsessions is his love of velvet. In the episode "The Label Maker" (#98), new girlfriend Bonnie takes him to her apartment for the first time. He is overwhelmed by her velvet couch. Bonnie asks George if he is a fan of velvet. George informs her that he would drape himself in velvet if it were socially acceptable.

In the episode "The Doodle" (#106), George is dating a woman named Paula. When Elaine tells George that Paula "like-likes" him, he is happy. Elaine adds that Paula does not consider looks important. George becomes upset with this revelation because the implication is that George is not good-looking. George continues to date Paula but he no longer cares about how he presents himself, or how he dresses, since Paula does not care what he looks like. George is going through one of his typical self-pity trips—if Paula doesn't care what he looks like, why should he care? Paula doesn't care that George has not shaven or that his shirt is untucked. He is depressed and comments to her that she doesn't care at all how he looks. She tells him that he could even wear sweatpants to Lincoln Center and she would not care. George is excited about this prospect. His excitement reaches its zenith when she tells him that he could drape himself in velvet for all she cares.

Later in this episode, George wears an outfit made of velvet. Jerry thinks this is very peculiar. He asks George if Paula has seen him wearing his velvet outfit. Not only has Paula seen George in the velvet outfit, George informs Jerry that they just had sex. George believes he has found the perfect person for him and declares that his search is over. Sarcastically, Jerry responds that the search for the right psychiatrist needs to begin. Unfortunately, George's hope for true love with Paula is destroyed when he observes her eating his discarded peach pits.

In a particularly funny skit in "The Doll" (#27) episode, George becomes obsessed with one of Susan's dolls from her rather extensive collection. Various collections such as this are another example of obsessive-compulsive behavior. Most people would find Susan's obsession with dolls very odd. And most collections are very odd (remember George's father collected the *TV Guides*), that is, unless they have monetary value. George would find out later (in "The Foundation," episode #135), during the reading of Susan's will, that her doll collection was worth 2.6 million dollars.

Initially, George's problem with her dolls is due to the great amount of space that they occupied. As George looks around the room at them, one in particular bothers him. Among them is one that looks exactly like George's mother, Estelle. Susan refuses to acknowledge the similarity.

The doll problem increases when Susan insists that a number of her dolls join her and George in bed when they sleep at night. One of these is the one who looks like his mother (and it really did look like her!). Understandably, George is uncomfortable sleeping in the same bed with his girlfriend and his "mother."

George brings the doll of his mother over to Jerry's. He tells Jerry that the doll is freaking him out. George admits to Jerry that he almost threw it into the incinerator but couldn't because the guilt would eat at him. George has become obsessed with the doll and he sees it as a symbolic representation of his mother and begins to work out his "issues" with his mother with the doll instead. Jerry tries to calm George. As he leaves Jerry's apartment he runs into Elaine in the hallway. Elaine screams when she sees the doll.

On his way back home, George stops at the coffee shop. He sets the doll down on one of the chairs at his table. In his mind, the doll begins to talk like his mother and criticizes the way he eats and the clothes that he is wearing. George angrily gets up from his table, grabs the doll and yells out, "C'mon, let's go. Let's go." A woman customer tells the cashier (Ruthie) "That man should really be in a sanitarium." Ruthie nods her head in agreement.

Proving that George's obsession is not his alone, his father, Frank (at Susan and George's apartment), sees the doll that looks like his mom and freaks out. Just as with George, in Frank's mind the doll is speaking to him as Estelle would. He lunges toward Susan to take the doll from her. He then twists the doll's head completely off.

In contemporary society it is important to protect personal information (especially one's social security number) as identity theft has become a very serious social problem—one that sociologists and criminologists have been studying for some time now. And for good reason, as identity theft is one of the fastest-growing crimes of the twenty-first century. Identity theft occurs when someone attains bits of information about another person and attempts to represent him- or herself as that person. Identity thieves usually take out credit cards, apply for loans, open utility accounts, purchase cars, or any number of other options, in the names of the persons whose identities they have stolen.

The victims of identity theft face potential huge financial bills and a disastrous credit rating. However, there exists an even worse fate to people who have their identity stolen: criminal identity theft. This occurs when an identity thief commits a crime but presents him- or herself as the person whose identity has been stolen. The victim of identity theft now faces a criminal record—one that they may not become aware of for months or even years.

George is obsessive in regard to his secret bank code. He wants to keep it secret, primarily because of safety issues. There is nothing deviant about wanting to be safe. And after the brief discussion of identity theft, it should be clear that keeping personal information to oneself is a good rule. However, as discussed in the episode "The Secret Code" (#117), George's obsession to keep his bank code a secret includes reasons beyond identity protection.

The secret code becomes an issue for George when he mentions to Susan that he needs to go to the ATM to get some cash. Susan offers to do it for him because she is going to the ATM anyway. She tells him to just give her his bank card and secret code. He refuses. She gets upset. George retells this story to Jerry. Jerry points out to George that considering he is about to marry Susan and that married couples share everything, he really should share his secret code with her. At first, George attempts to justify his actions by passing the buck to the bank and their policy of telling their customers to never give out their bank information to anyone. Of course, the secret behind George's obsession with his bank code lies with his fear of losing his individuality. George does not want to share everything just because he and Susan are a couple. He wants some self-identity to remain intact.

This obsession starts to get to George. He almost *needs* to tell someone. He decides to tell J. Peterman's dying mother his code (since she could not tell anyone) when no one else is in the room. She momentarily awakes from her nearly comatose state and yells it out, "Bosco! Bosco!" Peterman runs into the room and asks his mother what she is trying to say. Mrs. Peterman repeats, "Bosco." She dies immediately afterwards. J. Peterman is convinced that his mother's dying word must have some significance. George sits by quietly. Peterman speculates on a rumor that he once heard while he was a boy growing up in Costa Rica that his mother had taken a lover. Peterman speculates that perhaps his mother's lover's name was Bosco. Peterman is now obsessed with the significance of his mother yelling out "Bosco" on her death bed. George, meanwhile, in an attempt to keep his code secret, refuses to alleviate Peterman's suspicions (and Mrs. Peterman's good name) by telling him the true meaning of the word "Bosco." This is just one way that one person's obsession can affect others.

Kramer has his share of obsessions as well. As revealed in "The Calzone" (#130), Kramer engages in a rather peculiar habit. He decides that he will only wear hot clothes—those that came right out of the dryer. He quickly runs out of quarters to feed the dryer, and thus, his obsession. He starts to put his clothes in Jerry's oven. Then on one rainy day, Kramer asks the counter guy at the calzone place if he would put Kramer's clothes in the oven to dry off. They come out burnt and smoking. Kramer gets into an argument with the counter guy and he gets kicked out (and banned) from the calzone shop. George had been dependent on Kramer to get calzones for him and Mr. Steinbrenner (George had been banned earlier).

Cut off from his calzone supply, which he was sharing daily at lunchtime with Mr. Steinbrenner, George asks his boss if he might like something different than a calzone. Interestingly, Mr. Steinbrenner reveals one of his own excessive compulsive behaviors in his response to George's query. Steinbrenner informs George that when he finds something that he really likes, he will stick to it. In fact, Steinbrenner admitted to eating the exact same lunch, turkey chili in a bowl made out of bread, from 1973 to 1982.

Borderline Illegal Deviant Acts

A great deal of deviant behavior occurred throughout the nine-year run of *Seinfeld*. A number of minor infractions of social norms have been discussed earlier in this chapter, and in the next chapter a number of actual criminal violations will be presented. Borderline illegal deviant acts serve as the segue between these two topic areas. Borderline deviance generally refers to behaviors that are not quite illegal and those behaviors that may actually be illegal but are not prosecuted before a court of law.

In the episode "The Secretary" (#95), Jerry discovers that his dry cleaner Willie and his wife Donna are wearing the clothes that he has dropped off at their business. Jerry first notices Willie wearing Jerry's Hounds-Tooth jacket at the movie theater. Willie tries to deny it and proclaims that such a thing would violate the "dry cleaner's code" of ethics. Jerry counters that a dry cleaner shouldn't need a "code" to tell you not to wear other people's clothes. Willie continues to deny wearing Jerry's jacket. But Jerry has evidence; he whips out the movie stub from the jacket and shows Willie. Jerry has proof that someone wearing his jacket had attended the movie in question. (Note: The type of evidence that Jerry uses here is derived from the research method that uses unobtrusive measures. See chapter 1 for a discussion on research methods.)

Willie knows he's been busted. Jerry informs Willie that he will be taking his business elsewhere. Jerry demands his mother's fur coat back, but he can't find the stub. Willie tells Jerry that without the stub it will be impossible for him to find the coat and that it could be at any one of the fur warehouses. Jerry tells Willie that he will be back later with the stub. Later, Jerry is at a department store with Elaine and notices Donna wearing his mother's fur coat. Jerry confronts her and retrieves the coat.

Jerry believes that Willie and Donna are treating the dry cleaning business as a department store full of clothing to be worn whenever they please. This is a clear example of deviant behavior because people put their trust in professionals, whether they are doctors or dry cleaners. There are many expected and implied norms of professional behavior. Clearly, Donna and Willie crossed the line and are guilty of deviant behavior. However, are they guilty of theft, which would be a criminal offense?

Jerry most likely crosses the line of legality in "The Merv Griffin Show" (#162). In this episode, Jerry dates an extremely attractive woman named Celia, who has a great toy collection that she inherited from her father. The toys are priceless and have never been played with; so, of course, Jerry is preoccupied with them. Celia forbids him to play with the toys. Jerry and Celia have great sex, but still he wants to play with the toys, especially the G.I. Joe with the original frogman suit. Celia keeps saying "yes" to sex, but "no" to his playing with her (other) toys!

One night Celia is complaining of a headache. Jerry gives her medicine that causes drowsiness. Sure enough, she passes out. Jerry takes advantage of Celia by playing with her toys. Jerry brags to George about all the great stuff she has, and he is dying to go over there. They plot a plan where they bring turkey and wine to her house. She gets drunk and sleepy from the turkey (because of the chemical tryptophan found in turkey). After she passes out, Jerry and George play with her toys.

Elaine is appalled by Jerry and George's behavior—that is, until she finds out that Celia has an Easy-Bake Oven that has never been used. Soon, Elaine and Lou (a coworker) have joined in on the drugging and taking advantage of a woman after she has passed out just to play with her toys. Jerry, George, Elaine, and Lou have all justified their deviant behaviors, but they are guilty of deviance nonetheless. They are all well aware that Celia does not want her toys played with.

George nearly crosses the line of legality in his attempted fraud schemes. Fraud involves the illegal taking of someone's property. There is no threat or act of violence with fraud. Quite contrary, the fraudster is attempting to pull a "fast one" over someone by duping them with false information. The fraudster may even offer to front money or property as a form of enticement to the potential victim. There are many types of fraud, including healthcare fraud, telemarketing fraud, insurance fraud, and credit card fraud.

In the episode "The Implants" (#59), George is willing to commit credit card fraud in an attempt to get a reduced rate on a flight to Detroit. George wants to go to Detroit with his girlfriend Betsy to attend the funeral of her Aunt Clarice. He cannot afford the high-priced airfare. Kramer suggests that George ask for a "death in the family" fare which provides a 50 percent discount. Kramer convinces George to purchase two tickets on his credit card. One of the tickets is for Kramer who wants the miles for his frequent flyer program. Kramer tells George to cancel his flight after the miles have been posted; that way, George does not have to actually pay for Kramer's ticket.

George thinks this sounds like a great idea and the two of them go off to the airport. George tells the counter clerk at the airline that he would like a bereavement rate ticket to Detroit for himself and Kramer. The clerk informs George that he must first pay the full fare and then return to any of the counters with a copy of the death certificate and he will receive a refund for half of his fare. George is surprised to learn that a copy of the death certificate will be required. He begins to realize that there is a flaw with his plan. George is unable to get a copy of the death certificate. So instead, he has his picture taken by the coffin and attempts to use the photo in order to get his airline bereavement rate. The airline declines his request. George is responsible for the full fare. Furthermore, because George purchased "super-saver" tickets, which are nonrefundable, he gets stuck with the cost of Kramer's airline ticket as well. In short, George pays twice as much with his scheme than he would have paid if he had simply purchased his one full price fare.

In the episode "The Boyfriend (1)" and "The Boyfriend (2)" (#34 and #35), George is again involved in fraud. This time he lies to Mrs. Lenore Sokol at the unemployment office. A number of people and businesses attempt to defraud the government. They may file false insurance claims to receive benefits they do not deserve. Some people lie to the unemployment office and claim they are looking for work when they really are not. This behavior is clearly deviant. George is one of those people who are willing to lie about their job search in order to maintain or extend their "benefit period" (the time period they receive checks).

In this scheme, George creates a fictitious company, named Vandelay Industries, and claims that he has an interview with them in order to extend his benefits payments. A lot of people do this,

ink they can get away with providing a false com-
use a friend's phone number. The friend will have to
eme and agree to answer their phone as if they were
representing the fictitious company. This is certainly deviant
behavior, and it is illegal. Of course, if the plan never gets imple-
mented, a crime may never occur and therefore it becomes a "borderline illegal" act.

George provides Mrs. Sokol with a false name of the person who
supposedly interviewed him. George gets caught in his own deceit
when Kramer, who is not "in on" the fraud, answers Jerry's phone in
a "normal" manner. As Elaine and George try to steer Kramer's
answers, he continues to speak to Mrs. Sokol on the phone and
informs her that she has called a phone number of a private person
who lives in an apartment and not some type of business.

Kramer's whole life would appear to be deviant. He seldom works
and yet leads quite an adventurous lifestyle. In the episode "The Pothole" (#150), he takes part in the "Adopt-a-Highway" campaign.
Mile Marker 114 on the Arthur Berkhardt Expressway is Kramer's
jurisdiction. Typically, the highway department expects the people
who adopt the highways to give a financial contribution toward the
maintenance of it. On other occasions, adopters take responsibility
for physically cleaning their stretch of highway themselves.

Kramer is quite the proud "father" of his piece. With a gleam in
his eye he shows Jerry a Polaroid photo of his name on the roadway
sign. Kramer is shown cleaning "his" highway. The big pieces of
trash, cinder blocks, air conditioners, and shopping carts, he just
threw in the woods. The smaller pieces of trash he bagged. He took
down the posted speed sign because it had been spray painted over
to read 165 miles per hour. He planned to clean up the sign and
return it. Kramer's next move is his most deviant and possibly criminal. He decides to create "comfort" lanes on his stretch of the
highway by widening the lanes. Late at night, Kramer paints over
two of the divider lines and converts a four-lane highway into two
luxury wide lanes. A huge traffic jam results the next morning during
rush hour because of this. He realizes he will have "his highway
mile" taken away from him.

Losing his adopted highway is just one problem that Kramer
faced on *Seinfeld*. In the episode "The Diplomat's Club" (#108), he is
forced to confront his true demon—gambling. There are many forms
of gambling and nearly everyone has gambled at least once in their

lives. Gambling includes such things as buying lottery tickets, betting in office pools on sport events, church bingo, and casino gambling. Some forms of gambling are legal, while others are not.

Gambling is a complicated issue in contemporary society. On the one hand, there are such concerns as crime, youth participation, fraud, con games, and lost potential revenue for the government from illegal gambling. However, gambling has become a major growing industry in the United States and is responsible for contributing to the general society by providing jobs and tax revenues in areas where gambling is legalized such as on Indian land. Las Vegas and Reno are the cities that they are because of legalized gambling.

But gambling can produce a number of pathological and obsessive behaviors. Compulsive gamblers will bet until they have nothing left: savings, family assets, personal belongings; anything of value may be pawned, sold, or borrowed against. In desperation, compulsive gamblers may panic and turn to illegal activities to support their addictions. The gambling problem is so serious in the United States that there is a program called "Gamblers Anonymous," which is run like Alcoholics Anonymous and is designed to treat compulsive behavior.

Kramer had his gambling problem under control for almost three years when the gambling bug bites him again in "The Diplomat's Club." As an indication of just how serious a problem Kramer has, he begins betting on the arrival and departure times of planes at the airport. He gambles with a rich cowboy from Houston named Earl. Kramer loses and he loses big. He runs out of money. Earl is willing to give Kramer one more chance but he needs to see cash up front. Kramer informs Earl that he has to call his banker, who turns out to be Newman. Kramer tells Newman that he needs some money, fast. Newman figures out that Kramer has been gambling again.

Kramer tells Newman that he is down $3,200. Newman, like most people, does not have that kind of money at home. But Kramer is after something better; he wants Newman's prized possession. Newman says, "Oh no, no, not the bag!" Kramer responds, "Oh help me, man, I'm desperate!" The prized possession that Newman owns is the mailbag of the postal worker whom he replaced—David Berkowitz (the "Son of Sam" killer)! Earl is indeed impressed with this collateral and allows Kramer to continue betting.

Eventually Kramer does win his money back and makes a profit. But then Earl finds out that Jerry was responsible for delaying the flight in Ithaca, the flight Kramer made all his money on. Earl calls Kramer a cheat. Kramer is lucky that he is in a public place. Many times people who are cheated seek a violent revenge. This comedic episode manages to both entertain the audience and inform them of the dangers of gambling. However, with the government's backing and the proliferation of gambling, it is clear that in the near future many more Americans will suffer from the consequences of betting over one's head.

Chapter 8

Crime and
Social Control

*"Good Samaritan Law? I Never Heard of It.
You Don't Have to Help Anybody. That's What
This Country's All About."—Jackie Chiles*

Formal norms are known as laws. Laws are norms that have been written by a political authority with designated punishments established when they are violated. When a law has been broken, a crime has been committed. The judicial system provides certain officials the power to enforce laws.

Law and Social Control

All societies have laws and they all have a means of enforcing them. Social control refers to the processes and methods used by a society to secure its members' conformity to social norms. There are two general categories of social control: formal and informal. Formal social control (or direct social control) is accomplished by the "outside" social control agents of society. These social control agents include members of the judicial system (for example, police, courts, and prosecutors) and also parents, family, friends, and employers. Formal sanctions, or punishments, can be employed when people break the law. Sanctions may include a speeding ticket for driving too fast or a prison sentence for committing murder.

Informal social control (or indirect social control) is accomplished through "internal" socialization. That is, individuals have learned, through the socialization process, the rules of society and voluntarily abide by them. These people have "internalized" the rules of society. In order words, all people are capable of committing crimes on a regular basis, but most people do not (nor do they violate major folkways and mores) because they know better. They believe in the legitimacy of the law. For example, most people don't litter. They know that throwing trash and cigarette butts out the window of a car is a disgusting form of behavior. It is also against the law. If everyone abided by this simple law, "Adopt-a-Highway" programs would be unnecessary.

Most laws that are created are designed for the public good. According to one of the earliest sociological giants, Emile Durkheim, laws represent the general moral sentiments of a society. Durkheim also believed that crime and deviance serve a functional role in society because they help to unite its members. When a crime is committed, especially a serious one, public outrage is directed toward the violator. Citizens demand justice. The law, at least in theory, provides the mechanism to deliver justice. Thus, when violators are punished, society has reaffirmed its sense of morality.

The four main characters of *Seinfeld* were involved in a great deal of criminal activity. In fact, it was the violation of a law that led to the ultimate downfall of the four friends. The series concludes with Jerry, Elaine, George, and Kramer being incarcerated for violating the "Good Samaritan Law" (to be discussed later in this chapter).

As a general rule, crime is divided into three broad categories: street crime, white-collar crime, and victimless crimes. There are a number of examples of all three categories in *Seinfeld*. The following represent an interesting sampling of the various types of crimes.

Street Crime

The FBI divides street crime (or predatory crime) into two categories: violent offenses and property offenses. Violent offenses (or crimes against the person) include murder, rape, assault, and robbery; property offenses include burglary, larceny-theft, and motor vehicle theft. On *Seinfeld* there were examples of both categories of street crime.

Violent Offenses

The most serious offense against a fellow human being is murder. None of the regular characters on *Seinfeld* committed murder, but the topic of serial killing appears in the episode "The Masseuse" (#73). In the opening stand-up routine Jerry touches upon a number of issues of sociological interest. First, the serial killer never seems to kill his neighbors. We know that because it's always the neighbors who are interviewed by the media and the police and who report that the alleged killer was always so quiet. Jerry points out that these same neighbors complain about the stereo being too loud but the sounds of a chainsaw coming from their neighbor's basement is not disturbing.

"The Masseuse" episode centers on the serial killer Joel Rifkin. Elaine was dating a guy named Joel Rifkin at the same time when the news was filled with stories about the serial killer Joel Rifkin. And although they were obviously not one and the same person, it causes Elaine, and eventually Joel, a great deal of misery and discomfort. For example, Elaine's coworkers joke with her that she "better keep on his good side" and "I wouldn't sleep with my back to him if I were you." Elaine, frustrated by all the teasing, snaps back at her coworkers that she has had enough.

Elaine discusses with Jerry and Kramer her problems dating a guy with the same name as a serial killer. They review some of the information that they have on Rifkin, such as the fact that he strangled eighteen victims. Kramer offers a bizarre theory of serial killers. He notes that Rifkin, like the "Son of Sam," was adopted. Kramer concludes that adoption leads to serial killing!

Kramer is wrong, of course. Research shows that serial killers have long histories of violence that started in childhood in the form of abuse toward animals and weaker kids. Serial killers are usually white males. As adults they are generally social outcasts and have trouble relating to women. They slay their victims, one at a time, over a period of weeks, months, or even years. Criminologists and sociologists have identified a number of specific categories of serial killers, including the "mission-oriented killer" whose murders are motivated to rid the world of specific types of undesirable people, such as prostitutes. These murderers are aware of their actions and the consequences of their behaviors. Joel Rifkin is an example of this type of killer.

Perhaps the most violent of all social groups in the United States are America's street gangs. As a gang researcher myself, I know all too well the real dangers posed by gang members to the stability and general healthy welfare of the community. When I teach my university course on street gangs I do like to mention a particularly relevant *Seinfeld* episode, "The Van Buren Boys" (#148). This gang provides a number of basic elements of gang life, such as the importance of group loyalty, the use of secret hand signals, and initiation rites.

In this episode, Kramer is at Lorenzo's pizza place when he is backed into a corner by members of a street gang—The Van Buren Boys (VB Boys). Still holding the garlic shaker that he was using to sprinkle garlic on his pizza, Kramer has eight fingers showing (the other two are covered by the shaker). Turns out, Kramer was flashing their gang sign—eight fingers—for Martin Van Buren, who was the eighth president of the United States, the man they most admired. The VB Boys think that Kramer is an OG (original gangster, or an original member of the gang) because he is flashing their secret gang sign. The VB Boys immediately back off Kramer and let him go about his business. This is common behavior for gangs, to show respect to fellow gangsters and disrespect toward rivals.

Robbery is another serious violent offense. The FBI defines a robbery as the taking or attempted taking of anything of value from the care, custody, or control of a person or persons by force or threat of force or violence and/or by putting the victim in fear. A robbery is an act of violence because it involves the use of force to obtain money or goods.

A number of robberies occurred on *Seinfeld*. In "The Soup Nazi" (#116), Elaine purchases an antique armoire and tries to move it into her apartment. Unfortunately, it is Sunday and the super informs her that there is no moving in on a Sunday. So now, Elaine has this wonderful armoire but has no way of getting it inside. She knows it's not safe to leave it outside all night so she asks Kramer to watch it for her. He agrees to do it. In return, Elaine agrees to buy Kramer some soup from the "Soup Nazi." Shortly after Elaine leaves Kramer, two street "thugs" approach him. They take a liking to the armoire and decide to take it. When Kramer attempts to stop them, he is threatened with violence and backs off. The thieves leave with the armoire.

Kramer is visibly shaken by the whole experience. When Elaine returns she is upset with Kramer for losing the armoire. Kramer tries to explain to her that it was a very frightening experience and that his life was in danger. He then asks Elaine for the soup, which she did not get because she upset the Soup Nazi who then banned her from the soup shop for one year.

In the episode "The Robbery" (#3), Jerry returns home from a gig in Minneapolis and finds that his apartment has been robbed. He yells out for Elaine, who has spent the weekend at Jerry's place because she needed a break from her roommate. Jerry's TV and VCR were stolen—a frightening experience that leaves the victim vulnerable. Jerry wonders how he could have been robbed; after all, he just purchased a top-of-the-line lock for his door. Unfortunately for him, Kramer left the door opened, not just unlocked, but completely open after he returned to his own apartment. Elaine was at the store and returned to Jerry's apartment to find it robbed. Now Jerry has to deal with the consequences. Lacking insurance, Jerry is out the total cost of the stolen property.

George was once victimized in an "upscale" type of robbery. In the episode "The Subway" (#30), George is well-dressed and riding the subway on his way to a job interview. A very attractive woman sits next to him, assuming that he is well off financially speaking. She begins to flirt with him. Typical with most men under these conditions, George pretends that he is a wealthy business man. The train makes a stop and the woman gets off, but she suggests to George that he should join her. He agonizes over his dilemma: should he go on the job interview because he needs the work, or should he go off with this attractive woman who seems to be offering something else that he needs.

George and the woman go to a hotel room. She tells George to make himself comfortable while she changes in the bathroom. In his mind, George wonders what he should do—Should he take off his clothes? Is she taking off her clothes? She walks out of the bathroom wearing a nightie. She then handcuffs him to the bed. He believes he is in for some wild kinky sex. She returns to the bathroom temporarily and returns fully dressed. He had been set up. When she goes through his wallet, she yells at him for having so little money. She steals his new suit and leaves the room. George is left handcuffed to the bed, a victim of robbery, in part because of his own stupidity. Of course, being stupid is not against the law (maybe it should be) and that does not give someone the right to take advantage of those who are easily manipulated.

Another type of violent offense is assault and battery. Although many people believe that "assault and battery" refers to one single crime, they are actually two separate offenses. Battery requires an offensive touching, such as slapping, hitting, or punching a victim. Assault does not require actual touching, but it does involve either attempted battery or intentionally frightening the victim by word or deed.

In the episode "The Rye" (#121), Jerry is dragged into one of George's desperate attempts to get Susan's parents to like him. George and his parents are invited to dinner at the Ross's home. As polite invited guests are supposed to do (remember chapter 2) when invited to dinner, the Costanzas bring a marble rye bread as a gift. The Costanzas stop at Schnitzer's to get the rye because it is the best and they want to impress the Rosses. Well, the Rosses forget to bring out the bread, and Frank is so insulted that he sneaks it out of the house after the dinner party is over. George is so embarrassed about this "theft" that he figures if he could replace the "stolen" marble rye with another one, the Rosses would never know the difference (in actuality they did know that Frank stole the bread). George plots his strategy to replace the missing rye.

George sets up a distraction to keep the Rosses busy (a hilarious horse and buggy ride piloted by Kramer and powered by a horse with a terrible gas problem because Kramer had been feeding it Beef-A-Reeno from large economy size cans). Jerry is supposed to get a marble rye at Schnitzer's and sneak it over to the Ross's house where George will be waiting. While at Schnitzer's, an old lady (Mabel) one place in line ahead of Jerry orders the last marble rye. Jerry offers Mabel twice the amount she spent on the bread, but she refuses to sell it. Jerry then offers Mabel $50 for the $6 rye, and still she refuses. Mabel leaves the bakery. Jerry follows behind her on the sidewalk. Suddenly, Jerry lunges toward Mabel and robs her of the rye bread!

This is not one of Jerry's better moments in the show. He is guilty of at least battery and robbery. Despite Jerry's willingness to commit a crime and the horse-and-buggy ride set up by Kramer, George never does successfully sneak the rye back into the Ross's apartment. And, in a later episode, Mabel will remember Jerry robbing her of the rye and will cast the deciding vote to impeach Jerry's father as the condo president in their Florida retirement complex.

Property Offenses

Among the more common types of property offenses is auto theft. The high frequency and seriousness of this larceny are responsible for its treatment as a separate category in the Uniform Crime Rate.

Jerry's car is stolen on two occasions. The first time is in the episode "The Alternate Side" (#28). Jerry and George enter Jerry's apartment discussing their recent discovery that Jerry's car was stolen from right in front of his building. As statistics show, car theft is very common. Anyone who has seen the movie *Gone in Sixty Seconds* has a clue how easy it is for car thieves to steal *any* car they want. Statistics mean little to victims of car theft. These people want to know what happened to their car. George suggests to Jerry that he call his car phone. So, Jerry calls his car phone and the thief answers. He finds out that the thief did not have to cross wires or anything clever like that to steal the car because the keys were left right on the front seat. Turns out, Sid, the guy in the neighborhood who moves parked cars on the block, left Jerry's keys in his car.

A number of other criminal behaviors associated with the use of automobiles are just as common. Many people exercise poor judgment while driving: they drive recklessly, too fast or too slow, ignore traffic signals, and disobey lower speed limits in construction zones. Many motorists do not even park their cars legally. They may park in front of fire hydrants, in loading zones, in handicapped spots even though they are not handicapped, or fail to put money in the meter.

In the episode "The Scofflaw" (#99), parking ticket violators are highlighted. One police officer has spent most of his career trying to catch the elusive "white whale" of scofflaws. The cop almost caught the scofflaw one day until Kramer inadvertently distracted him by yelling "pig" at a passing motorist who was littering. Kramer attempts to apologize to the cop the next day. The cop explains to Kramer that he has been after this scofflaw since 1979 when he first ticketed his brown Dodge Diplomat for parking in a church zone. The fine was never paid and since that first incident, that scofflaw has piled up more parking tickets than anyone in New York City. The cop was about to catch this criminal when Kramer interferes with his work.

Days go by and once again the police officer comes across the elusive white whale. He is ready to move in for the kill, finally. Just then, however, another disturbance—caused by George crashing his car into another—occurs and the white whale drives off, again. The cop yells, but the scofflaw drives on. Kramer, who runs out of the coffee shop when he hears the sounds of two cars colliding, recognizes the whale—it is Newman!

Kramer later confronts Newman with his discovery. Newman admits that he is the notorious scofflaw and that he is tired of always looking over his back, worried that he will some day get caught. Kramer convinces Newman to turn himself in to the court of law. Newman agrees. As Newman stands in front of the judge, she is obviously upset with his extensive list of violations. The judge scolds him and orders him to keep his car in a garage. Newman breaks down and cries. He tries to tell the judge that he can't afford a New York City garage, but the judge insists or else the court will impound his car.

In the episode "The Little Kicks" (#138), Jerry and Kramer go to the movies to see a special preview of *Death Blow*. Jerry was able to get a third ticket for Kramer's friend Brody. Brody happens to be a low-life criminal involved in both violent and property offenses. In this particular case, Brody records the movie to sell bootleg copies. Jerry is uncomfortable with Brody "stealing" this film. Kramer tells Jerry to relax, that Brody is a bootlegger and that he records films all the time. Midway through the movie, Brody gets ill (from eating so much candy that he snuck in) and asks Jerry to finish taping the movie for him. When Jerry refuses, Brody reveals to Kramer and Jerry that he has a gun under his jacket.

Without many other options, Jerry does finish recording the movie. At 3 AM Brody comes to Jerry's house looking for the tape. In the morning, Jerry expresses his great concerns about the whole bootlegging ordeal. Brody returns to tell Jerry what a great job he did and offers him another "gig." Jerry is too afraid to say "no" to Brody to his face but tells Kramer about it after Brody leaves Jerry's apartment (with a baseball bat that he borrowed from Kramer). Kramer thinks Jerry should be happy that he got another paying gig. Jerry is worried about doing time in jail for bootlegging. Jerry does not end up taping another film. Interestingly, George offers to do it for Jerry in an attempt to impress a hottie (Anna) in Elaine's office who likes "bad boys." George gets caught and is processed at the police stations, where he breaks down and cries. Anna is not impressed by George's tears of fear and breaks up with him.

Another form of theft is passing bad checks. A "bad check" involves the cashing of a bank check, to obtain money that is knowingly and intentionally drawn on a nonexistent or underfunded bank account. It is a type of fraud because the perpetrator is attempting to deceive someone in an attempt to gain funds. In the episode "The Little Jerry" (#145), Jerry is guilty of "bouncing" a check at a bodega. The owner, Marcelino, taped Jerry's check on his cash register with all the other bad checks.

Because he unintentionally passed a bad check, a humiliated Jerry wants to make amends with Marcelino. Jerry goes to the bodega to talk with him. Sure enough, right on Marcelino's cash register under a sign that reads "Checks no longer accepted from:" is Jerry's check. Adding to his humiliation is the fact that the check has clowns on it (part of those ridiculous check options that banks like to throw in every now and then). Jerry offers to make amends and even pays a "service fee" to cover any inconvenience he may have caused Marcelino. Unfortunately for Jerry, Marcelino keeps the check posted on the register because it is a "matter of policy."

White-Collar Crime

The term *white-collar crime* was coined by sociologist Edwin Sutherland. It is an umbrella term that encompasses a great number of crimes committed by consumers, professionals, and corporations. Consumer white-collar crimes include such acts as embezzlement, padding expense accounts, credit card fraud, insurance fraud, and mail fraud. Conservative estimates of the cost of consumer fraud are five times higher than the combined economic costs of all street crimes. Politicians seldom direct attention toward stopping white-collar crimes (and for good reason, as many are guilty of a variety of them); instead, they focus on street crime. The Enron case is one example of the impact crooked corporate leaders can have on the lives of thousands of people who placed their trust in the company. Many people were financially ruined. White-collar crime not only involves great financial loss, but also is the cause of the loss of a great number of lives (e.g., deaths caused by unsafe products).

Most people do not focus much attention on white-collar crimes. This pattern holds true in *Seinfeld* as well, as there are far fewer references to white-collar offenses than street offenses.

In the episodes "The Cadillac (1)" (#124) and the "The Cadillac (2)" (#125), embezzlement is illustrated. Jerry innocently purchases a brand-new Cadillac for his father (Morty) in the episode "The Cadillac (1)." Morty's so-called friend, Jack Klompus, doesn't believe that Jerry makes enough money from his stand-up comedy to be able to purchase such an extravagant gift for Morty. Jack is actually jealous of Morty but cannot admit it. With the seeds of jealousy sown, Jack decides to discredit Morty and uses any means necessary to convince people that Morty is up to no good.

At a tenants committee meeting, Morty, as the president of the condo association, stands behind a lectern and bangs his gavel to get the meeting started. Jack is still visibly upset with Morty. A committee member, Herb, wonders why it has taken so long to start the restoration of the fence at the Briarwood gate. Morty explains that he is still waiting for the best bid before he okays the project. Jack mutters something under his breath. Morty inquires what Jack has to say. Jack publicly accuses Morty of embezzling funds from the treasury. Morty is enraged that Jack would accuse him of stealing. Morty demands proof. Jack uses Morty's brand new Cadillac as proof. No one in the condo association believes that Jerry can afford to purchase a Cadillac for his father. (They don't think he is funny enough to earn that kind of money as a comedian!) Morty later explains to his wife Helen that the board is trying to impeach him because of the "embezzlement scandal."

In "The Cadillac (2)" the suspicion of Morty's embezzling grows over, of all things, his late arrival to dinner. Morty and Helen are used to eating dinner at 4:30 PM in order to catch the early bird special. Morty explains to Jerry that it's a great deal; you get tenderloin, a salad, and a baked potato for $4.95. But Jerry is not ready for a big dinner at 4:30; he thinks it's way too early and promises to pay for his parents' dinner if they go later. His mother reluctantly agrees. She is aware of the repercussions from the condo community—anyone who eats after the early bird special is either flaunting their wealth or guilty of something.

As Jerry, Helen, and Morty arrive at Scott's restaurant, a few people are milling around outside. Jack and his wife Doris walk out just as the Seinfelds arrive. Jack points out their social deviance (missing the early bird special) and makes a comment about how it must be nice to have so much money that he can afford to eat after six. Jack gathers other community members around to point out the Seinfelds' late arrival to dinner in their fancy new Cadillac.

Jack is working to get Morty impeached from his position as the condo association president. At first, there are not enough votes to kick Morty out of office. And even though he is completely innocent of embezzlement, Jack is able to convince quite a few people that something is amiss, as evidenced by Morty's sudden lavish lifestyle. When the time comes to vote, it suddenly dawns on Mabel Choate, one of the tenant board members, where she remembered seeing Morty's son, Jerry—he was the one who robbed her of her rye bread when she was in New York visiting her daughter (see chapter 7). Mabel changes her vote to "in favor" of impeachment. The other members all follow suit and Morty is officially dismissed as condo

president. A smug Jack Klompus smiles in triumph at Morty's dis-
honor. Jack, as the vice president, takes over as president. Thus,
Morty is convicted of a "crime" that he did not commit.

In the episode "The Package" (#139), another white-collar crime,
mail fraud, is illustrated. This "scheme" begins with Jerry using a
screwdriver to try to operate his stereo. George takes his picture—
because he is flirting with a woman named Sheila who works at a
film development store. Kramer tells Jerry to get his stereo fixed. Jerry
informs him that he has tried to have it repaired but it keeps coming
back with the same problem. Kramer thinks Jerry should get a
refund, but as Jerry points out, the warranty has expired. Kramer
hatches a scheme so that Jerry can get compensated. He breaks the
stereo into many pieces and places them in a box and mails it to
Jerry. Kramer wants Jerry to claim that the stereo was damaged
during delivery. He purchases the postal insurance so that Jerry can
receive a refund, thus allowing Jerry to purchase a new stereo
through fraudulent means.

Jerry is about to "get away" with this crime (that Kramer put into
action) when Newman, his arch enemy, observes a photo of Jerry
taking a screwdriver to his stereo before delivery. It makes Jerry look
like maybe he tampered with the stereo purposely to file a false
claim. Newman calls Jerry in to the Post Office to discuss this possible mail fraud. Newman shows him the photo that he confiscated
from the photo processing store. Newman is convinced that he is
about to bring his adversary to his knees. He goes in for the kill and
asks Jerry, isn't this your signature on the mailing package? And as it
turns out, it is not, because Jerry's Uncle Leo had actually signed for
the package. As a result, the case is closed pending further evidence.

Victimless Crimes

The term "victimless" is a little misleading when describing this general category of crime. Victimless crimes refer to illegal behaviors in
which all the direct participants are consenting adults. Whether
labeled "victimless" or not, these consenting adults *are* engaged in an
illegal act. The most common types of victimless crimes are prostitution, gambling, and illegal drug use. The concept of "victimless
crimes" does not mean that there is never a victim, but rather these
crimes do not require a victim. Thus, at any given time, there may be
someone exchanging money with a prostitute and expecting some

type of service. Generally these transactions occur without anyone being "victimized." However, there are many scenarios that could lead to someone being victimized with a prostitute: the customer and prostitute both risk being physically harmed, they both risk being robbed, they both risk getting a sexual transmitted disease (STD), and, of course, they both risk being arrested.

There are very few references to drugs in *Seinfeld* and none of the main characters use illegal drugs, nor is it ever implied. There are, however, episodes that deal with prostitution and gambling.

In the episode "The Maid" (#175), Jerry inadvertently gets involved with a prostitute. Jerry hires a maid named Cindy. She cleans his apartment, and he leaves her money. Before long, Jerry and Cindy have sex. As Cindy is leaving Jerry's apartment one day, she picks up the money that Jerry always leaves for her on the counter, and gives him a big kiss good-bye. Eventually Cindy reaches the point where she comes over just for sex and does not clean the apartment. Kramer enters Jerry's apartment as Cindy exits Jerry's bedroom. She picks up her money from the counter. She says thanks and good-bye to Jerry and leaves his apartment. Jerry is bewildered. He realizes that he is paying for sex. Kramer calls him a john, a term used to describe male customers of prostitutes. The next time Cindy comes over Jerry refuses to pay her because she did not clean. Cindy expects to be paid because she did have sex with Jerry. With her scam exposed, Cindy angrily informs Jerry that she does not want to be his maid or girlfriend any longer.

Jerry is approached by a man who identifies himself as Maxwell from Maid to Order, the company that Cindy works for. He is acting like a pimp and asks Jerry about the money he owes Cindy. Jerry does not want any problems and offers Maxwell the money. He declines the money and tells Jerry to pay Cindy directly. While driving down the street Jerry sees Cindy walking on the sidewalk, wearing a really short skirt. He pulls over and offers her the cash that he "owes" her. Just then, a police cruiser pulls up with lights on. The police assume Jerry is trying to proposition a hooker.

In the episode "The Wig Master" (#129), George is having trouble with prostitutes at the Jiffy Park where he has parked his car at a discounted rate. On one occasion George finds a used condom on the floor of his car and lipstick on the dashboard. The attendant blows him off and offers George a few free shirts. Kramer also has his car parked at the Jiffy Park. And while George is arguing with the atten-

dant, Kramer is told that his car is not available because the keys have been misplaced. The attendant offers him the use of a Cadillac—a Mary Kay pink Eldorado Cadillac.

George begins to interrogate a hooker about what might be going on at the Jiffy Park. She thinks George is a cop. George attempts to reassure her that he is not a cop and offers her some money to answer some questions. Just then, Susan walks by and asks George what he's up to. He tries to explain his innocence but Susan doubts his story. George demands his car but the attendant tells him it will take a couple of days to get his car out because other cars are parked in front of his. George is well aware of the criminal activity going on at the Jiffy Park and is trying to get out ASAP.

This episode ends with Kramer returning to the parking lot to pick up the "loaned" Cadillac. The wild clothes he is wearing makes him resemble a pimp and the Cadillac looks like a pimp-daddy car! As he looks inside the car he sees a prostitute with her john. Kramer starts to argue with the hooker and the client runs away. The hooker yells at Kramer because he cost her money. She assaults Kramer and he defends himself. Just then, a police officer appears and yells for Kramer to freeze. To the police officer, Kramer appears to be a pimp fighting with one of his girls. As Kramer tries to explain he is not a pimp, the police officer frisks him.

In the episode "The Susie" (#149), Kramer's friend Mike Moffit has become a bookie—someone who takes illegal bets. Mike is the guy who once called Jerry a phony and Jerry has not completely forgiven him for the comment. Mike is trying to make amends with Jerry. Mike tells both Jerry and Kramer that he is a bookie and wonders if either of them would like to place a bet. Kramer, as we know (see chapter 7), has a gambling problem so he initially declines. Jerry simply wants nothing to do with Mike or gambling.

Kramer's addiction gets the better of him, and he places a $100 bet on the Knicks over the Pacers in an NBA basketball game in the Garden. Kramer informs Jerry that he placed the bet under Jerry's name, so Jerry will have to cover the bet. Jerry is upset with Kramer that he used his name to place a bet. Kramer justifies his behavior by utilizing an odd version of reason; namely, that he could not place the bet in his own name because he has a gambling problem. Jerry ends up winning big on the bet. But Mike can't cover! While Jerry gets ready to unload the groceries from his car, Mike walks by and informs Jerry that he does not have the money to cover the bet.

Jerry explains to Mike that as a bookie, he has to be able to cover bets that he loses. Jerry calls Mike a phony for pretending to be a bookie that cannot perform the role properly. Mike begs Jerry to give him until Friday to cover the bet. He offers to help Jerry unload his groceries from Jerry's car trunk. Jerry is having trouble closing the trunk and Mike offers to help. Instead, Mike gets his hands slammed by the trunk, and he screams out in pain.

Both of Mike's thumbs are broken, and now he is wearing two hand casts. Mike is now afraid of Jerry and asks Kramer to intervene. Mike thinks Jerry roughed him up on purpose because he did not cover the bet. Jerry explains to Kramer that it was just an accident. Just as the person who places a bet risks being injured when they cannot cover a bet, a bookie also risks being a victim in this victimless crime.

Placing a bet on a ballgame is quite common in both the legal and illegal gambling worlds. Placing bets on cockfighting is deviant and criminal in any arena. And yet, cockfights, dogfights, and other forms of illegal events are staged for people to bet on. In the episode "The Little Jerry" (#145), Kramer has a rooster that is a good fighter. Marcelino runs an illegal cockfight ring in the back of his bodega. Marcelino convinces Kramer to enter "Little Jerry" (the name of his rooster) in a fight and if Little Jerry wins, Marcelino will take Jerry's bad check off his cash register. Unbeknownst to Kramer, Marcelino has brought in a "ringer" rooster from Ecuador. This rooster has 68-0 record. Kramer attempts to stop the fight by jumping in the ring to protect "Little Jerry," but he ends up getting pecked violently several times by the rooster. Once again, a victim is found in this "victimless crime!"

Formal Social Control Agents

When informal social control, or self-control, fails to produce conformity to the law of the land, formal social control agents must take action. Society's first line of defense against crime comes from law enforcement agencies. When the police make an arrest it is up to the prosecution to present evidence that will lead to a conviction. The accused is allowed to hire a defense lawyer to protect his own needs and self interests. A judge and/or jury will make a decision as to whether the accused is guilty or innocent. If a person is found guilty of a crime, the judge will sentence the criminal in accordance to the guidelines established by law.

Law Enforcement

The police have a tough job. Most of the time, they respond to incidents that have already occurred. They must find a way to piece bits of information and various clues together in an attempt to find the perpetrator of the crime.

If Jerry were a police officer he'd most likely want to be the sketch artist. In the opening monologue of "The Trip (2)" (#42), Jerry describes the primary advantage of being a chalk outline guy. Namely, that it's not dangerous because the criminals are long gone. The chalk outline provides a number of valuable clues (for example, the direction the bullet came from). But Jerry is right that the chalk outline guy seems to have one of the safest jobs in law enforcement.

Police that take reports from victims of robbery are also removed from the criminal. They take information from victims to try to help relocate their lost property and valuables. After Jerry was robbed in "The Robbery" (#3), a policeman comes to Jerry's apartment to fill out a report. Elaine is also there. The police officer diligently fills out his report and asks Jerry a number of standard questions, such as what items were stolen, when the crime occurred, and so forth. The officer informs Jerry that they will do their best to recover the stolen items and will inform him if and when the stolen property is recovered. Jerry asks if they ever find the stolen goods and the policeman admits that they generally do not. And that's the reality of a being a robbery victim—you seldom ever get your stuff back.

There are occasions when people are victimized and the police (as well as other members of society) utilize a "blame the victim" style to investigating the crime. Although this can be a serious problem, in *Seinfeld* a variation of the "blame the victim" law enforcement mentality is illustrated in a very humorous manner. In the episode "The Bottle Deposit (2)" (#132), Jerry has his car stolen by his mechanic Tony, who has developed an emotional attachment to it. The investigative detective goes over to Jerry's apartment to ask him a few questions. Eventually the detective asks if Jerry had treated the car properly. He drills Jerry on his driving habits (e.g., riding the clutch, zipping over speed bumps). Jerry does not see how that is relevant. After all, his car was stolen, what difference should it make that his maintenance schedule was not followed. The detective tries to explain to Jerry that he has seen this before. The mechanic forms an emotional attachment and fears that he is going to lose the car, he panics, and then does something rash. Once again the police leave Jerry's apartment and inform him it's not too likely they will recover his car.

The police do, of course, solve many crimes. When they find a suspect they interrogate her. A common ploy is the old "good cop, bad cop" routine, where one cop acts like they are trying to help the suspect, and the other cop comes down with hard questions in an intimidating manner. This technique may generate results, but as in the case with Kramer ("The Trip [2]"), when he is accused of being the "Smog Strangler" the bad-cop routine almost leads to an innocent person admitting to a crime he did not commit. Kramer feels so intimidated by the interrogation process that he nearly confesses to being a serial killer.

The police use a variety of techniques in the attempt to get to the truth. A polygraph machine (a lie detector test) is one option. In the episode "The Beard" (#102), Jerry is attracted to a female police officer (Tierney). They make small talk and eventually she references a scene from the television show *Melrose Place*. Anyway, Jerry tells her that he never watched the show. Tierney doubts Jerry's answer and jokes with a fellow police officer that they should give him a polygraph test.

The next day, Jerry returns to the police station. He is strapped into the polygraph machine and interrogated about *Melrose Place*. Before long, he buckles under the pressure and blurts out a reference to the show that only regular viewers would know about. He was busted! At the end of the "The Beard" episode, the four main characters meet at Jerry's to watch *Melrose Place* together, never before knowing that all of them had been watching it secretly in private.

Lawyers

When the police make an arrest, the case is turned over to the prosecutor. The better the evidence gathered by law enforcement, the better the chance the prosecution has in gaining a conviction. Whereas the police are driven by policy and enforcement of laws, the prosecutor is usually an elected public official and is therefore often guided by certain political realities. Thus, prosecutors often exercise personal discretion in their decision to go ahead with any specific case. In a court of law, the prosecutor is directly challenged by the defense attorney.

In *Seinfeld* there is little attention given to the role of the prosecution until the two-part conclusion of the series. On the other hand, one defense attorney, Jackie Chiles, makes a number of appearances—usually related to some trouble that Kramer was involved with. (The character played by Jackie Chiles was meant to be a parody of Johnny Cochran.) Jackie uses every dirty trick in the book. He has his own doctors for his clients to see, and he employs an extreme interpretation of the Constitution. For example, in the episode "The Maestro" (#113), Kramer sneaks coffee into a movie theater, and he spills it on himself and gets burned. Kramer decides to sue the coffee store (Java World) that sold him the coffee because it was too hot. Imagine, people being shocked that their coffee is hot! This episode is clearly mocking the real case where a woman spilt coffee on herself and then had the nerve to sue a major fast-food company. (And worst of all, there are all kinds of idiotic and frivolous law cases like this in "sue-happy" America.)

Kramer hires Jackie Chiles. Kramer admits to stuffing the cup of coffee under his shirt to sneak into the theater. Sneaking in food to a place that sells food is a clear violation of proper behavior. After all, people can't bring their own food to a restaurant or their own booze to a bar, so why would Kramer (or anyone for that matter) think it is acceptable to sneak in coffee to a movie theater? Kramer asks Jackie if that will be a problem (in his suit against the coffee maker). Jackie assures him that it's the movie theater with the problem. Jackie argues that Kramer has constitutional rights as a consumer

Kramer's bone of contention with Java World is that they put the top on for him. Therefore, in Kramer and Jackie's minds, it's Java World's fault that Kramer spills coffee on himself.

Kramer ends up "burning" Jackie when he agrees to the very first offer the coffee company makes him. Java World has not even finished explaining its proposed settlement when Kramer agrees to accept it (free coffee in all their stores for the rest of his life).

The Courts

The courts symbolize an attempt to legitimize the government and its social control apparatus—the criminal justice system. Ideally, the courts are a place where evidence is brought forth and honest and impartial decisions are made.

From the perspective of the *Seinfeld* series, it is a court of law that brings an end to the deviant and criminal lifestyles of Jerry, George, Kramer, and Elaine. The four characters are on a flight to Paris when their private jet, provided by NBC, develops mechanical troubles and is forced to land in Latham, Massachusetts. The pilot assures them that the plane will be repaired, and they will be safely on their way to Paris before long. The four contemplate what to do to pass the time. All of a sudden a carjacking takes place right in front of them. An armed robber forces an overweight motorist out of his car and robs him of his wallet. Kramer films the incident. The four characters mock the guy being robbed. Interestingly, a police officer is nearby and does nothing about the carjacking. Instead he approaches the four characters, whom he arrests for violating Article 223-7 of the Latham County Penal Code. The four have never heard of the law before. The cop informs them it's new and that it is referred to as the Good Samaritan Law.

The law was modeled after the French law that was passed after Princess Diana was killed and all those photographers were just standing around (taking pictures) and not assisting in the rescue attempt. Jerry, Kramer, George, and Elaine are the first arrested under the new law. When the four are told of the seriousness of their violation, they contact their lawyer—Jackie Chiles. Over the phone, Jerry explains to Jackie their situation.

> *Jackie*: "Uh huh. Good Samaritan Law? I never heard of it. You don't have to help anybody. That's what this country's all about. That's deplorable, unfathomable, improbable. Hold on. Suzie [his secretary], cancel my appointment with Dr. Bison and pack a bag for me. I want to get to Latham, Massachusetts, right away."

When the local prosecutor learns that high-profile lawyer Jackie Chiles is taking the case, he realizes that the whole town will be swarmed with media. But that also means full motels and lots of business for the local community. The district attorney acknowledges that they must win the case no matter what. They believe that the biggest issue to surround the case will center on character. The DA orders his staff to find out everything they can on the four friends.

The DA's office finds plenty of evidence to discredit the character of Jerry, George, Kramer, and Elaine. Its investigation leads to a steady stream of past characters and guest stars that the four suspects have encountered throughout the years. Each of the witnesses has stories to tell that reflect negatively on "The New York Four." The judge assigned to this case is Arthur Vandelay. George is excited because Art Vandelay is a name that they had used before in a fictitious manner. George tells Jerry that he thinks the judge's name of Vandelay is a good sign.

But it is not a good sign. By the time Judge Vandelay hears from all the witnesses, the character of the four defendants is ruined. The judge sentences them to one year behind bars.

Many die-hard *Seinfeld* fans were disappointed in the series' finale, but it would have been impossible to create any finale to this fantastic show that would make everyone happy. Instead, the primary disappointment was the failure of "famed" lawyer Jackie Chiles to prove his clients' innocence. The film that Kramer took of the carjacking does reveal their bad character, but it also reveals that the carjacker had a gun, and therefore it was not reasonable to risk assistance and intervention. Kramer's video also shows the face of the carjacker, so they actually assist the police in the capture. And, there was a cop on the scene to notice that the four characters did nothing to assist a victim and yet he did nothing as well!

From a sociological perspective, however, a lesson can be learned from this flawed defense—the law is not perfect. Some innocent people are sent to prison and some guilty people are free and roaming the streets.

Chapter 9

Race and Ethnicity

"Look to the [Black and White] Cookie, Elaine!"—Jerry

The field of sociology dedicates a great deal of study to racial and ethnic issues. Cooperation and conflict are both characteristics of interracial and interethnic contact between diverse groups of people. Categorizing groups of people into distinct racial and ethnic groups is a long-standing tradition. People have always identified with specific groups to the point where saying "we" becomes a common trademark of self-identification. Modern governments of the world like to make such categories "official." In the United States, categorization of people occurs officially with the US Census Bureau's collection of statistical data.

Defining Race and Ethnicity

Sociologists that employ statistical data to support their theories and observations rely heavily on official data from governmental sources, especially the Census. Consequently, sociologists use the same categories of people as the US government. It is important to note that these categories are *socially* created. In essence, we are all of the same race—the human race.

The terms *race* and *ethnicity* are often used interchangeably, but that is a mistake. A racial group refers to a category of persons who

169

share socially acknowledged *physical* (based on biologically transmitted traits) differences (such as skin color) that distinguishes them
from others. Skin color differences among people are the result of
living in different regions of the world—people who live in regions of
intense heat developed darker skin (from the natural pigment
melanin), which provides protection from the sun. In more moderate
climates people developed lighter skin. The great diversity of racial
traits found among the people of the world today is the result of
migration and intergroup mating practices. The children of interra-
cial/ethnic parents inherit physical traits from both ancestry groups.

In the United States, a number of racial groups are identified by
the Census Bureau. These include white, black, Pacific Islander,
Asian, and Native American. Within these broad categories are a
number of other distinct groups known as ethnic groups.

An ethnic group is a category of persons that perceive themselves
(and are perceived by others) as distinct because of *social* and *cultural*
differences. Ethnic groups possess such shared characteristics as
nationality, geographic residence, religion, or language. An ethnic
group is like a subgroup of a larger racial grouping. For example, the
racial category of Asian can be divided into such ethnic groups as
Chinese, Japanese, Filipino, Vietnamese, and Laotian. The His-
panic/Latino population presents a different type of classification
scheme as some are dark-skinned and others are light-skinned.
Among the diverse American Hispanic ethnic groups are Mexican
Americans, Cuban Americans, and Puerto Ricans.

Membership in both racial and ethnic groups is involuntary and
lifelong; it is handed down biologically from parents to their children. However, as more and more people marry and procreate with
partners outside their ethnic and racial group, humans are becoming
more amalgamated—especially in the United States. Many people
today are not sure which racial or ethnic grouping to check on a
census questionnaire. In other words, if an individual has one white
parent and one black parent, is the child white or black? The census
has attempted to keep up with the changing racial and ethnic
makeup of its citizens by allowing such options as the category of
"Other" for those who do not like, or do not fit, into the predetermined categories.

Discussing Race

Discussing racial and ethnic issues is potentially explosive. People are very sensitive and weary of discussing race. And for good reason, when one considers the long history of oppression forced upon the "weaker" groups by the militarily and politically "stronger" groups. Currently, ethnic and racial strife, conflict, and warfare exist throughout the planet. Is it any wonder people are on edge while discussing race?

When I teach sociology courses on race and ethnicity I always share the *Seinfeld* episode "The Wizard" (#171). (It is this very fact that led to the idea of writing a book on the sociological relevance of *Seinfeld*.) This episode does a wonderful job of illustrating the delicate nature of discussing race, even when it's between friends, who assumingly, are not racist. "The Wizard" also helps to illustrate the difficulty in relying on skin color as a means of identifying a racial membership. As the four characters on *Seinfeld* will demonstrate, you can't always tell someone's "color" just by looking at them.

George and Jerry are together at Monks coffee shop. Elaine walks in with her new boyfriend, Darryl. She introduces Darryl to George and Kramer and soon after, Darryl leaves. Jerry asks Elaine about her ex-boyfriend, David Puddy. Elaine informs Jerry that she has given up on Puddy, but she is curious about Jerry's reaction to her new boyfriend.

> *Jerry*: "What? About you datin' a black guy? What's the big deal?"
> *Elaine*: "What black guy?"
> *Jerry*: "Darryl. He's black, isn't he?"
> *Elaine*: "He is?"
> *George*: "No, he isn't."
> *Jerry*: "Isn't he, Elaine?"
> *Elaine*: "You think?"
> *George*: "I thought he looked Irish."
> *Jerry*: "What's his last name?"
> *Elaine*: "Nelson."
> *George*: "That's not Irish."
> *Jerry*: "I think he's black."
> *George*: "Should we be talkin' about this?"
> *Elaine*: "I think it's OK."
> *George*: "No, it isn't."
> *Jerry*: "Why not?"

George: "It would be okay if Darryl was here."
Jerry: "If he's black."
Elaine: "Is he black?"
Jerry: "Does it matter?"
Elaine: "No, course not. I mean, I'd just like to know."
Jerry: "Oh, so you need to know?"
Elaine: "No, I don't need to know. I just think it would be nice
  if I knew."
Waitress (reaching for the check): "Should I take that?"

Jerry, Elaine, and George were so uncomfortable and self-conscious just discussing race that when the waitress, who is black, reaches for the check they all tip her heavily, as if to lift some sort of guilt for discussing race.

Elaine is now curious. She is attracted to Darryl regardless of his race, but now that Jerry planted the seed in her mind that he might be black (for those readers who cannot visualize Darryl, he is "light-skinned" and, quite frankly, it is very difficult to determine his race based on his skin color), she wants to find out. Rather than simply asking Darryl his race (and is that a "politically correct" question to ask someone you have just recently started dating?), Elaine decides to look for clues. Her clues all come in the form of various stereotypes attributed to certain racial groups. As Elaine approaches Darryl's apartment she hears loud rap music being played and smiles knowingly, as if thinking, yep, he must be black. Elaine knocks on the door and Darryl lets her in.

Elaine: "Great music."
Darryl: "Oh, it's my neighbor. They blast that stuff twenty-
  hours hours a day. I hate it. [He pounds on the wall that
  separates the two apartments.] Yo, yo, turn it down!"
Elaine (looking at pieces of art in Darryl's apartment): "Oh, wow,
  these are nice. Do they have any cultural significance?"
Darryl: "They're African."
Elaine (once again thinking she has figured out that he is
  black): "Right, African."
Darryl: "Well, not Africa, actually. South Africa."
Elaine (puzzled): "South Africa."
Darryl: "My family used to live there, but, uh, we got out
  years ago, for obvious reasons. You know how it is."
Elaine (more confused than ever): "Maybe."

The reference to South Africa confuses Elaine because as recently as the early 1980s the white minority was still dominating the black majority. Blacks were victims of discrimination and judicial injustice (apartheid). When "The Wizard" first aired (1998) the white minority was being pushed off their lands and being victimized by social injustice. Thus, Elaine still does not know whether Darryl is black or white. She seeks input from George while they sit at Monks. He still insists that Elaine simply asks Darryl what race he is. George also suggests that maybe Darryl is "mixed." Elaine questions George whether or not "mixed" is the "right" word for a child of an interracial couple. Not sure what language is appropriate to use, George is once again uncomfortable, as is Elaine.

Elaine continues her attempt to find out Darryl's race by means other than a direct question. Elaine buys Darryl a Wizard, an electronic device. But she does so just so that she can help him fill out the warranty information card that comes with it. This next scene is very significant from a sociological standpoint because it illustrates the growing discomfort among Americans to respond to questions that ask the respondent to identify his race and/or ethnicity. Elaine starts to fill out the warranty and gets to the question about race:

> *Darryl*: "Isn't that optional?"
> *Elaine*: "It certainly should be. It's nobody's damn business!
>   But they really would like to know."
> *Darryl*: "All right, I'm Asian."
> *Elaine*: "What?"
> *Darryl*: "Just to mess with 'em."
> *Elaine* (laughing awkwardly): "Oh. Right. Good one."

Elaine gets distracted from her quest when he looks at the next question and replies that his annual income is "over a hundred thousand."

Elaine tells Jerry she doesn't care anymore about Darryl's race. They are now going out to dinner at Spanish restaurants. She reasons that she is safe that way; she views Spanish restaurants as some sort of neutral buffer between white and black. As we shall learn soon, Elaine has inadvertently sent a message to Darryl, who unbeknownst to the audience at this point, is also curious about her race.

The issue of race continues to resurface. Half-clues spring up over and over when Elaine and Darryl are together. One day the two of them are at Monks and the waitress asks Darryl if he wants coffee. Darryl says "yes." The waitress then asks if he is black. There is a short pause and Elaine comes to full attention to hear Darryl's response. However, the waitress simply offers a follow up question, "Or should I bring some cream?" Meanwhile, Darryl observes an elderly conservative-looking couple gesturing towards him and Elaine. Darryl asks Elaine whether or not she saw what just happened.

> *Elaine*: "What?"
> *Darryl*: "God, there are still people who have trouble with an interracial couple."
> *Elaine* (excitedly): "Interracial? Us?"
> *Darryl*: "Isn't that unbelievable!?"
> *Elaine*: "Yes, it's awful! They're upset because we're an interracial couple. That's racism."
> *Darryl*: "I don't feel like eating."
> *Elaine*: "Me neither. Well, maybe this turkey club."

Darryl is upset because of the way the old white couple looked at him and Elaine. Older people are more likely to hold conservative racist and sexist views, as tolerance to diverse people has only been taught on a consistent basis for the past few decades. Elaine reacts differently than Darryl. She is not bothered by this example of racism because she finds the idea of interracial dating kind of new and exciting. People who are really victims of racism do not find it exciting. It can be bothersome in mild cases and dangerous in extreme conditions.

One of the many "unofficial rules" about dealing with diverse people are to be careful not to offend them. The use of certain words and slang is forbidden by members of one racial group when talking to members of another racial group. Elaine thinks it is okay for her to address the black waitress at Monks in a more "comfortable" manner, now that she is dating a black man.

While Elaine is sitting at a table at Monks, waiting for Darryl, the waitress offers her a menu. The waitress complains to Elaine about the number of hours she has worked and Elaine states, "I hear ya, Sister." The waitress is offended and repeats Elaine's "improper" usage of the word "Sister." Elaine tries to defend herself by proclaiming that she is dating a black man—implying that it should be okay for Elaine to say "Sister" to a black woman even though she is white. As Darryl walks in, Elaine points him out to the waitress as a sign of confirmation.

> *Waitress*: "He's black?"
> *Elaine*: "Yeah."
> *Darryl*: "I'm black?"
> *Elaine*: "Aren't you?"
> *Waitress* (as she leaves): "I'll give you a couple of minutes to decide."
> *Darryl*: "What are you talking about?"
> *Elaine*: "You're black. You said we were an interracial couple."
> *Darryl*: "We are. Because you're Hispanic."
> *Elaine*: "No. Why would you think that?"
> *Darryl*: "You're name's Benes, your hair, and you kept taking me to those Spanish restaurants."
> *Elaine*: "That's because I thought you were black."
> *Darryl*: "Why would you take me to a Spanish restaurant because I'm black?"
> *Elaine* (becoming uncomfortable with the conversation): "I don't think we should be talking about this."
> *Darryl*: "So, what are you?"
> *Elaine*: "I'm white."
> *Darryl*: "So, we're just a couple of white people?"
> *Elaine* (almost disappointedly): "I guess."
> *Darryl* (equally disappointed): "Oh."
> *Elaine*: "Yeah. So do you want to go to the Gap?"
> *Darryl* (getting up and leaving with Elaine): "Sure!"

Thus, Elaine and Darryl both find out, through direct dialogue, that they were both white. At first they are disappointed. But then, introducing a stereotype of white people, they are happy to go off and shop at the Gap!

Racism

Racism refers to any attitude, belief, behavior, or social arrangement that leads to one group being denied equal access to goods and services in favor of another group on the basis of race. Racists believe that their race is superior to all other races; consequently, they believe

that racist tactics are justified in order to protect their own best interests. Any person, of any race, is capable of being a racist. No one is
born a racist. Racist behaviors are learned through interaction with
others. Prejudice, negative stereotyping, and discrimination are
examples of racism.

Prejudice and Negative Stereotyping

Prejudice refers to negative beliefs and attitudes regarding a group of
people. A common type of prejudice is the stereotype, an oversimpli-
fied, exaggerated mental picture of a group of people. In both cases,
prejudice and stereotypes refer to *beliefs* held by a person of one
group toward all persons of another group. Discrimination, on the
other hand, refers to actual negative *action* or *behavior* that is directed
toward a person, or group, because of race.

It is generally assumed that stereotypes are negative connotations
of people, but that is not always the case. Thus, is "Germans are
known for their efficiency" a racist comment? It is not a negative
stereotype; after all, being labeled "efficient" should be construed as
a compliment.

The episode "The Chinese Woman" (#90) illustrates the debate
over whether or not the use of a stereotype is automatically an
example of racism. Elaine and Jerry enter Jerry's apartment. There is
a phone message waiting for Jerry from George. Jerry attempts to
return George's call but he has a problem reaching him. Jerry,
instead, reaches a woman named Donna Chang, apologizes for
dialing the wrong number and hangs up. Jerry immediately regrets
hanging up so quickly because, as he explains to Elaine, he loves Chinese women. Elaine tells Jerry that he just made a racist comment.
Jerry replies, "If I like their race, how can that be racist?"

When Jerry attempts to call George a second time he reaches
Donna Chang again. It turns out Donna's phone line has been
crossed with George's line so she is getting all of his calls. Kramer
enters Jerry's apartment while he is still on the phone with Ms.
Chang. Kramer wants to know who Jerry is talking with and Elaine
informs him that it is a Chinese woman. Kramer is very excited and
professes his love for Asian women. When Jerry gets off the phone
he tells Kramer and Elaine that he has a date with Donna. She has
seen Jerry perform at a comedy club and is a fan. Jerry is very excited
because he has a date with a woman from the Pacific Rim for the first

time in his life. Interestingly, Jerry and Donna agreed to meet at a Chinese restaurant. Elaine thinks that going to a Chinese restaurant is a little racist, but Jerry informs her that it was Donna's idea. Jerry thinks Donna must be very assimilated to American culture, especially if she is willing to eat at an American Chinese restaurant.

Jerry has never met Donna Chang. They have only spoken on the phone once, yet he is making many stereotypical assumptions about her. He arrives at the restaurant and a very good-looking blonde woman approaches him and introduces herself as Donna Chang. Jerry is shocked and disappointed. He questions how *she* could be Donna Chang. Donna quickly realizes that Jerry must have thought she would be Chinese because of her last name. Donna admits that the family name was not originally Chang, it was Changstein.

Later, Jerry talks to Elaine about the date. He tells her how disappointed he was that Donna was not Chinese. He also complains that Donna is guilty of "false advertising" because she does a lot of things that are stereotypical of the Chinese. Besides suggesting the Chinese restaurant, she references her acupuncture class, and she occasionally says things like "that's ridiculous." Elaine wonders why Jerry would still want to date her. Jerry admits to Elaine that he is going to see Donna again because she is, after all, a woman, and an attractive one at that.

Jerry is not the only person in this episode to be duped by Donna Chang and her "false advertising" of a "Chinese self." George's parents are thinking about getting a divorce. Estelle, George's mother, tries to call George, but because the lines are still crossed, she reaches Donna Chang. After talking with Donna, Estelle decides not to proceed with the divorce. George is glad that his parents are not divorcing—not because of any familial sentiment, but because he dreads the idea of double holiday time with his parents. George wonders what made his mother change her mind. Estelle explains that it was the advice of a Chinese woman that did the trick.

Estelle is going by her own stereotypical view of the Chinese, that they have some sort of insightful life philosophy. It seems that Donna gave Estelle a few bits of wisdom from Confucius. Estelle is so grateful that she insists on meeting her. So, Jerry and Donna drive to Queens to meet with Frank and Estelle. When Estelle meets Donna she is very upset. Stating the obvious, Estelle tells Donna that she is not Chinese. Donna acknowledges that fact and adds that she is from Long Island. Estelle is flabbergasted. She thought that she was getting advice from a Chinese woman not someone from Long Island. She feels duped and insists that she is not about to take advice from a woman from the Island. Jerry suggests to Donna that she might want to consider changing her name.

Jerry and Estelle were working on a stereotypical view of Chinese women. In both cases they were "positive" stereotypes—at least in the minds of Jerry and Estelle. Jerry was working on a notion that Chinese women are all nice and sweet and make great girlfriends and wives. Estelle believed that Chinese women are wise and therefore their advice is worthwhile and significant. Estelle also demonstrates a negative stereotype toward people from Long Island—that their advice has less meaning than a Chinese person's advice. These are just a few examples of what can go wrong when people work with certain stereotypical assumptions of other people.

Racist stereotypes *are* negative. Negative stereotypes affixed to a group of people extend to individuals from within the racial grouping. In addition, a negative encounter with one person of a certain racial group may lead to a generalization that all members of that group share the same negative attribute. For example, if a Southerner meets a rude New Yorker, he or she may conclude that all New Yorkers are rude. It is true that some New Yorkers are rude, but certainly not all New Yorkers. Many people from New York think that all Southerners are rednecks. (Note: when people from the Northeast use the term *redneck* it is meant as a derogatory term, whereas in the South, it is considered, by many, as a badge of honor.) Again, it is true that some Southerners are rednecks, but certainly not all Southerners.

In the episode "The Sniffing Accountant" (#68), Jerry manages to disparage all people from South America—the whole continent! Jerry, Kramer, and Newman all have the same accountant, Barry Prophet, who has invested their money. They begin to get suspicious of the accountant because he is sniffing all the time and he goes to the bathroom a lot—both characteristics of a cocaine user. Based on these stereotypes and other "clues," Jerry, Kramer, and Newman decide that they want their money back from Prophet. Jerry decides to call his office. Kramer and Elaine are in Jerry's apartment when he makes the call. When Jerry is informed that Barry is out of the office and that he went to South America, Jerry is visibly upset. Jerry and Kramer immediately assume the worst. In their minds, South America is a continent of and for drugs. Jerry believes that people who go to South America all come back with drugs. It is true that in some cases some people come back to the United States with drugs taped to their bodies, or that they have swallowed balloons of drugs to be "flushed out" of their systems when they go to the bathroom. However, as Elaine points out, just because some people go to South America for drugs that is no reason to impugn an entire continent. Jerry admits that he is willing to impugn South America based on the limited information that he has of the continent.

The discussion between Jerry and Elaine reflects the "classic" manner in which a stereotype works. Yes, there are some drug runners going back and forth to South America, but they represent a very small percentage of such travelers.

Many racists are so "color blind" that they cannot (or will not) distinguish individuals from the larger racial group. In other words, a racist will say something like, "Well, you know, they all look alike." In the episode "The Diplomat's Club" (#108), George is accused by his boss, Mr. Morgan, of having a racial bias. George is trying to get on Morgan's good side, because George thinks he's on "thin ice" with him. George offers up what is meant to be a compliment to Morgan by saying that he looks like former boxing great Sugar Ray Leonard. George thinks that Morgan must hear that all the time because of their resemblance. Morgan views George's comment as racist and comments to George that he must think all black people look alike. George tries in vain to convince Morgan that he meant nothing racial about his comment.

Morgan does look a bit like Sugar Ray Leonard, but George's comment backfires. George tries to solicit help from his coworkers who overheard his comments, but they all shy away from him. They realize the sensitive nature of discussing race as well as the fact that their boss viewed such a comment as racist; it is not surprising that none of George's coworkers came to his rescue.

George shows a copy of a photo of Morgan to Jerry, Elaine, and Kramer, trying to get someone, anyone, to verify his belief that Morgan does look like Sugar Ray, and that George is, therefore, not a racist. Jerry agrees that there is at least a resemblance between the two but suggests to George that he still should not have said anything. George tries to convince Jerry that he is not a racist. George even states that he would have "marched on Selma"—if it was on Long Island.

George wants to prove to Mr. Morgan that he is not a racist. He tries to think of a black friend of his that he can hang out with in Morgan's presence. But, as Jerry points out, he doesn't have any black friends. Then again, except for Jerry, Elaine, and Kramer, George doesn't have *any* friends. Eventually, George calls an exterminator that Jerry once used because he is a black man. George takes the exterminator to dinner where Morgan is dining and tries to pass the exterminator off as a good friend. Morgan quickly realizes George and the exterminator are not friends. Morgan is really angry now, because he believes George is trying to bribe a black man to be his friend just to look good in front of him. Morgan gets up from his table and leaves. George offers to pay for the check. The waiter, who is black, tells George that Sugar Ray Leonard can eat at that restaurant for free whenever he wants. George, feeling vindicated, runs after Mr. Morgan so that he can hear the waiter call him Sugar Ray.

In the episode "The Soup Nazi" (#116), a very peculiar man runs a soup stand. It serves the best soup in New York. The only problem is, the guy running the stand insists on very specific and regimented ordering procedures. Anyone who does not order properly is denied service in a very emphatic manner: "No soup for you!" As a result, customers secretly refer to the man as the Soup Nazi. But Kramer believes that the Soup Nazi is merely misunderstood. Kramer and the Soup Nazi are friends. The Soup Nazi likes Kramer because he is the only one who understands the hard work involved in making great-tasting soup. Kramer has come to understand that the Soup Nazi expects perfection from his soup, so how could he expect anything less from his customers?

The Soup Nazi has his issues. He yells at a customer for speaking in Spanish and denies him soup. In the end, after Elaine distributes copies of all the Soup Nazi's recipes (which she obtained when he so generously replaced her stolen armoire with one of his own—the one that held all his secret recipes), he gives away his remaining soup, closes shop, and moves to Argentina—another stereotypical reference to the place where some Nazis moved to after World War II. There have been consistent rumors that Hitler actually escaped from his death bunker in Germany and moved to Argentina where he lived secretly for years after the war.

In the episode "The Checks" (#141), Kramer's stereotypical view of the Japanese as wealthy people would cause great distress to three Japanese tourists. Kramer befriends the three tourists while they are sightseeing in New York. Kramer shows them around the city and takes them shopping. Misunderstanding the currency exchange rates, Kramer believes that his new Japanese friends are wealthy because they have thousands and thousands of yen. They buy Kramer a new suit. Kramer later justifies his acceptance of the suit from the Japanese because they are known as gift-givers. Not wanting to offend them, he accepts the suit. In no time, Kramer has encouraged them to spend all their money. They are so broke that they cannot afford their suites at the Plaza Hotel.

So, Kramer invites them to stay with him in his apartment until it is time for them to return to Japan. Kramer does not have three other beds for his guests so he has them sleeping in his chest of drawers. Kramer goes over to Jerry's apartment to borrow some pillows and explains to Jerry and Elaine what is going on. Jerry is shocked that Kramer has them sleeping in a dresser. Once again, Kramer reveals his stereotypical views of Japanese. He has heard that the hotel rooms in Tokyo are so small that sleeping in drawers will make the Japanese tourists feel right at home. Jerry just looks at Kramer with amazement and proclaims that Kramer is about to cause an international incident. Kramer just smiles and heads back to his apartment.

The three tourists meet with Japanese television executives in New York (the same executives that Jerry and George are trying to sell their television idea for *Jerry*) to serve as a focus group to attest to the comedic value of Jerry Seinfeld. Instead, the tourists complain about how poorly they have been treated. Kramer did not quite cause an international incident but the producers quickly turn down *Jerry*.

Hundreds of years ago, Native Americans were victims of genocide perpetrated by Europeans, and, later, Americans. Genocide is the intentional attempt to exterminate a race of people by a more dominant population. There are numerous examples of genocide, past and present. The Native American populations of North and South America were decimated by European explorers and settlers between the sixteenth and twentieth centuries. The use of warlike Indian imagery in sports represents just one type of racism that Native Americans have been forced to endure.

In "The Cigar Store Indian" (#74), Jerry is guilty of many inadvertent racist comments and uses of symbolism that disparage Native Americans. In this episode, Jerry purchases a cigar store Indian (which in itself is politically incorrect) to give to Elaine as a "peace offering" gift for an earlier fight they had. When Jerry shows up at Elaine's apartment with the gift, she is hosting a poker game for her girlfriends. A card accompanies the gift. Jerry tells Elaine to read it out loud. So, Elaine complies. In the note, Jerry suggests that he and

Elaine "bury the hatchet" and smoke a peace pipe. One of Elaine's friends, Winona, gets up from the table to go home. She looks uneasy with the whole "peace offering" gift. As Winona walks by Jerry and Elaine to leave, Jerry begins to rock the Indian statue back and forth, making stereotypical Indian chants: "Hey-yah, ho-ah, hey-yah, ho-ah." Winona leaves angrily.

Jerry, still not quite gripping the severity of his faux pas is informed by Elaine that Winona is a Native American. Jerry did not mean to offend Winona; he even wants to date her. He goes over to her apartment to apologize. Eventually she agrees to come down to the street to meet with him. Winona explains to Jerry that she is very sensitive to the whole "Indian" stereotype issue. Jerry attempts to reassure her that he is a good guy and that he is sensitive to racial issues. He asks her if she would like a bite to eat, and she agrees.

Jerry mentions to Winona that there is a really good Chinese restaurant somewhere nearby but he cannot remember the exact address. Noticing a mailman, who is crouched to the ground emptying a mail box, Jerry excuses himself and approaches him to ask where the Chinese restaurant is. Jerry assumes, that as the local mailman, he most certainly will know. The mailman stands up and turns toward Jerry and Winona. He is Chinese. And now he is upset. The mailman interprets Jerry's comment as racist and lays in on Jerry for making a stereotypical comment. Jerry attempts to convince him that it was not a racist statement. Meanwhile, Winona is observing all this and once again thinks the worst about Jerry.

Just when Jerry is sure that things cannot get worse, a cab drives by with Kramer and the cigar store Indian inside it. Elaine did not want the statue and gave it to Kramer who just happened to drive by when Jerry was talking with Winona. Kramer compounds the problem when he yells out war-whoops. Winona is so offended she storms back into her building.

Winona is a forgiving person and offers Jerry one more chance to prove he is not a racist. He is on guard for everything that he says. They agree to go to dinner at the Gentle Harvest.

> *Winona*: "Ooh, I love that place, but it's usually so crowded. Can we get a table?"
> *Jerry*: "Ah, don't worry. I made reser—" (Jerry catches himself and stops.)
> *Winona*: "You made what?"

Jerry: "I uh, I uh, I arranged for the appropriate accommoda-
tion. And then Knicks tickets, floor seats."

Winona (looking at the tickets): "How did you get these?"

Jerry: "Got 'em on the street, from a scal—[catches himself
again]—A, uh, one of those guys."

Winona: "What guys?"

Jerry: "You know, the guys, that uh, sell the tickets for the
sold-out events."

Winona: "Oh."

Jerry is beginning to realize how many words have double mean-
ings which, when taken out of context, can be deemed as offensive
to certain members of the population. Things get really touchy for
Jerry and Winona when she asks Jerry to return the *TV Guide*—the
one with Al Roker on the cover. Winona had given it to him earlier
to replace the one that Elaine took (and subsequently lost) from
Frank Costanza. Jerry says that he cannot return it to Winona
because Elaine had already given it to Frank. Winona insists on its
return, claiming original ownership. Jerry informs Winona that you
can't give something to someone and then take it back. After all, that
would make her a . . . Jerry stops himself. Winona presses him—that
would make her a what? An Indian Giver? Jerry pretends to be unfa-
miliar with that term. Nonetheless, Winona is upset.

Discrimination

Discrimination refers to actual behavior that treats people unequally
on the basis of an ascribed status (a characteristic that someone is
born with), such as race, ethnicity, or gender. Discrimination can
take place on two distinct levels: individual (or interpersonal) and
institutional levels.

Most people understand what is meant by individual discrimination. It is discrimination that one person implements against
another individual. For example, as mentioned earlier in this
chapter, Mr. Morgan accused George of being a racist. This was an
interpersonal complaint that Morgan had against George.

Institutional discrimination refers to social arrangements and
practices that favor one group over another. Minorities have long
complained that the social system works against them and favors the
white majority. Sociologists have shown that systematic and institu-

tional forms of discrimination exist in many social institutions, including the judicial system, housing, banking, insurance, police and fire response times to certain neighborhoods, and so on. For example, in real estate, there is a fairly common type of institutional racism employed called *racial steering*. Racial steering occurs when white customers are shown homes in white neighborhoods and black customers are shown houses in racially mixed or all-black neighborhoods.

In an attempt to balance past injustices, "quota" systems have been established in a variety of social institutions in an attempt to help minority members get ahead in society.

Another type of institutional racism is known as *redlining*. Redlining can be defined as the refusal to service people who live in certain neighborhoods. Generally speaking, the neighborhoods that are "redlined" are the lower SES neighborhoods. People who live in these neighborhoods are often faced with the reality that taxicabs will not pick them up and pizzerias will not deliver food to them.

In the episode "The Pothole" (#150), Elaine is a victim of redlining, not because of her race, but because of her neighborhood. Elaine places an order with China Panda, a Chinese restaurant. When she gives her address she is told that they don't deliver below 86th Street. Elaine calls a second time and disguises her voice and gives a false address in the delivery zone. She waits outside an apartment building for the food. The delivery guy wonders why she is on the street instead of inside her apartment. Elaine assumes he will just walk away but, instead, he waits to see what Elaine is going to do. When she cannot get into the building, she turns and looks at him, and admits defeat by handing the food back to him. As the delivery guy walks away Elaine declares that she is a victim of "address discrimination."

"Address discrimination" is very real. Car insurance, property insurance, tax rates, and more are all determined by location. If you live in a high-crime area, you pay a higher rate of insurance. Live on the wrong side of town? Brace yourself for various forms of institutional discrimination.

There exists in (any) society a number of subgroups that are filled with rage toward members of other racial groups. These subgroups are known as hate groups. Hate groups openly display their disdain for people who are not like themselves. Among the more violent in America are the Aryan Nation, the Ku Klux Klan, and various violent factions of skinheads.

In the episode "The Limo" (#36), a classic stereotypical portrayal of a hate group is presented. Things start off innocently enough for the four main characters, but by the end of this episode, they are all in danger of being murdered by a hate organization called the Aryan Union.

George is at the airport to give Jerry a ride home. There's a big problem: George's car broke down on his way in. So now, they are both at the airport faced with a decision as to the best way to get home. Noticing a group of drivers holding signs up for arriving passengers, Jerry makes a comment to George that he knows O'Brien's chauffer will be waiting a long time because O'Brien did not make the flight out of Chicago. O'Brien was really upset because he had to get to Madison Square Garden. George jokes that they should take his limo. And eventually, they do.

George pretends to be Donald O'Brien and Jerry pretends to be Dylan Murphy (a fictitious name that Jerry made up to go along with the prank of George acting as O'Brien). The driver tells the two that he has the four passes to Madison Square Garden. George and Jerry assume that the passes must be for a Knicks-Bulls game since O'Brien was coming from Chicago and said he was going to the Garden. Jerry and George decide to invite Elaine and Kramer to join them.

When the chauffeur makes an unexpected turn, George inquires what is going on. The chauffeur informs them that he is picking up the other two members of the party. These two people, Tim and Eva, are local comrades of O'Brien. Luckily for George and Jerry, Tim and Eva have never met O'Brien. Eva gushes over George (because she thinks he is O'Brien) and tells him how much she loves his book *The Big Game*. Eva brags that she has memorized the whole book. She is a little embarrassed about her admiration of it but admits that it has changed her life. She admires the way the major players are identified and concludes that O'Brien is a brilliant man. Acting out the role of O'Brien (as he sees it) George says that it's just a game. Tim points out how humble O'Brien is, after all, in the epilogue, he wrote that the fate of the world depends on the outcome of this game.

At this point, Jerry and George are still unaware of who O'Brien really is and what he is really all about. Eva offers George a copy of his speech that she has received from O'Brien's secretary. George starts to read it; it is filled with racist ideology blaming the Jews and the blacks for destroying white America.

Suddenly there is a loud bang. George thinks it was a gunshot. The limo pulls over. Eva falls on top of George because she is willing to die for him. Tim leaves the car to see what's going on. It was just a flat tire. Tim assures George and Jerry that he and Eva are prepared to handle anything. Tim opens a briefcase filled with firearms.

Meanwhile, Elaine and Kramer are waiting for Jerry and George, assuming that they are on their way to a basketball game. But Kramer questions why George and Jerry are using fake names. A friend of Elaine's walks by and tells her that he is heading to the Garden to protest a neo-Nazi rally. Dan tells Elaine and Kramer that the head of the Aryan Union, O'Brien, is flying in from Chicago to speak. Kramer begins to suspect that Jerry *is* O'Brien. Elaine calls Kramer stupid for even thinking such a thing. Elaine tells Kramer that Jerry may be neat, but he's not a Nazi. Elaine has described a rather unusual, and seldom used, stereotype of Nazis.

The limo reaches Elaine and Kramer. They join Jerry, George, Tim, and Eva in the limo. Kramer points to Jerry and says hello O'Brien. Kramer then looks at George and calls him Murphy. Tim and Eva finally begin to suspect something is wrong. The phone rings; it's the real O'Brien! Tim and Eva contemplate what to do, but decide to let the four out of the limo. By this time, the protestors have surrounded the car and assume O'Brien is inside. They rock the car. A number of news crews are at the scene. George is shown in front of a news camera with an on screen graphic that states: "Donald O'Brien, Leader of the Aryan Union." George yells out to the crowd that he is not the real O'Brien, but by this point, the media has already splashed his picture with a caption declaring him the head of Aryan Union.

Bridging the Racial Gap

Interethnic and interracial contact is a reality of social life. The great diversity that exists in the United States mandates that people find some way to interact peacefully with each other. Sociologists generally acknowledge three broad solutions toward a more harmonious racially diverse society. One solution is amalgamation—the physical blending of two or more diverse and previous distinct groups. This is accomplished when racially diverse individuals procreate, resulting in children that are a racial blend. There is an increase in racially mixed marriages as society has increasingly become accepting toward these once taboo relationships. Since none of the characters on *Seinfeld* ever get married or have children, there are no relevant examples to share.

A second approach toward racial harmony involves assimilation—the cultural blending of two or more previously distinct groups. This approach involves cultural conformity. All the diverse groups make up a "melting pot" where they are blended together culturally. Old cultural ways and heritages are to be abandoned in favor of the new culture that people have chosen to join. Historically, the dominant group does not change its cultural ways—minority groups are expected to do all of the conforming. Modern versions of assimilation recognize that the majority group must also conform, at least to some degree. American society is filled with examples of assimilation from the diversity of music, arts, clothing, and food to a growing acceptance of diverse outlooks and perspectives on social life.

A third possible solution toward racial harmony involves cultural pluralism, or multiculturalism. Under this ideal, all groups are treated equally and share equally in the scarce resources of society. Pluralists believe that all racial and ethnic groups have something to offer society and therefore all cultures should be maintained. Of course, the only way this system will work is if people are tolerant to those who are different from them. Cultural Pride Days are an example of multiculturalism. American Irish citizens established St. Patrick's Day, and Italian Americans established Columbus Day as a means of showing pride of their cultural heritage. Many other groups do the same thing.

Puerto Rican Day in New York City is a major event, complete with a parade, music, dancing, ethnic food, and a sense of cultural pride. For some people, cultural celebration days are simply nuisances that must be tolerated. Many motorists and local people complain about the traffic congestion as a result of such celebrations. An example of a cultural pride day appears in "The Puerto Rican Day" (#176). One man complains about the traffic jam caused by the parade and wonders how long he will be inconvenienced. Elaine responds with a stereotypical comment that Puerto Ricans are very festive people and therefore the parade could last awhile. Elaine is just as upset as others. She likes to get home early on Sundays so that she can unwind and prepare for the coming week. Attitudes like this do not help to foster harmony among diverse groups. It would be nice if people accepted cultural differences of others; if they did, we could all bridge the racial and ethnic gap.

In the episode "The Dinner Party" (#77), Jerry attempts to illustrate to Elaine just how diverse groups such as whites and blacks *can* get along. Jerry and Elaine are at the Royal Bakery to pick up a chocolate babka for a dinner party that they were invited to. Jerry also orders a black and white cookie to eat in the bakery while they wait for George and Kramer to return from the liquor store (they were getting wine for the party). Jerry loves his black and white cookie and he attempts to explain its charm to Elaine, which is that nothing mixes better than vanilla and chocolate.

> *Jerry*: "And yet, somehow, racial harmony eludes us. If people would only look to the cookie all our problems would be solved."
> *Elaine*: "Your views on race relations are fascinating. You really should do an op-ed piece for the *Times*."
> *Jerry*: "Um, um. Look to the cookie, Elaine. Look to the cookie."

Jerry notices a black man who is also eating a black and white cookie and nods approvingly at him. The black man nods back at Jerry in a positive manner. Has Jerry found the answer to racial harmony via the black and white cookie? Could it be that simple? No! After Jerry finishes the cookie his stomach begins to bother him. Elaine asks what's wrong with him. He reluctantly admits that he thinks it was the cookie that upset his stomach. He tells her that is stomach feels like David Duke and Louis Farrakhan were both inside of him. Elaine is now slightly disillusioned: "If we can't look to the cookie, where can we look?"

Well, world leaders, and even sociologists have not found a way to solve racial problems throughout the world. Did anyone honestly think *Seinfeld* was going to solve racial strife? Perhaps we should look again to the black and white cookie. After all, even Bette Midler attests to the power of the cookie. In the episode "The Understudy" (#110), Midler raves about the power of the black and white cookie. While recuperating in her hospital room, Bette asks Kramer to get her a black and white cookie saying, "If I don't get a black and white cookie, I'm not going to be very pleasant to be around."

Look to the cookie.

Chapter 10

Marriage and Family

"Elaine, Ya Gotta Have a Baby."—Carol

As young adults age, they begin to feel societal pressure to conform to the norm of getting married and starting a family. In the episode "The Soul Mate" (#136), Elaine is entertaining some girlfriends, including Carol, the woman whom the gang visits in an earlier episode ("The Hamptons") to see Carol and Michael's first child, Adam. In "The Soul Mate," Elaine, Lisa, and Gail are standing around Carol as she changes the baby's diaper. Carol mentions that you aren't even bothered by the smells because it comes out of your own baby. Elaine politely says, "That's sweet." The women now turn their attention to Elaine and criticize her single lifestyle. They think it is time for Elaine to settle down, get married, move to the suburbs, and raise a family.

> *Gail*: "Being a mother has made me feel so beautiful."
> *Carol*: "Elaine, ya gotta have a baby!"
> *Elaine* (trying to change the subject): "Oh hey, you know, I had a piece of whitefish over at Barney Greengrass the other day—"
> *Lisa*: "Elaine. Move to Long Island and have a baby already."
> *Elaine*: "I really like the city."
> *Carol*: "The city's a toilet."

Elaine retells her day's events to Jerry and George and the pressure she felt from her girlfriends. Mocking Carol, Elaine emphasizes her voice and says, "Elaine, ya gotta have a baby."

Jerry: "Why do you invite these women over if they annoy you so much?"

Elaine: "They're my friends, but they act like having a baby takes some kind of talent."

Jerry: "C'mon, you want to have a baby."

Elaine: "Why? Because I can?"

Jerry: "It's the life force. I saw a show on the mollusk last night. Elaine, the mollusk travels from Alaska to Chile just for a shot at another mollusk. You think you're any better?

Elaine: "Yes! I think I am better than the mollusk."

There are many reasons why Elaine's friends pressure her to have a baby. In particular, they are pointing out the importance of marriage and family and its role in culture. In this chapter, the significant social institutions of marriage and family are discussed.

Social Expectations

The family is a major agent of socialization. The earliest indoctrination to society's norms and expectations come from the family, especially the child's parents (or guardians). The first group that an individual is a part of is the family; because of this the family is a primary group. The "we" feeling and a sense of belonging begins within the family structure. Consequently, the role of the family and its influence on individuals, especially when they are young, is typically immense. Children that are raised in a loving, nurturing environment are more likely to be well-adjusted adults. The family is also a social group that possesses the same characteristics as any other social group: rules, norms, the provision of sanctions, a hierarchy, a leader(s), and so on.

The social institution of marriage has existed in a variety of forms throughout the history of mankind. Sociologists define marriage as a (relatively) enduring, socially approved sexual and economic relationship between at least two persons for the purpose of creating and maintaining a family. In some societies, marriage practices have allowed, or even required, people to have more than one spouse at a time. This type of marriage system is referred to as polygamy. In the United States, as well as most other industrialized nations, monogamy is the system that is encouraged, or even mandated by law. Monogamy involves one person being married to one other person at any given time.

In the United States, as well as in many other societies, the notion of romantic love preceding marriage is idealized. This children's nursery rhythm reflects the traditional American view of the "proper" way of doing things: "First comes love, and then comes marriage, soon after, comes the baby carriage."

Romantic Love

We "love" many things. We also use the word "love" very nonchalantly to describe a variety of feelings. For example, it is common for people to say things like "I love football," "I love a cold beer on a hot summer's day," or "I would love to get an A on my final exam in sociology."

Romantic love is much different than the generic use of the word. Romantic love involves a deep physical and emotional attraction. Romantic love is valued in American culture because it is considered a prerequisite to marriage. Social psychologists compare falling in love to getting high on drugs. The falling-in-love process generally begins as a "weekend habit." As the process continues, it becomes serious—often without the realization of the participants, who become increasingly more psychologically dependent on each other. Romantic lovers see only the good in their partners; they either ignore each other's flaws or refuse to deal with them because they are *so* in love. The lovers discover that no one else gives them the same "high" that they experience with their loved one. The lovers enjoy each other's company so much that they begin to crave it. They are "gaga" for each other! Romantic lovers even experience withdrawal distress when they are separated from each other.[13]

Falling in love may occur suddenly or slowly. No one knows for sure what internal processes occur that trigger romantic love feelings. The lovers themselves often give varied, contradictory, and unilluminating answers to the question, Why do you love each other?

It is important to note that romantic love usually only lasts a few years. After time, the lovers begin to acknowledge each other's flaws and little quirks. Things that once were simple and charming annoyances (for example, when men leave the toilet seat up) become irritations that often lead to shouting disagreements or fights. In order for any relationship to survive the long run, couples must learn to go beyond the limits of romantic love. Couples must learn to base their relationship on shared goals, a lasting commitment, and compromise. Many marriages fail because couples marry simply because they were in love. Being "in love" should be just one of many reasons why someone would want to marry, certainly not the only reason.

Without question, the "high" one experiences when they are romantically in love with another person (who shares the same feelings) is exciting, thrilling, and rewarding. Thoughts of the other continuously intrude into the minds of people in love. They can't help but think about their lovers. In the episode "The Soul Mate" (#136), Kramer is gaga for a woman named Pam. The problem is that Pam is Jerry's girlfriend. There is supposed to be an unwritten "law" between friends, you never "steal" their love interest away from them. To even attempt such a thing is unforgivable. Initially, Kramer abides by this code of conduct and worships Pam from a distance out of respect to Jerry.

The minute that Kramer meets Pam (at Jerry's apartment) he falls for her. Kramer explains to Newman his dilemma. Newman acknowledges that Kramer has fallen for "forbidden love." Newman advises Kramer to confront Jerry directly, man to man, as best friends. So, Kramer takes the high road and discusses with Jerry his extreme attraction to Pam. Kramer admits to Jerry that he loves her. He loves her voice, her name, and her hair. He considers her a dreamboat.

After hearing all the praise that Kramer heaps on Pam, Jerry suddenly thinks he could be gaga for her. Funny how a little competition leads a person to realize just how good of a partner he has. Kramer informs Newman that Jerry wants Pam more than ever. Newman, who despises Jerry, wants to help Kramer win Pam over, so they devise a plan. Newman, who is good at writing love poems, is going to help Kramer win Pam over through literature and poetry— a smart move considering the fact that Pam works at a bookstore.

Kramer and Newman institute their plan. They go to Pam's bookstore. Kramer innocently approaches her and makes small talk. Newman hides behind a bookcase and whispers to Kramer things to say. With Newman's help, Kramer wins her over. Jerry is now the disappointed one as he has lost his girlfriend. Pam attempts to explain her own feelings to both Jerry and Kramer and admits that she has feelings for them both. Jerry and Kramer argue over who loves Pam more when suddenly Kramer asks Jerry whether or not he really thinks that Pam would want him to be the father of her children. Pam informs the two friends that she does not want to have children. Jerry and Kramer look at each other in puzzlement. No children?! They both assumed that one day they would have children with the woman that they love.

Having children is just one of the many things that couples need to talk about before they get married. And if one person wants children and the other does not, there is an obvious impasse to overcome. The romantic viewpoint of another quickly changes when a major dispute over certain issues (like having children) come to bear on the relationship. Being gaga with someone can quickly change to "go-go"—as in, I am going to get out of this relationship.

When people are in a romantic relationship, they can use three powerful words—"I love you"—on a regular basis. It is quite reassuring to say to someone "I love you" and know that you will be getting the same response in return. On the other hand, saying "I love you" for the first time can be risky and dangerous to one's self-esteem if the response given by the other is not what was expected. The episode "The Face Painter" (#109), provides a perfect illustration of the dangers of saying "I love you" for the first time.

In "The Face Painter" George is dating a woman named Siena— as Jerry mocked George about her name, he's dating a crayon. Elaine and George are at Jerry's apartment. George announces that he is thinking about "making a big move." He wants to tell Siena that he loves her. Jerry inquires whether George is confident in the I-love-you return. George admits that it's a fifty-fifty proposition. As if George needed any more pressure, Jerry tells him that he is potentially setting himself up for a major letdown. But George is excited to make the big move regardless of the consequences, especially in light of the fact that he has never told a woman that he loved her. Jerry and Elaine are shocked to hear this.

Poor George, he has never told a woman that he loved her. And he is about to say it to a woman that he's not even sure loves him back. Anyone who has ever said "I love you" to someone and did not get the "I love you, too" return is surely rooting for George. The big night arrives. George and Siena are sitting in George's car listening to the Devils-Rangers play-off hockey game on the radio. In an attempt to prove his love to Siena, George tells her that he could have gone to the game with his friends but chose to keep his date with her instead. George then says, "Because I, I love you." Siena, who obviously does not share George's feelings ignores his proclamation of love and suggests that they get something to eat because she is hungry.

Ouch! Shot down big time. There is no return from a response like Siena's. The only thing to do is to reevaluate the relationship. Logic would dictate that they should both run, quickly.

But this is George we are talking about, and there is a reason why he is such a lovable loser. He thinks he can, he thinks he can. Unfortunately, most little engines cannot climb high mountains, and they learn their lesson. Not George. When Kramer informs George that Siena is deaf in one ear (George did not know this) he suggests to George that maybe Siena never even heard his proclamation. George believes he has new hope. George excitedly prepares himself to proclaim his love once again. The next evening George and Siena are sitting in his car again when he tells her that he loves her. Siena responds, "Yeah, I know. I heard you the first time." Double-slammed! There is no returning from that embarrassing scene. It is clearly time for George to abandon any hopes of a romantic relationship with her.

Couples routinely break up and fall out of love. There are times, however, when one, or both, members of that relationship begin to miss what they once had. They begin to rewrite past history in light of their current miserable and emotional state of mind. Just as people who first fall in love view the other in romantic ideals, the revisionist also begins to think of the other only in a positive, romantic manner. The episode "The Pick" (#53) provides an excellent example of romantic revisionist love.

In "The Pick," George is reminiscing about his ex-girlfriend Susan. George shares his feelings about Susan with Elaine and Jerry, who both know the "truth" about George and Susan's past relationship. He tries to convince himself and Jerry and Elaine that they were in love with each other. They tell George, no you weren't. George wants her back. His friends remind him that he didn't even like her when they first dated. But George is in denial and pursues her once again.

A lot of people want something, or someone, just because they can't have it, but that feeling often changes once the object of desire has been attained. George and Susan do get back together. And from the department "Be careful what you wish for," George ends up regretting getting back together until the day of her tragic death.

Marriage

In most Western cultures, marriage follows romance. Two people fall in love, go through some sort of courting procedure, and then commit to one another through marriage. Societies that promote marriage based on romantic love leave it up to the two people to find each other.

In other cultures love has nothing, or little, to do with marriage, and families help to find their sons and daughters a life-long partner through an "arranged marriage." In these cultures it is believed that love will follow the marriage. Marriage is not an ideal but a reality. Partners are matched to each other based on more tangible needs (property, power, to end a feud or war, etc.) than romantic ideals.

In the episode "The Little Jerry" (#145), Elaine and Jerry are at a cockfight at 3:30 AM in the back of a bodega. Elaine mentions to Jerry that she is considering marrying a man she just recently met. Jerry wants Elaine to stop and think about the ramifications of a "love-less" marriage. However, as Elaine explains to Jerry, after taking stock in her life and observing her current surroundings, what is she clinging to in her single life that is so important? Elaine has concluded that her single life is not working out for her so why not get married?

Societal marriage patterns are deeply influenced by cultural norms and values. For example, in the United States, marriage is limited to one person married to one other person at any given time— monogamy. There are a number of legal restrictions as well. For example, the incest taboo forbids marriage between people who are too closely related to one another (such as siblings). Presently, only the state of Massachusetts allows a marriage between members of the same sex. The other forty-nine states and the federal government do not legally acknowledge same-sex marriages. Following the 2004 elections, many states passed amendments to their state constitutions forbidding same-sex marriages.

In American culture, a "courtship" period (when two people date and get to know each other well enough to decide whether or not to commit to each other in either a civil or religious ceremony) is generally followed by an engagement proposal, the engagement period, and then finally, the wedding.

Many couples are in love with each other, and yet, they don't all get married. Why is it that some people want to get married and others do not? In the episode "The Engagement" (#111), Jerry, George, and Kramer ponder these two opposing viewpoints.

Jerry and George are at Monk's coffee shop discussing their failed relationships. They begin to think that maybe there is something missing from their lives, specifically, marriage and a family. Jerry (reflecting society's expectations of what constitutes a man) feels that they are not even "real" men because they are not married with children. They both think it is time to make a change, specifically to commit to a woman and raise a family. Jerry vows to stop breaking up with women for stupid reasons—something he is known to do. Many people are like Jerry. They find picky reasons to end a relationship. Jerry worries that when he is sixty years old he will still be having lunch with George, "like two idiots." Reaffirming Jerry's newfound interest in marriage and family, George tells Jerry that when they are sixty they should be having lunch with their children. They both decide that they are pathetic and that they need to be like "normal" people (who get married and raise a family). Jerry thinks that it would be nice to actually care about someone else other than himself. George agrees with him and contemplates pursuing (yet again) his ex-girlfriend Susan. (Remember: George and Susan were off and on for years.) George and Jerry tell each other that they are both serious about establishing a loving relationship with someone special.

And so, with that conversation the famous pact is made between George and Jerry to get their respective acts together and settle down with a nice woman and start a family. George would in fact pursue Susan's affection immediately. He is ready to become one of the 90 percent of Americans who can be expected to get married. After some convincing, Susan accepts George's wedding proposal. George calls his parents and they are ecstatic. George is finally acting in a manner that makes his parents proud.

Meanwhile, Jerry meets up with Kramer after his life-altering conversation. Kramer is another life-long bachelor and offers Jerry a very different perspective on this social norm. After Jerry explains to him that he and George believe that there is something missing from their lives, Kramer bursts Jerry's commitment bubble.

> *Kramer*: "So, then you asked yourselves, 'Isn't there something more to life?'"
> *Jerry*: "Yes. We did."
> *Kramer*: "Yeah, well, let me clue you in on something. There isn't!"
> *Jerry*: "There isn't?"
> *Kramer*: "Absolutely not. I mean, what are you thinking about, Jerry? Marriage? Family?"
> *Jerry*: "Well—"

Kramer: "They're prisons. Man-made prisons. You're doing time. You get up in the morning. She's there. You go to sleep at night. She's there. It's like you gotta ask permission to use the bathroom. 'Is it all right if I use the bathroom now?'"

Jerry: "Really?"

Kramer: "Yeah and you can forget about watching TV while you're eating."

Jerry: "I can?"

Kramer: "Oh, yeah. You know why? Because it's dinner time. And you know what you do at dinner?"

Jerry: "What?"

Kramer: "You talk about your day. 'How was your day today? Did you have a good day or a bad day? Well, what kind of day was it?' 'Well, I don't know. How about you? How was your day?'"

Jerry: "Boy."

Kramer: "It's sad, Jerry. It's a sad state of affairs."

Jerry: "I'm glad we had this talk."

Kramer: "Oh, you have no idea!"

Kramer has highlighted many of the negative aspects of marriage and with that Jerry begins to seriously reconsider his ideas of love, commitment, and raising a family. Of course, George has already gone full throttle forward on the pact made between them.

When a couple decides to get married, a number of rituals are generally followed. Most important is the wedding ceremony itself. There is a popular belief that wedding ceremonies are more important to women than they are to men. Some women dream of their wedding days from the time they are little girls. Choosing a best man, a maid/matron of honor, along with ushers and bridesmaids are among the many decisions facing the happy couple.

Another ritualistic tradition of the wedding ceremony is giving a toast. The toast is usually given by the "best man." There are no steadfast guidelines to giving a toast. Generally speaking, the idea of giving a toast is to pay homage to the wedding couple. Telling a couple of jokes, sharing information about how the couple got together and making some comment about how wonderful it is that two previously distinct families are now joined together are among the basic topics that may be covered in a toast.

A reference to a toast that George once gave at a wedding is revealed in the episode "The Opera" (#49). (The reason for this will be apparent shortly.) In this episode, George, Jerry, Kramer, and Elaine are all preparing to go to the opera. Jerry is not into operas, he wonders why everyone needs to sing all the time. Kramer makes a point to say that operas are very exciting and that people often dress formally. So, George and Jerry decide to wear tuxedos. George arrives at Jerry's apartment wearing a very small tuxedo that does not fit properly. Jerry makes a wisecrack about it. George mentions to Jerry that he has not worn the tux in six years when he made a toast at a friend's (Bobby Leighton) wedding.

Reminiscing about that toast, Jerry says it was the worst toast that he has ever heard. Apparently George cursed continuously throughout the toast. Jerry says that it reminded him of a Redd Foxx record. Jerry mentions that everyone was in stunned silence at the end of the toast and that no one even drank from their glasses to toast the couple. George does not think his toast was so bad. He believes that he was just "warming" up the crowd. Jerry disagrees and tells him that his toast was most likely the worst one in history. The father of the bride was so upset that he put George in a headlock and threw him out of the wedding.

As George learned at Bobby Leighton's wedding, the violation of a social norm is generally followed by a sanction (punishment). In this case, George was rudely escorted from the wedding because of his improper wedding toast.

Some people look to marry a person who has many of the same qualities that they possess, especially in terms of race and social class. This birds-of-a-feather-stick-together approach was once mandated in the United States as miscegenation laws existed in many states (especially in the South) until 1967 when the United States Supreme Court ruled them unconstitutional. Miscegenation laws prohibited marriage between races. People who marry within their own race, religion, or ethnic group are following what sociologists call the *endogamy* marriage pattern.

On the other hand, there are people who abide by the opposites-attract premise to relationships and marriage. When people from opposite racial, religious, or ethnic groups marry they are participating in a marriage pattern referred to as *exogamy*. An example of an exogamous marriage occurs in "The Betrayal" (#164) episode. Elaine's friend, Sue Ellen, an upper-class white woman, is about to marry Pinter, who is from India. The wedding is called off when Sue Ellen finds out at her wedding that, years earlier, Elaine slept with Pinter (known to Elaine as Peter).

For the past few centuries, marriages in Western culture have generally been restricted to opposite-sex partners. For the past decade, a concerted effort to legalize same-sex marriages has been led by gay-rights organizations. In May 2004 Massachusetts became the first state to legalize same-sex marriages. A predictable conservative backlash, spearheaded by Christian coalition groups and President George W. Bush, has led to an attempt to pass an amendment to the United States Constitution to mandate that only heterosexual couples have the right to marry.

In the episode "The Subway" (#30), Elaine is invited to a lesbian wedding. She is at Jerry's apartment with George and Kramer. The four of them are getting ready to head to the subway where they will eventually head off in different directions and experience different adventures. Unsure of the wedding protocol for lesbian marriages, George asks Elaine how they work out the bride and groom. He wonders if they flip a coin. Elaine thinks George is an idiot for asking such a question. George thinks he has asked a legitimate question. He then wonders if it is a politically incorrect question.

George, like most people, does not know the answer to that and many other questions related to same-sex marriages. Assumingly, once same-sex marriages become more common, the participants will establish a number of traditions, most of which will be similar to opposite-sex marriages.

Elaine is now riding the subway on her way to the wedding. She is carrying a bulky wedding gift and is upset with the fact that a man would not give up his seat for her. (In this era of gender equity, is a man *still* expected to give up a seat to a woman?) Another female passenger comments to Elaine that in the past men would give up their seats for women but now "we're liberated and we have to stand." Elaine and the woman continue their small talk. Eventually Elaine mentions that she is on her way to a wedding. The woman asks several questions including what type of work "he" does. When Elaine informs this stranger that there is no "he" only two "shes" because it is a lesbian wedding, the woman is flabbergasted. The woman is especially shocked to hear that Elaine is the "best man." The woman walks away from Elaine; she is not prepared for a world where same-sex partners are allowed to marry.

This woman's attitude toward a lesbian marriage reveals a certain sentiment in American society. For some people, especially the younger generation, there is a growing tolerance and/or full acceptance of gay marriages. For many others, however, the idea of a gay marriage is just too much for them to handle. They are not in favor of individual rights and prefer instead creating a marriage model that all others must conform to.

Some couples like to live together before they get married. They believe that living together first serves as a type of trial marriage. They also hope (and assume) that if they "survive" a *cohabitation* period that when they get married their marriage has a greater chance of success. Sociologists have conducted studies for years to find out whether couples who live together before marriage have a higher success rate than those who do not cohabitate first. Initially, studies indicated little statistical difference. However, more recent studies have shown that couples who cohabitate before marriage actually have a higher rate of divorce and report lower levels of happiness than couples who do not cohabitate before marriage.

Perhaps Jerry and his girlfriend Meryl found the best alternative to a traditional marriage—a fake marriage. This fake marriage occurs in the episode "The Wife" (#81). Jerry and Meryl are really chummy and have been sleeping with each other for some time. They kid each other about hogging the bed and the covers and count the number of "I love yous" they give to one another.

One morning, Jerry finds a locket in a jacket that he has not worn in a while. So, Jerry and Meryl decide to stop by the dry cleaners on their way to breakfast to see if Marty (the dry cleaner) knows anything about the locket. Looking at it, Marty happily proclaims that it was his wife's. His wife died eight years earlier, and the locket has great sentimental value to him. Apparently, the locket slipped off his wrist and into the jacket pocket. Marty is so pleased with the safe return of this valued piece of jewelry that he offers Jerry and his family 25 percent off all their dry cleaning from this point on. Jerry tells Marty that it is not necessary, but he insists on the generous offer.

Looking to seize an opportunity for her own dry-cleaning discount, Meryl mentions to Marty that she should also be included because she is Jerry's wife. Marty looks at Jerry in a stunned manner; he did not know that Jerry was married. Jerry decides to play along with Meryl and says that yes, she is his wife, Meryl Seinfeld. Marty extends the dry cleaning discount offer to Meryl, and Jerry and Meryl continue their lovey-dovey behavior for each other for the benefit of Marty.

What started out as a little joke, so that Meryl could get herself a discount on dry cleaning, develops into a full-fledged fake marriage between Jerry and Meryl. They began acting like a married couple at home and in public. While Jerry tells Kramer about his discount, he includes the part of the story about Meryl. Jerry tells Kramer that he loves using the expression "my wife." Once he started saying it, he could not stop. He tells Kramer to use the expression my wife in a sentence. Kramer says, "My wife has an inner ear infection." He smiles with approval. Kramer likes saying "my wife" did this and "my wife" did that. Kramer now has a different view of marriage than that explained earlier in this chapter.

Eventually the fake marriage falls apart. Whenever couples get married their actions have a ripple effect on many others, especially the immediate families of the couple. Jerry's parents call him from Florida because they heard about the "marriage" through Uncle Leo—who found out one day while he was at the cleaners and over-heard Marty say something to Jerry about his wife. Jerry and Meryl fight over little things like a misplaced can opener. And Jerry, true to his nature on *Seinfeld*, becomes attracted to another woman and Meryl finds out about it. Meryl is understandably upset. Jerry decides it is time to end the pretend marriage and tells her that he wants a "divorce." Jerry attempts to soften the breakup by saying he just wasn't ready for the responsibilities of a fake marriage.

And so, Meryl drifts away, like so many other women in Jerry's life. But at least Jerry was able to enjoy a fake marriage and was not faced with a real divorce and the many costs related to it.

Since Jerry was involved in a fake wedding, he did not have to deal with the legal, social, and emotional consequences of a divorce. Nearly half of those couples who do marry will face a divorce. Second marriages have an even higher rate of divorce. Divorce is a topic discussed on *Seinfeld* but applicable to secondary characters only. For example, in the episode "The Chinese Woman" (#90), George's parents, Frank and Estelle, are contemplating divorce. Jerry and Elaine saw Frank with a mysterious caped man in Manhattan. They wondered why a man would wear a cape. This mystery man was no caped crusader—he was Frank's divorce lawyer.

Whenever a couple breaks up and they are parents, the children will obviously be affected. Sometimes a divorce is a healthy solution for a bad family situation. Consequently, the children may be better off after their parents divorce. In most cases, the family is torn apart and the children are shuffled from one parent to the other. As an adult son of Frank and Estelle, George's only concern is how his parents' divorce would negatively affect him. George explains to Jerry the downside of his parents' potential divorce in terms of time costs to George. He is worried that he will have to spend twice as much of his time to visit his parents because they will be living apart. Much to George's selfish delight, Frank and Estelle do not follow through with the divorce.

One major cause of divorce is adultery. It is the worst violation of the marriage bond and is nearly always viewed as an unforgivable violation of trust. Jerry emphasizes the seriousness of adultery in the opening monologue of "The Junior Mint" (#60) episode when he points out that you can't just *have* adultery—you *commit* adultery. Furthermore, you cannot commit adultery unless you already have a commitment. Jerry also points out that some people even cheat on the people that they are cheating with. These are the lowest of the low people of society.

In the episode "The Good Samaritan" (#37), George thinks that he has committed adultery when he slept with a married woman named Robin. Robin and her husband, Michael, got into an argument when George said, "God bless you" to Robin after she sneezed and Michael failed to make the gesture (see chapter 2). Robin wanted to have an affair with George. George thought it was very "adult" to have an affair and so he did have sex with Robin. Feeling a little guilty, George mentions to Robin that he just committed adultery. Robin points out to George that *he* hasn't commit adultery (he is not the one married) but that *she* has (because she is the one who is married).

George realizes right away that he has made a mistake. His mistake would become more problematic after Robin and Michael get back together, as Michael threatens George that he would "sew his ass to his face." As any coward would do, George leaves the city. He takes off for three weeks with Jerry.

Family

The family is defined by the US Census Bureau as a household with two or more people related by blood, marriage, or adoption. Sociologists employ a slightly more liberal definition of the family to include couples (gay or straight) who cohabitate and economically cooperate with one another. Marriage is not required for two (or more) people to constitute a family.

There are a couple of distinct categories of the family that interest sociologists. First is the distinction between the "family of orientation" and the "family of procreation." The family of orientation refers to the family to which one is born (or adopted) into and raised. The family of procreation is the family that is formed when individuals marry (or cohabitate) and start their own family.

A second distinction is made between the nuclear family and the extended family. The nuclear family consists of the immediate family members—generally, siblings, parents, and possibly others that live together or in close proximity. The extended family refers to a larger kinship circle of family members who live together or in close proximity. In the United States, the most common family form is the nuclear. This is especially true with middle-class families. Worldwide, the extended family form is more common.

The characters of *Seinfeld* held true to family patterns found in the United States. The four main characters all live by themselves (thus, disqualifying them from constituting their own family). They were raised in a nuclear family orientation, and we learn very little about their extended families.

Elaine's Family of Orientation

In the episode "The Jacket" (#8), the audience is introduced to Alton Benes, Elaine's father. Alton is a brilliant writer and a retired military man. Elaine has a tough relationship with him. He's a very dominating man with an intimidating presence. Elaine is supposed to have dinner with him and nearly begs Jerry and George to join her as kind of a buffer.

Jerry and George agree to meet Elaine and Alton at the Hotel Westbury. When Jerry and George arrive, Elaine is not there yet. Jerry and George awkwardly try to make small talk with Alton, but his callous attitude and remarks make them very uncomfortable. They now need Elaine to be a buffer!

Elaine finally arrives at the hotel lobby while Alton is in the restroom. She asks Jerry and George if everything is okay because her father can make some people a little uncomfortable. Alton returns to lobby.

Alton: "Well, look who's here."

Elaine: "Oh, hi, Dad."

Alton (kisses Elaine): "Hello, dear. Who's the lipstick for?"

Elaine: "No one."

Alton: "How's your mother?"

Elaine: "Fine."

Alton: "How about you? Are you working?"

Elaine: "Yeah, I'm reading manuscripts for Pendant Publishing. I told you ten times."

Alton: "Pendant? Those bastards. All right, boys. We'll go to that Pakistani restaurant on 46th Street. You're not afraid of a little spice, are you?"

The dialogue between Elaine and Alton reveals quite a bit of information. Alton does not really pay attention to Elaine's life (she told him ten times where she works), he disapproves of her style (too much lipstick), and (apparently) Alton and Elaine's mother are divorced. I never found any other reference to Elaine's mother throughout the *Seinfeld* series. The audience certainly never meets her.

We also learn that Elaine has a sister, but we never meet her either. Elaine's sister's name, Gail, is mentioned in the consecutive episodes "The Airport" (#52) and "The Pick" (#53). In the episode "The Airport" Jerry and Elaine are flying back to New York together from St. Louis. Jerry had a gig in St. Louis and the club gave him an extra ticket, which he gave to Elaine. As they are driving the rental car back to the St. Louis airport Jerry mentions to Elaine that things worked out pretty well for the both of them—he had a good show and Elaine was able to visit with her sister.

In "The Pick," Elaine decides to send out a Christmas card with her picture on it. Kramer took the photo. He did a pretty good job too. Except for one little problem—Elaine's nipple is revealed. Elaine never noticed the exposed nipple in the photo until Jerry draws her attention to it. She is extremely upset. She begins to realize all the people she mailed the card to, including her parents, grandparents, sister, and nephew.

We learn more about Elaine's family, both immediate and extended, because of "nipple-gate" than any other reason. Near the end of "The Pick" episode, Gail calls Elaine to ask if she realizes how old her nephew is. It seems that her nephew, who is an adolescent, developed quite an attraction to the card and has hidden it somewhere for his own private viewing.

Kramer's Family of Orientation

The only family member of Kramer's we ever met is his mother, Babs. We are introduced to Babs Kramer in "The Switch" (#97) episode. Kramer and his mother have been estranged for years (it is never explained why) but they are reunited in this episode.

Kramer can thank George for the reunion. George is dating a model named Nina. He is amazed by how much food she can eat and yet stay so slim. Kramer informs George that she is most likely bulimic. George is upset by this potential reality; and not because of any concern for Nina's health, but because he feels it's a waste of money to feed someone who is just going to throw the food up. Jerry refers to it as "refunding" food. George wants confirmation. He knows that Nina always goes to the restroom after she finishes eating, so he figures he needs help from the "inside." He needs a bathroom matron.

Jerry looks at Kramer. Kramer shies away. George is suspicious. Finally Kramer acknowledges that his mother is a matron at one of the upscale restaurants where George and Nina dine. Kramer reluctantly agrees to bring George to meet Babs so that George may solicit her help.

The reunion between Babs and Kramer goes very well. When they first meet she shouts out Kramer's first name—for the first time on the series—Cosmo! George can't wait to tell it to Elaine and Jerry. George later arrives to Jerry's apartment. Elaine is there. George tells them Kramer's first name and they all laugh aloud. When Kramer walks into the apartment, they laugh at him. He realizes that George has let the cat out of the bag. But then he shares the "breakthrough" regarding his name. He describes how his whole life he was ashamed of his first name. However, with a new sense of identity (and most likely his renewed relationship with his mother), he decides he will no longer run away from his name, he will no longer run away from who he really is. He is going to be Cosmo Kramer from this point on.

Kramer feels as though a huge burden has been lifted off his shoulders. He is comfortable with who he really is. He walks around the neighborhood proudly arm-in-arm with his mother. People yell out "Cosmo!" and Kramer happily acknowledges them and his complete familial identity.

George's Family of Orientation

The *Seinfeld* audience is quite familiar with George's parents Frank and Estelle, as they are regular characters. George, like Kramer and Jerry, is an only child, which is one of the contributing psychological explanations for the selfishness that these three continuously display. (Note: There is one reference to George having a brother in the episode "The Suicide" when he states to Rula, a psychic, "Pauline? Wait a minute. I got it. My brother once impregnated a woman named Pauline." We never hear mention to a sibling for George at any other time. George most likely makes his comment in direct answer to Rula's question, "Who's Pauline" because he *wants* to believe in the psychic. There is no reason to believe that he really did have a brother.

George's parents did not do a very good job raising their son as he turned out to be quite neurotic. In the episode "The Merv Griffin Show" (#162), it is revealed (in George's home movies) that George's parents were still changing diapers on him at age seven and a half!

George constantly complains to his friends about his parents, and it seems that they were often fed up with him as well. In the episode "The Doll" (#127), Frank converts George's old bedroom into a billiard room. Problem is, George's old room is really too small to use a pool stick in. George should not have taken it so personally. After all, he is a grown man, why would his parents keep a room in their house for him? A billiard room is a logical choice.

In the episode "The Junk Mail" (#161), George's parents constantly "blow off" their own son. Frank and Estelle are just as sick and tired of George as he is of them. For example, George calls his parents on the phone and they pretend that there is a Chinese food delivery person at the door. Estelle even uses a fake, stereotypical Chinese voice to say "Chinese food."

George doubts very much that people his parent's age are eating Chinese food after dark because "that's like swallowing stun grenades." Jerry points out to George that whenever anyone orders Chinese takeout, there are always leftovers. George agrees and drives out to his parents' house the next day for a visit and inspection for Chinese containers. In other words, he is spying on them. His parents are not happy to see him. Frank abruptly stands up and tells George that they were on their way to a catered affair. Frank and Estelle leave very shortly after George arrives.

After his parents leave the house, George takes a look in the refrigerator and discovers that there are no leftovers. He is getting very suspicious. He decides to wait for his parents to return and confront them directly. He waits quietly in the kitchen. When his parents arrive he asks why they ditched him. George is not prepared for his parents' response. Frank tells George that they love him but even parents have limits. Estelle is sick of all of George's breakups, firings, and the weekly Sunday phone calls. Frank informs George that they are cutting him loose because it is supposed to be their time to enjoy life. George is in shock by this development. He discusses this with Jerry who tells George it's what he's always wanted. George replies to Jerry that he is not ready yet to be cut free from his parents.

George's relationship with his family of orientation is dysfunctional to say the least. His parents are wacky and George has many "issues." Imagine how difficult it was for George when he once ("The Puffy Shirt" #66) had to move back in with them because all he had left to his name was $714. And as Jerry points out, it's never a good sign when an adult has to move back in with his parents. It's like probation or rehabilitation.

Jerry's Family of Orientation

As to be expected, the *Seinfeld* audience learns the most about Jerry's family. Throughout this book, numerous references have been made to Jerry's parents, Helen and Morty, as well as Uncle Leo. Leo and Helen are siblings. We meet Nana, Jerry's grandmother, in a couple of episodes. In one, "The Kiss Hello" (#103), Nana needs help opening a bottle of ketchup. Nana confuses the past with the present and asks Leo if he ever gave his sister the $50 that his father gave to Leo to give to Helen.

We hear of and see many other members of the extended Seinfeld family as well. In the episode "The Pony Remark" (#7), Jerry and his parents attend a small family reunion that is being hosted by Manya and Isaac, second cousins of Helen. He doesn't really want to go because, after all, he has only met with them a few times in his whole life. But Jerry, as a good son, tags along with his parents to keep his mother happy. Jerry brings Elaine with him as well. The family is sitting around a couple of tables put together. Uncle Leo talks continuously about his son Jeffrey. Jerry cracks jokes to keep the mood light. Everything is progressing nicely until Jerry makes a wisecrack against ponies. Manya gets angry and tells everyone about her childhood in Poland when she and her siblings had ponies. Just a couple of days later, Manya dies. Jerry worries that his pony comment caused her untimely death.

As mentioned earlier, Jerry is an only child, so his nuclear family consisted of just three members. Jerry, apparently, had a good childhood and was raised by loving parents. They always supported Jerry and were there for him whenever he needed them. From the perspective of an adult son, Jerry, in "The Puffy Shirt" (#66) episode, wonders why anyone is ever intimidated by parents. When you are fully grown your old room seems so small and your parents seem so small that you wonder why you were ever so scared of them while you were growing up.

It seems that Jerry was never really scared of his parents. He sought their approval and as he became more successful he attempted to present them with lavish gifts. As we know, Jerry purchases a Cadillac for his father—something Morty always wanted. However, in the episode "The Money" (#146), Helen and Morty, concerned that Jerry does not really make enough money to afford such a gift, decide to sell the Cadillac and give the money back to Jerry. They sell the car to Jack Klompus. Of course, Jerry attempts to buy it back from Jack, who insists on driving it one more time. Jack drives it into a swamp and the car is ruined. Thus, in effect, Jerry purchased the car twice for his father and still Morty does not end up with it.

Oddly, Morty's favorite gift from his son is a t-shirt that reads "#1 Dad." It is a drastically undersized shirt that Jerry got from Kramer, who got a dozen shirts for a buck. Jerry brings it with him to Florida during one of his visits to his parents. Morty starts referring to himself as "#1." He even sleeps in the shirt. Helen worries that the tightness of the shirt is cutting off Morty's circulation.

The Family of Procreation

Starting one's own family is the dream of nearly all people. Most married couples want to have children and, generally speaking, there is pressure from other family members for the newlywed couple to start planning a family of their own—the family of procreation.

There are many different family forms including one where couples have decided that they do not want children. They voluntarily choose to remain childless. Other couples wish to have children, but for some medical reason are unable to. In cases like these, couples may choose to adopt. In the episode "The Yada, Yada" (#153), Beth and Arnie, friends of Elaine's, are hoping to adopt. As part of the many standard procedures involved in any legal adoption case, a great deal of paperwork must be completed. Interviews of close friends of the potential adopting parents is also a routine procedure. Elaine is interviewed and lets it slip that Arnie has a bad temper. Her comment, in effect, leads to the adoption agency denying Beth and Arnie a child.

When a woman becomes pregnant it common for her best girl-friend(s) to throw a baby shower. In the appropriately named "The Baby Shower" (#15) episode, Elaine throws a shower for her friend Leslie. For some unspecified reason, Elaine admits to Jerry that she has a need for Leslie's approval. Elaine is not comfortable throwing a baby shower in her apartment (her roommate has Lyme disease!) so she asks Jerry if it's okay to use his apartment. Jerry is a little reluctant and teases Elaine about the rituals that surround a baby shower. He wants to make sure such parties never erupt into drunken orgies of violence or hazing of the fetus. Elaine assures Jerry that no such rituals will be performed.

At the shower all the women talk about settling down. They tell Elaine that she needs to have a baby and move to the suburbs. As described at the beginning of this chapter, Elaine's friends place a great deal of pressure on her. For the vast majority of the population this is "normal" behavior and single people like Elaine are often targets of teasing by married-with-children friends.

Having children is so mundane that, worldwide, many children are born every second of the day. But for the parents of a baby, having their own child is the pinnacle of their lives. As Jerry points out, having children *does* represent the "life force." Without children, humanity ceases to exist.

On the other hand, because of extreme overpopulation, the world would be much better off if the number of babies entering the world were drastically reduced. The four main characters of *Seinfeld* certainly did their part to keep population in check as none of them had a baby.

Chapter 11

Religion

"Happy Festivus: A Festival for the Rest of Us!"—Frank

Perhaps no other social institution commands as much attention, commitment, and loyalty as religion. Highly religious people find the communal ritualistic behaviors of religion and its ceremonial rites of passage primary sources of identity. The maintenance of a self-identity often goes hand-in-hand with religious identification. When people attain their identity primarily from religion, they ignore, or pay less attention to, societal forces. Because of this, power groups have long used religion as a social control mechanism. Thus, as Karl Marx once said, "Religion is the opiate of the masses."

In order to distinguish aspects of life that are religious and aspects of life that are secular, French sociologist Emile Durkheim introduced the terms *the sacred* and *the profane.* Sacred items are those things which are set apart from the everyday and are shown reverence. They are symbols of a higher authority, or belief system—they are religious. Examples of sacred items would include a rosary, a holy book, a menorah, a prayer rug, and religious statues (especially those blessed or deemed holy symbols).

Profane items are the mundane, everyday items that people use or come into contact with. The profane refers to secular items such as clothing, food, staplers, tape dispensers, televisions, and so on.

Although many people may offer definitions of religion, the sociological definition of religion would be something like this: Any set of answers to the dilemmas of human existence that makes the world somehow meaningful; a system of beliefs and rituals that serves to bind people together into a social group. Thus, a particular religion has followers of "like-minded" people who, through ritualistic behaviors, reinforce key beliefs and ideals about life and an afterlife.

Ritualistic behaviors and constant reinforcement of beliefs lead many people to assume that they have the "right" answers regarding God or gods. People with deep-rooted religious beliefs generally develop an intolerant behavior toward people with different views. (For an easy example of this, tell someone who believes heavily in the existence of God that there is no God and see how they react.) Religious intolerance has lead to discrimination, persecution, and discrimination.

Theism

There are two types of theism. Monotheism refers to a belief in one God. Examples of monotheistic religions include Islam, Judaism, and Christianity. Polytheism refers to a belief in many gods and includes such world religions as Hinduism, Taoism, and some variations of Buddhism. Slightly confusing matters is the fact that some Christians (e.g., Catholics) believe in one God composed of three entities. This Trinity includes the Father, the Son, and the Holy Spirit.

Surveys conducted in the United States consistently indicate that nearly 90 percent of Americans believe in one "true" God. However, just because most people believe in God, that does not mean they have consistent views of his (or her) role in their lives, or their role in his life. In other words, there are great inconsistencies among people in their interpretations of how God affects their daily lives.

In the episode "The Pilot" (#63), Jerry and George are working together on a television pilot idea for NBC. George displays his unique form of a "fear of success." He is actually worried that if the pilot is picked up he will become rich and famous. He decides to talk to a therapist about his fear. The psychiatrist, Dana, points out the obvious positive benefits of the series being picked up, specifically, that George will be rich and successful. George tells Dana that God will never let him be successful and happy and that God would strike him dead before that would happen.

Dana: "I thought you didn't believe in God?"
George: "I do for the bad things."
Dana: "Do you hear what you're saying? God isn't out to get you."

We begin to see why George is so neurotic and suffers to the extreme that he does. He self-inflicts a great deal of pain in his life. George is afraid of success because he believes only in a vengeful God, one that will surely knock him down before he'll ever find fame and fortune.

Some religions (e.g., Calvinism) teach that God has preordained those who will go to heaven or hell. Therefore, people look for "signs of grace" from God. They justify their advantageous position in the social world as a type of religious intervention. Monarchies during Medieval Europe were based on a similar principle known as the divine right of kings.

Other religions (e.g., Catholicism) teach that salvation in the afterlife is open to anyone who leads a "proper" life on Earth. Abiding by church and societal laws, donating money to the church, and helping others is the primary ticket to heaven.

As a result of the great diversity in religious beliefs, there exist major divisions of thought as to what constitutes a "proper" lifestyle. This diversity is directly responsible for wars between nation-states at the macro level and intrapersonal conflict between members of society at the micro level.

To avoid interpersonal conflict while dating, most people prefer to date those who have similar religious beliefs as themselves. The more religious a person is, the more important it will be to date someone of similar faith (or lack of faith for secularists and humanists). Elaine has dated men with different religious ideals than her own, and the end results were never good.

One of the most frequently returning characters on *Seinfeld* is David Puddy. Elaine dates Puddy off and on for years. However, it is not until one of the last episodes of the series that we learn that Puddy is highly religious. In the episode "The Burning" (#172), Elaine borrows Puddy's car and notices that all the preset buttons on his car radio are set to Christian rock stations. She drives to the coffee shop to meet Jerry and George, and tells them about this. George comments that he likes Christian rock because the message is so positive. Elaine wonders whether Puddy actually believes in something spiritual or if maybe he was just too lazy to change the presets on the radio (it was a new car). Elaine admits that she would rather date a dumb and lazy guy than a religious guy because she would have an easier time understanding lazy and dumb.

George suggests that Elaine change the presets on Puddy's radio to see if he notices. Elaine agrees to the plan and reprograms his stations. She returns the car to Puddy. She borrows it again and Puddy has switched the channels back to the religious stations. Once again, Elaine meets George and Jerry at the diner and complains to them about Puddy being religious. She is so upset that she pries a "Jesus fish" off his bumper. Jerry wonders why Elaine is so disappointed that Puddy is a spiritual person. Elaine believes that she was misled and admits that she dates him because he seems so one-dimensional.

Elaine eventually decides to ask Puddy if he is religious. At his apartment Elaine and Puddy engage in this conversation:

Elaine: "So, you're pretty religious?"
Puddy: "That's right."
Elaine: "So, is it a problem that I'm not really religious?"
Puddy: "Not for me."
Elaine: "Why not?"
Puddy: "I'm not the one going to hell."

Elaine is now troubled on many levels. She had preferred a simple and shallow relationship with Puddy and now she finds out that Puddy believes she is going to hell and, furthermore, Puddy is not worried about it. As a secular person, Elaine is not really worried about whether or not she may be going to hell, but she is disappointed in her boyfriend's attitude toward her lack of religiosity. Elaine wants Puddy to care that she is going to hell.

In many cases where couples have different religious views, they will attempt to find some sort of compromise. One partner may in fact attempt to "save" a partner they believe is heading down the wrong path. In this same episode, Puddy does agree to Elaine's insistence that they go see a priest for counseling. The priest assumes that Elaine and Puddy are married and tries to reassure them that many couples of interfaith marriages have difficulty. When Elaine informs Fr. Curtis that they are not married he informs them that they are both going to hell (for having sex outside of marriage).

Puddy is shocked and upset that he can not pick and choose which of God's commandments he wants to follow. Many people share

Puddy's delusion. And Elaine actually feels vindicated and better about herself because Puddy is also condemned to hell along with her.

Most religions that teach the existence of one true God generally teach that an equal antiforce also exists. In other words, there cannot be good without evil. It is evil that tempts humans to stray from religious teachings. Evil is usually expressed in terms of the devil. The devil may, or may not, have horns, hoofed feet, and a tail, but evil surely exists among us.

In one of the funniest *Seinfeld* episodes, "The Face Painter" (#109), an El Salvadorian priest (Father Hernandez) confuses Puddy for the devil. Puddy, as a New Jersey Devils hockey fan, is wearing face paint purposely designed to make him look like a devil. He is also wearing a Devils team jersey that adds to the visual effect. Puddy will meet up with this priest shortly after he exits Madison Square Garden with Kramer, Elaine, and Jerry.

The Devils have just won a play-off game and Puddy, to put it mildly, is very excited about his team's victory. Puddy is taunting his friends, who are Rangers fans, and mistakenly steps out into oncoming traffic. Puddy is almost hit by a car. Because he is on the passenger's side of the car, Puddy screams at the passenger. He begins to pound on the car.

> *Puddy*: "Hey, what are you doing?! Watch where you're driving, man! Don't mess with the Devils, buddy. We're number one, we beat anybody! We're the Devils! The Devils!! Haaa!!!"
>
> *Father Hernandez* (as Puddy runs off): "El Diablo! Dios mio! El Diablo!"

It is never clearly explained how, but Elaine finds information about Father Hernandez and shares it with Jerry at a funeral for a friend. Father Hernandez was visiting from El Salvador and has now gone loco after his encounter with Puddy dressed as the devil. The priest refuses to leave the church basement out of fear of the devil.

"The Face Painter" concludes with Elaine visiting Father Hernandez in his basement church room. He has not been doing well; he is extremely distraught. He needs a miracle (defined secularly as a statistically rare occurrence). It has been raining outside so Elaine is wearing a long white hooded raincoat. Another priest at the church informs Father Hernandez of Elaine's arrival. As she enters the room and approaches Father Hernandez, she is backlit by the sunlight coming through the window—she appears to be glowing. Upon seeing Elaine, Father Hernandez says, "Oh. La Madonna! Madre de Christo! Yo estoy lista!"

Father Hernandez believes that he had just been visited by the Madonna, the mother of Christ. His "miracle" has occurred. Often when people search for spiritual answers they allow their minds to see what they need to see, rather than to see reality. Periodically we hear of people who see visions of spiritual leaders on buildings, rock formations, and even a grilled cheese sandwich. (In November 2004, a ten-year-old grilled cheese sandwich that some say bears the image of the Virgin Mary sold on eBay for $28,000! GoldenPalace.com, an online casino, placed the "winning" bid on this sandwich with a bite taken out of one end. And to think, George Costanza was mocked for eating an éclair that was thrown in the trash because Jerry considered food with a bite taken from it as trash!) Psychologists offer therapy to people who claim to have "visions" or claim to hear "voices" (from God or otherwise) because such people are assumed to be suffering from some sort of psychological impairment such as schizophrenia.

"The Face Painter" episode and "The Burning" present conflicting images of Elaine and Puddy. Elaine, the nonbeliever in "The Burning," was viewed as the Madonna in "The Face Painter." Puddy, who believes in God and considers himself a religious person in "The Burning," is mistaken for the devil in "The Face Painter."

Organized Religion

There are a number of world religions that exist in an organized fashion. Hinduism, Buddhism, Judaism, Confucianism, Christianity, and Islam are the major worldwide religions. Sociologist Ernst Troeltsch, a student of Max Weber, first developed a system to classify religious groups based on a church-sect distinction. A church may be defined as a relatively large, well-established religious organization with a formal hierarchy (including professional clergy), an established set of rules and procedures, and a relatively diverse membership. A church is well-integrated into society.

A sect is a relatively small religious group that sets itself apart from society and is relatively dogmatic and places high demands on its homogeneous membership. Sects are not well integrated into society. Sects are offshoots from a church. They encourage members to withdraw and avoid society's negative influences (as deemed by the sect leaders). New members of sects are those people who were disenchanted from the rules or bureaucracy of the church they were raised in and its allegiance to a "corrupt" social system.

In between churches and sects are denominations. A denomination is close to a church, with the main difference that a denomination does not hold a monopoly nor does it have official state recognition. Denominations are usually on good terms with the government.

Religion is very important to many people. In some cases, individuals feel pressure from their families to marry someone within the same religion. The primary concern is centered on children and how they should be raised if they are born with parents of two different faiths.

In the episode "The Conversion" (#75), George's girlfriend (her name is never given) wants to break up with him because of religious differences. She comes from a strict family that insists she marry someone who is Latvian Orthodox. George explains to his friends that he feels so strongly for this woman that he is thinking about converting. Jerry thinks George is crazy, but Elaine finds it romantic. George reasons the whole process must be quite simple, maybe make a donation, have a ceremony, and poof—conversion! Building on the romantic aspect introduced by Elaine, George decides to surprise his girlfriend upon successful completion of the conversion.

George, who is obviously not a very religious person, feels that the conversion to the Latvian Orthodox religion is no big deal. Elaine has George believing that the conversion will be romantic, rather than spiritual as religion is supposed to be. Jerry reminds George that his conversion will have dire repercussions with his parents.

Well, George decides to go ahead with the conversion. He meets with Latvian priests to discuss it. They ask George a number of questions to test his true commitment and desire to convert. George tells the priests that he likes their hats. He feels that their hat conveys a solemn religious look that is very important in a faith. George is hoping for an express conversion but the priests insist that he learn more about the religion by reading about it and then they will test him.

George and the priests are interrupted by Sister Roberta's entrance into the room. Sr. Roberta is supposed to be taking her final vows the following Thursday. (Her plans are almost derailed when she meets Kramer, or the "Kavorka"—see chapter 6.) George leaves with the books and heads over to Jerry's apartment. Jerry reminds

George yet again about his parents' reaction to his conversion. George plans on "taking the vow of silence" approach—in other words, he hopes to hide it from his parents.

The conversion date nears and an announcement of George's conversion is visible on a sign in front of the Latvian church. A friend of Estelle Costanza's reads the message and immediately informs her about her son's impending conversion. George, who is living with his parents at this time, is confronted by them when he arrives home. They fear the Latvian Orthodox religion is some type of cult and believe that they have brainwashed George to join. George assures them that the religion is legitimate and the reason he is converting is because of a woman. Frank steadfastly distrusts the Latvian religion, he is convinced they are involved in animal sacrifice and warns George to leave the squirrels alone!

George quickly realizes that he has not learned all of the teachings and fears that he will fail his last test. So, he cheats. As a result, he passes with an amazingly high score, and the conversion takes place. George cannot wait to tell his girlfriend about his secret conversion. At Monk's coffee shop George tells her the big news and how he did it just for her. She is flattered but drops a bomb on him; she is going back to Latvia to live with some relatives for a year. She says good-bye and adds a little salt to George's wound by saying, "Oh George, you are so sweet. Don't ever change."

In the Hindu religion, the concept of *karma* is very important. Karma is a religious belief that one's behavior in this life will determine one's position in the next life. Thus, if someone leads a good life (by helping others), he or she may not be rewarded in this life but will be in the next life and return to earth as a higher life-form.

In contemporary society, many people have adopted a secular interpretation of karma (or what I call postmodern karma). The pop culture usage of karma is usually expressed in such ways as "What comes around goes around" and earning "karma points," which means that if someone accumulates enough karma points (through various good deeds) she will be rewarded in this life as well as in the next. A couple of *Seinfeld* episodes address the issue of karma.

In the episode "The Cadillac" (#124), Jerry returns home from his highest-paying gig ever. Kramer is stunned after Jerry reluctantly agrees to show Kramer just how much money he earned. Kramer wonders what Jerry is going to do with such a big paycheck. Jerry jokes that he is going to donate a large portion of it to charity. (Many religions teach that this is a method of gaining entrance to heaven; it is also an effective way of maintaining the religious hierarchy.) Kramer is pleased by Jerry's response. But Jerry then informs him of his true intent for the money; he is going to buy his father a brand new Cadillac. His father has always wanted one and now that he can afford to do it, he is pleased to make his dad happy. Kramer smiles at Jerry and tells him, "You're gonna score some big points with the man upstairs on this one." Jerry: "Oh, isn't that what it's all about?" Kramer and Jerry both smile in agreement; by Jerry's giving a nice expensive gift to his father, he will earn some great karma points.

In the episode "The Pitch" (#43), the concept of bad karma was illustrated. Newman trades his motorcycle helmet to Kramer for his radar detector. Unbeknownst to Newman, the radar detector is defective. At Jerry's apartment, Newman confronts Kramer over the speeding ticket he just received because the radar detector did not work. Newman is rightfully angry at Kramer and demands his helmet back. Newman also wants Kramer to pay for the ticket. Kramer refuses. Newman turns to Jerry for help. Jerry, of course, does not like Newman, so he takes Kramer's side of the argument and states, "Buyer beware!" Trying one last time, Newman asks for the helmet back. Kramer refuses and states, "We had a deal. There are no guarantees in life." Newman replies, "No, but there's karma, Kramer."

Newman is trying to use a form of guilt on Kramer by instilling a common belief into his mind that bad deeds usually lead to punishment. The karma aspect highlights the idea that punishments may not be incurred in this lifetime, but in the afterlife (for Christians) or in the next life (for Hindus). Regular viewers of *Seinfeld* will remember that the helmet Kramer receives in trade from Newman actually saves Kramer's life when crazy Joe Davola (see chapter 12 for a description of Joe) delivers a powerful kick to Kramer's head—and the helmet he is wearing saves him. Yet to be determined, however, is whether or not the bad karma that Newman warned Kramer about will take place at a later time. Readers of this book can decide for themselves the role of karma.

Religions are consumed with rituals and ceremonies. Ritualistic religious behaviors represent rites of passage and status within the religious community. Because Jerry is Jewish, and the star of *Seinfeld*, the audience learns quite a bit about Judaism. The religious ceremonies of Judaism are associated with major life transitions. Two major rites of passage are discussed on *Seinfeld*: the bris and bar mitzvah.

The bris involves the circumcision of boys shortly after birth to symbolize Abraham's covenant with God. In the episode appropriately named "The Bris" (#69), Jerry, Elaine, George, and Kramer are visiting their friends Myra and Stan Flick and their newborn baby, Steven, in the hospital. Stan and Myra ask Jerry and Elaine to be the godparents to the baby. Jerry and Elaine are rightfully honored by such a request and ask about their duties and obligations as godparents. They are told the most important thing is to help with the bris (circumcision).

The four friends return to Jerry's apartment. Elaine and Jerry discuss their new roles. Elaine must find a mohel—the person who performs the circumcision. She has no idea how to find one, so she starts looking through the phone book. Jerry's primary role is to hold the baby while the bris is being performed. Kramer tries to convince Jerry and Elaine that a bris is a barbaric ritual. Jerry tries to convince Kramer that the bris is a religious tradition. Kramer counters, so was sacrificing virgins. George tells Kramer it is a matter of hygiene. Kramer insists that the hygiene aspect is a myth. Furthermore, he tells his friends that sex is more pleasurable without a circumcision.

The day of the bris arrives. George, Jerry, Elaine, and Kramer join Stan and Myra, along with some other friends, for the solemn occasion. The mohel arrives. He is a near basket case and begins to worry the invited guests with his behavior. For example, he complains about the baby crying and Elaine leaving a wine glass too close to the edge of the table. Just as the ceremony is about to begin, Kramer grabs the baby from Myra. He is unsuccessful in his attempt to stop the ceremony. The mohel is upset and tries to restore order by invoking religious teachings. He describes how a bris is "a sacred, ancient ceremony, symbolizing the covenant between God and Abraham, or something."

The baby is taken from Kramer and handed to Jerry. The bris ceremony continues. George faints at the sight of the mohel's trembling hand with the knife. Jerry is nervous and bug-eyed. The next scene shifts to George's car with Jerry screaming about how the mohel nearly circumcised his finger. The mohel cut Jerry instead of the baby. At the hospital the doctors are able to reattach Jerry's severed finger tip. Stan and Myra, upset over the way Jerry and Elaine handled the bris ceremony replace them as godparents with Kramer because he was the one person who showed how much he cares about baby.

Another important rite of passage in the Jewish religion is the bar mitzvah for boys and the bat mitzvah for girls. This ceremony takes place at puberty and represents passage into adulthood. In the episode "The Serenity Now" (#159), Elaine attends the bar mitzvah of Adam Lippman, the son of her boss, Mr. Lippman. Lippman is a proud father. He proclaims that today his son is a man (as viewed by this rite of passage). Elaine congratulates Adam. Suddenly, Adam lurches at Elaine and zealously French kisses her. He yells out that he is a man.

Adam has taken his new status as a man in literal form. His religion may now consider him an adult by virtue of his bar mitzvah, but civil society does not. American society is predicated on the assumption of a separation of church and state. Meaning, among other things, that religious laws have no jurisdiction over civil (sociopolitical) laws. His behavior with Elaine was inappropriate because she is an adult and he is a child.

A couple of days after the kissing incident, Elaine confronts Adam on the inappropriateness of his behavior. Mr. Lippman is in the room with Elaine and Adam. She points out to Adam that he is only thirteen years old and regardless that the rabbi called him a man, he is not really a man. Adam is extremely upset to learn of the fallacy of his religious teachings: "Well, if I'm not a man, then this whole thing was a sham. . . . I renounce my religion!"

Elaine's secular intrusion of civil reality into Adam's religious world has caused him to question his faith. The lesson that Adam learns is a tough one. Sociologists constantly remind people that just because they believe something is true, it does not mean that it is true. Such evidence, that runs contrary to one's beliefs, is an example of what sociologists call "culture shock." Many people experience culture shock when they come into contact with diverse groups of people. This is one of the main reasons why most people prefer the company of others who think and believe as they do. "Like-minded" people form religions as a means of reinforcing belief systems that are congruent to an ideal way of life.

Ideals of proper behavior are handed down from one generation to the next through such religious ceremonies as the bris and bar mitzvah. In other cases, certain behaviors are forbidden and considered wrong, or even evil. For example, orthodox Jews forbid the eating of crustaceans—aquatic animals with skeletons outside their bodies, including shrimp, crabs, and lobster—because they are not kosher.

In the episode "The Hamptons" (#85), the four main characters are visiting friends in the Hamptons. Jerry's and George's girlfriends are also there. After taking a walk on the beach, Kramer returns to the beach house with enough lobster for everyone. (Initially, no one knows that he has obtained them illegally by stealing them from commercial lobster traps.) At the dinner table everyone thanks Kramer. However, Rachel (Jerry's girlfriend) refuses to eat any of the lobster because she is kosher. Kramer admires her religious commitment and tells Rachel that when she dies she will receive special attention.

Kramer has hinted to a "karma reward system" before (alluded to earlier in this chapter). He also respects Rachel's devotion to her faith. In fact, he will be responsible for stopping Rachel in her time of questioning her faith. Late at night, Rachel quietly enters the kitchen and opens the refrigerator looking for leftover lobster. Kramer is standing guard. He worries that she might be tempted to try some of it because everyone raved about it. Rachel pleads with him, but he will not relent. Kramer tells Rachel it would not be kosher for him to allow her to eat the lobster.

Kramer, because he respects her religious beliefs, is there for Rachel when she needed someone the most. George, however, does not share Kramer's respect for others' religious commitments. Upset that Rachel told his girlfriend Jane about his "shrinkage" problem (see chapter 6), he gets up early in the morning and makes scrambled eggs for breakfast. Everyone raves about how delicious the eggs are. George asks Rachel specifically if she liked the eggs. She nods approvingly, and George suggests to her that she might want to use a lobster bib while she eats her eggs. Rachel asks whether there is lobster in the eggs. George admits to his act of deviance. With that, Rachel storms out of the kitchen. Jerry follows her. George appears quite pleased with himself for "sticking it" to Rachel, even though he knew she *inadvertently* disobeyed the rules of kosher eating.

George does not harm Rachel because she is Jewish, but rather because she caused him personal harm. There are many occasions when people are discriminated against because of their religious affiliation. The attempted genocide of Jews by Nazi Germany represents an extreme form of discrimination and hatred. Discrimination against Jews is called anti-Semitism.

According to historian Yehuda Bauer, the term *anti-Semitism* was coined in 1879 by a professed anti-Semite, the German radical writer and politician Wilhelm Marr. The old term *Jew-hatred* had become obsolete because it only described traditional Christian hostility toward Jews. Marr, and other racists of his era, wanted an all-encompassing term, which did not contain the word *Jew*; he wanted a term that sounded more "scientific" to describe the hatred that many people had for Jews. Marr labeled the languages Hebrew, Arabic, and Aramaic (all of which were often used by Jews in the nineteenth century) as Semitic languages.

The topic of anti-Semitism is discussed in detail, and with humor, in the episode "The Showerhead" (#126). Jerry's Uncle Leo believes he is a constant victim of anti-Semitism. While having lunch together at Monk's coffee shop, Uncle Leo complains to Jerry about his hamburger. He believes that the cook must be an anti-Semite. Jerry tries to convince Leo that the cook has no idea whether the customers are Jewish or not and therefore certainly did not overcook the burger because Leo is Jewish.

It is generally accepted that people within the same group can make fun of their own heritage but people are not allowed to mock other heritages. This principle is applied to Jewish people in the episode "The Yada Yada" (#53). Jerry and George visit their friend and dentist, Tim Whatley. Whatley announces that he has converted to Judaism. Jerry welcomes him to the faith.

Jerry is not so pleased with Whatley's conversion after Tim tells a Jewish joke (that his workout at the health spa is a "Jewish workout"—he sits in the sauna). George and Jerry look at each other in disbelief. Whatley has only been a Jew for a couple of days and he's already telling Jewish jokes? During a dental visit at Whatley's office, Jerry confronts Tim about his jokes. Tim reminds Jerry that it's the Jewish sense of humor that has helped to sustain the Jewish people for three thousand years. Jerry tells Tim it has been five thousand years. Tim thinks five thousand makes the story all the better. Jerry is most likely off in his estimation as historians trace the beginnings of the Jewish faith to a period somewhere between 2000 and 1600 BCE.

When Whatley makes a Catholic joke, Jerry gets even more upset with him. Whatley believes he can still tell Catholic jokes because he used to be Catholic. As it turns out, Jerry is more offended at Whatley for his comedic immunity than his Jewish immunity. Jerry goes to a Catholic church to talk to a priest (Father Curtis) about Whatley. (In a hilarious scene, Jerry enters the confessional and is unsure how to sit down—he is supposed to kneel on the kneeler. Father Curtis explains to Jerry that is a kneeler not a chair.)

The priest asks Jerry to begin by telling him his sins. Jerry points out that he is Jewish and is happy to hear the priest inform him that's no sin. Jerry tells the priest that he believes Whatley converted to Judaism for jokes. The priest asks Jerry if this offends him as a Jewish person. The priest is surprised to hear Jerry respond that it offends him as a comedian.

Jerry does not receive the help that he anticipated. In fact, when Jerry tells a dentist joke (What's the difference between a dentist and a sadist? Newer magazines.) to Father Curtis, he gets offended and tells Tim Whatley. Whatley hits the roof in anger that Jerry is telling dentist jokes. In a return visit to Whatley's office, Jerry's exam turns very painful. Whatley punishes Jerry for his dentist joke. Whatley points out how "his people"—dentists—are a persecuted group and that they have the highest suicide rate of any profession. Jerry offends Whatley further when he asks, "Is that why it's so hard to get an appointment?"

A discussion about dentists between Jerry and Kramer cleverly draws parallels between the sociological analysis of racial and ethnic discrimination and prejudice to the field of dentistry. Jerry tells Kramer about his incident at Whatley's dental office. When Jerry refers to dentist as "those people" Kramer tells Jerry to listen to himself. Kramer repeats "those people." Kramer defends dentists as if they were an oppressed minority group. He argues that dentists came to this country like everyone else, following a dream, hoping for a good life. Jerry tries to point out that he is only talking about dentists. Upon hearing that, Kramer calls Jerry an "anti-dentite!" Kramer: "You're a rabid anti-dentite! Oh, it starts with a few jokes and some slurs. 'Hey, denty!' Next thing you know you're saying they should have their own schools." Jerry points out that they do have their own schools, and Kramer sees this as further evidence of their victim status.

Jerry later attends a wedding with his new girlfriend, Beth. He has admired Beth for some time but does not really know her that well. At the wedding, Jerry says hello to the father of the groom (Mickey), Mr. Abbott. Abbott tells Jerry that Whatley was one of his students. He is so upset with Jerry for telling dentist jokes that he warns Jerry that if this was not his son's wedding day, he'd knock his anti-den-tite bastard teeth out. Beth wonders what is going on. After Jerry brings her up to speed, Beth tells her own dentist joke ("What do you call a doctor who fails out of med school? A dentist"). Jerry laughs. He thinks he has found a kindred spirit in Beth. Mockingly, Jerry says, "Dentists." Beth replies, "Yeah, who needs 'em? Not to mention the Blacks and the Jews."

Jerry suddenly realizes what sociologists teach: racist jokes are not so funny when you are on the receiving end of one.

Seinfeld introduced the concept of "shiksappeal"—a quality that a non-Jewish female possesses that attracts Jewish men and teenage boys. As described earlier in this chapter, Elaine attended the bris of Adam Lippman, who then hit on Elaine because he thought he was a man. While Elaine explained to Adam her ideas as to what constitutes being a man, Mr. Lippman listened with great interest. He realizes that he possesses those very traits and thinks that Elaine is actually describing him. Suddenly, he lurches at her and French kisses her.

Elaine is in shock. First the son and now the father have put the moves on her. She goes to Jerry's apartment to talk to him, but she finds George there instead. George tells Elaine that Jewish men love her because she is a shiksa, a non-Jewish woman. Thus, Elaine has shiksappeal because Jewish men love the idea of dating a woman that's not like their mother. Elaine thinks George is way off base.

Elaine must have missed the sociological analysis of the marriage and dating pattern of exogamy (attraction and marriage between people of two different groups—in this case, religion). Even so, Elaine decides to confront Mr. Lippman with George's theory of why Lippman finds her attractive. She tries to reason with him that if he weren't Jewish, he would not be interested in her. He tries desperately to convince her that's not true. In an attempt to prove himself, Lippman denounces Judaism. Elaine mutters, "Oy vey!" Elaine's amazement over her shiksappeal leads her to see a rabbi—who in turn, also hits on her!

Alternatives to Organized Religions

Organized religions are generally straightforward about their intentions, practices, and goals. They are a part of the greater society. In fact, they often have great influence in the maintenance and development of society. Cults, on the other hand, represent a religion that is totally withdrawn from, and often in conflict with, organized religions and civil society. Cults promote values and beliefs that deviate immensely from the established norms.

Cults are led by charismatic leaders who generally claim that they have had a revelation or a message from God. The cult leader becomes a source of fresh ideas for those who seek answers to various life concerns. Cults tend to be unstable and are totally dependent on their leader for the continued establishment and growth of the group. Recruitment practices generally involve brainwashing the naive who are seeking simple answers to life's complicated issues.

In the episode "The Checks" (#114), the audience is introduced to the world of cults via the Sunshine Carpet Cleaners. George and Kramer are in Jerry's apartment. George is about to leave because he has to meet with these carpet cleaners. Kramer tells George that he has heard they are a crazy religious cult and that the carpet cleaning business serves as a means for them to get into people's homes.

Later at George's apartment, three guys dressed in bright yellow overalls are about to leave after having cleaned it. George is waiting for the "pitch" into the cult but the cleaners just pack up and leave. George is perplexed; he wanted to at least listen to what they have to say. He is now consumed with finding out why the cult rejected him—if indeed, they are a cult as Kramer claimed. He hires them again to clean the offices at Yankee Stadium, including the office of George's boss, Mr. Wilhelm.

A couple of days later, George and Jerry are in a meeting with Japanese television executives in an attempt to pitch their sitcom. Members of the Sunshine Carpet Cleaners appear from another room. One of the members is Mr. Wilhelm. George can't believe it.

Many people are not actively involved with organized religions. They lead good, respectable lifestyles, but they do not feel the need to conform to the rules of a heavily regulated hierarchical social institutions.

Humanists, for example, believe in the value of life here on Earth and are not convinced that there is an afterlife. Because of this, they value earthly life more than religious people do (because our humanly existence may be the only existence we ever experience). Karl Marx was a humanist. He wanted all people to be able to reach their full human potential. He tried to convince the proletariat that there is no guarantee of an afterlife and therefore, they should live life to the fullest in the here and now. Furthermore, Marx believed that the existing sociopolitical institutions and religious dogma interfered with humans ever being able to reach their full human potential.

Some people believe in the validity of such religious functional equivalents as astrology, tarot, palm reading, voodoo, Santeria, and a wide variety of other belief systems.

One of the most significant contributions to popular culture in this area from *Seinfeld* comes from "The Strike" (#166). In this episode, we are introduced to Festivus—a festival for the rest of us. Festivus is an alternative, secular holiday to the religious holidays that dominate American society in December. George's father Frank created Festivus. We first learn of it when Jerry, Elaine, and George discuss it at the coffee shop. George's father hates all the commercial and religious aspects of Christmas, so he made up his own holiday. Instead of a tree, Frank puts up an aluminum pole. Festivus also includes a "feats of strength" contest. For George it is always one big nightmare that results in Frank beating him yearly in the feats of strength. Having never heard of Festivus before, Elaine laughs uncontrollably as she learns about it.

Later (at Jerry's apartment), Kramer learns about Festivus when he hears Jerry greet George with a "Happy Festivus!" Kramer immediately wants to learn about it. George begs Jerry not to tell the story again, but Jerry does anyway. Elaine walks into Jerry's apartment and states, "Happy Festivus, Georgie." Kramer is amazed that Frank created his own holiday. He meets with Frank to learn more about its origin. Frank explains that many Christmases ago, he was trying to buy a doll for George. He reached for the last one on the shelf when another man also reached for it. They got into a fist fight over it when Frank suddenly realized that there must be some other alternative to organized religious celebrations such as Christmas.

The doll was destroyed. But on that day, a new holiday was born: "Festivus—A festival for the rest of us." Frank describes one other ritual of Festivus. At dinner, the family members gather around and tell each other all the ways in which they have disappointed one another over the past year. Frank tells Kramer that an aluminum pole is used instead of a tree but no tinsel because Frank finds tinsel distracting. Kramer loves the idea of Festivus and wants to join in the celebration.

Festivus takes on a life of its own. Kramer demands December 23 (the official date of Festivus) off from work at the bagel shop—where he had just returned to work after being "on strike" for years. The characters all greet one another with "Happy Festivus!" Festivus "miracles" pop up everywhere (really they are mundane events that Kramer labeled as "miracles"). Meanwhile, Frank basks in the glory of the rebirth of Festivus ("George's heritage"). George is reliving his childhood trauma.

At the Festivus dinner Frank greets his guests and family: "Welcome, newcomers. The tradition of Festivus begins with the airing of the grievances. I got a lot of problems with you people!" After the airing of grievances, Frank moves onto the "feats of strength." Sadly, George is the person that Frank decides to challenge. George does not want to participate. His mother yells encouragement. Frank proclaims this Festivus as the best one ever.

Chapter 12

Health and Mental Health

"Serenity Now. Insanity Later."—Lloyd Braun

We have all heard the expression, "Don't complain, at least you have your health." George will hear this expression from Debby in "The Scofflaw" (#99) episode. But the fact is most of us will get sick (often) even if it's just a cold. Typically, when someone suffers from a cold they go to the drugstore for some cold medication. But as Jerry explains in the opening monologue of "The Stranded" (#27), it is difficult to pick out the right medication. One option will state that it is "quick acting," but another one will say it is "long lasting." Jerry states, "When do I need to feel good—now or later? It's a tough question." In "The Stranded" episode, Jerry and George are at a drugstore looking over cold medicine alternatives:

> *George*: "There's a hundred different things here. What's the difference between these two? [George and Jerry each grab a box and look over the ingredients.] You got propylparabin?"
>
> *Jerry*: "Got it."
> *George*: "You got isobutan-30?"
> *Jerry*: "I got isobutene-20."
> *George* (thinking that his is better): "A-ha."
> *Jerry*: "You got sorbitant sesquioliate?"
> *George*: "Got it."
> *Jerry*: "I have aloe!"
> *George*: "You got aloe? I love aloe."

Jerry: "Where do they make yours?"
George: "Jersey."
Jerry: "White Plains."

George and Jerry look at each other, convinced of which product is "better" based on where it was made. George puts down the box that was made in New Jersey and grabs the one made in White Plains instead.

Reality tells us that if any one cold medicine is truly "the best," all the other alternatives would become obsolete; therefore, none of them are much better than the rest. In "The Andrea Doria" (#144) episode, Kramer, who distrusts the medical profession, goes to a veterinarian instead of a medical doctor for cough medicine. Kramer finds a dog with the exact same cough as his and takes him to the vet. Kramer ends up taking the dog pills and begins acting like a dog. (In a hilarious scene, Jerry teases Kramer, like a dog, by shaking his keys and says to Kramer, "Come on boy, want to go for a ride?" Kramer jumps up excitedly. As they ride in the car, Kramer begins to realize that Jerry is really taking him to a human doctor. Kramer "escapes" from the car and runs away, like a dog.)

What is Health?

According to the World Health Organization, health is defined as the ability to function effectively—physically, mentally, and socially. From this definition, it is clear that health is, at least in part, affected by social conditions. In other words, health varies from one society to another and from one group to another within the same society.

A sociological examination of the health of Americans is both encouraging and disappointing. On the positive side, the life expectancy of Americans has increased from about 49 years in 1900 to 77.6 in 2005, an increase of more than 50 percent. The infant mortality rate has dramatically decreased in the past century. Americans can thank science, medicine (the system developed for the purpose of treating illness), healthier living conditions, and a better diet. Developments in medicine include immunization against various diseases, penicillin, and other antibiotics.

On the negative side, the United States does not compare very favorably with the other nations in the industrial world. According to the National Center for Health Statistics (2005), there are more than 20 nations in 2005 with a higher life expectancy than the United States. At 81.9 years, Japan has the highest life expectancy in the world. The United States has the highest infant mortality rate in the industrial world (Japan has the lowest). Furthermore, despite easy access to nutritional food, the Centers for Disease Control and Prevention report that two-thirds of American adults are classified as either overweight or obese. National studies indicate that about 30 percent of American children are overweight or obese.

There is a great discrepancy in the healthcare Americans receive. Those who can afford healthcare have access to the best care available in the world. On the other hand, for the more than forty million Americans who are without health coverage (insurance), the cost of medical care is beyond their financial means.

Physical Health

The American obesity epidemic has not gone unnoticed. The media discusses it extensively, and the health profession warns of the harmful consequences of being overweight. As a result an entire industry has profited from creating and marketing a variety of dieting programs. The pharmaceutical industry promotes taking pills in conjunction with exercising. The average person, meanwhile, seeks to find the great balance between dieting and eating foods that still taste good.

The current diet craze centers on watching the number of carbohydrates that one consumes. In the 1990s, dieters watched their fat intake. *Seinfeld* provides an excellent example of this in the episode "The Nonfat Yogurt" (#71). Kramer has invested in a nonfat yogurt shop where everyone raves about how good the yogurt tastes. Only George seems to question how it is possible for something that tastes so good to not have any fat in it. Life experiences usually prove that if something seems too good to be true, it is. After days of regularly eating the nonfat yogurt, Kramer comments to Elaine and Jerry (in Jerry's apartment) that they both seem to be putting on weight. Elaine and Jerry weigh themselves and find out that they have put on seven and eight pounds respectively. Jerry blames the yogurt. Kramer insists that it's 100 percent nonfat yogurt.

Elaine and Jerry decide to take a sample of the yogurt to a lab and have it tested. As it turns out, it is loaded with fat. Jerry brings it to the attention of the local authorities and the shop is forced to stop selling yogurt advertised as nonfat. Naturally, the real nonfat yogurt turns out to taste terrible. Newman personally blames Jerry. He loved the old yogurt and vows to get even with Jerry.

Newman's sentiments reflect the thoughts and attitudes of many overweight Americans. They prefer food that tastes great over food that is good for them. (It is interesting to note that Wayne Knight, the obese actor who played Newman, lost well over one hundred pounds in the period 2002 to 2004 the old-fashioned way—he dieted and exercised.)

Being overweight does not mean that someone is sick. It does, however, add to complications in health. An overweight person who smokes and fails to exercise regularly is just asking for health problems—and they will most assuredly experience them.

"Being Sick"

"Being sick" is not simply a physical experience. Instead, a number of social factors contribute to one becoming sick. Furthermore, when someone claims to be sick, she must also abide by the role expectations associated with "being sick." When people are sick, they are dysfunctional (because the normal and natural state of affairs is for people to be healthy, productive members of society). Society must have healthy, functioning members perform roles and tasks necessary for the maintenance of society. As a result, society establishes some form of medical care to assist sick people back to health.

Sociologist Talcott Parsons defines the "sick role" as composing of two essential elements: (1) specifying who can claim to be sick, and (2) specifying a set of obligations that sick people must perform in order to become healthy again. Thus, someone with a simple headache or minor aches and pains is not expected to claim the sick role and take time off from work; while those who are sick must take care of themselves (e.g., resting, drinking plenty of fluids, seeing a doctor, taking the prescribed medicine) in order to become functioning members of society again. In other words, only truly sick people can claim to be sick, and sick people can expect sympathy for a limited period of time before they are expected to return to "normal."

There is a social taboo against claiming the sick role by those who truly are not sick; the sick role, after all, is reserved for those who are truly ill. This taboo explains why society has such a negative view of hypochondriacs—people who claim to have a sickness but in reality do not. Generally, hypochondriacs learn about symptoms of a disease, self-diagnose and then proclaim to others that they are sick. Hypochondriacs are very dysfunctional, counterproductive, and deviant members of society.

George displays a perfect example of a hypochondriac in the episode "The Heart Attack" (#13). In this episode, George, Elaine, and Jerry are at the coffee shop when suddenly George mentions that he thinks he's having a heart attack. Jerry and Elaine doubt George's claim. Jerry knows his friend all too well and therefore does not react with a sense of urgency. After a lengthy debate, they decide to take George to the hospital just in case.

The scene shifts to the hospital where the doctor tells Jerry (in the hallway and out of George's range) that there is nothing wrong with George. Jerry is not surprised by this and decides to have some fun with George. Jerry teases George that if things don't work out that he would like George's Black Hawks jacket. Jerry also teases George about calling his girlfriend, Susan Davis, for a date. George, acting all depressed, tells Jerry "go ahead." After all, if he's dying what does he care? He even begs Jerry to kill him with a pillow right now to get "it over with." Jerry jokingly pretends to smother George with a pillow when Elaine enters the hospital room. Jerry whispers to Elaine that George is really okay and that he is just fooling around. So Elaine decides to join in with the fun as well and asks George about renting his apartment.

The sick role also involves the taboo of proclaiming to be in extreme pain. While it is understandable that ill people will experience pain, prolonged pain is viewed as both personal neglect and the failure of proper medical care. Modern medicine is designed to mask pain while individuals recover, or while they are dying. Interestingly, social psychologists Anselm Strauss and Barry Glaser report that people who claim intense and worsening pain found that the medical staff begins to ignore them.

People *do* get sick. But, they are expected to play the sick role properly. This includes taking the necessary steps toward recovery and recuperation. Staying home in bed and resting is a sound recovery mechanism. People who claim the sick role because they are hypochondriacs or are simply faking it to get out of work or school risk many social sanctions. I remember one semester while teaching at the University of Nevada at Las Vegas (UNLV) a student called me on test day claiming to be sick. She coughed and sneezed and used a variety of techniques to support her claim for the sick role. I gave her the benefit of the doubt. But later that night, I saw her dancing at a nightclub with her friends. Busted! You cannot claim the sick role and then go out partying on the same day. She violated the rules of "role playing" (one's performance must be congruent to the role that one is claiming/playing) as presented in Erving Goffman's work on the *presentation of self*. Her social sanction (punishment) was the denial of a make-up exam.

Another category of people with an overly irrational approach to health are the germ-o-phobes. Now, this is not to suggest that germs are something to be laughed at; after all, germs are the cause of a great deal of sickness. As a rule, one should wash one's hands regularly, but especially after going to the restroom. Studies have shown that many people do not wash their hands in public restrooms. Some merely run water over their hands and do not use soap. The scary thing is, even if you wash your hands in a public restroom you are not safe from those do not. Think about it. When you exit a restroom you have to use the door knob to exit; if just one person has not washed their hands you have come in contact with germs. Scarier still is the realization that some of those people who do not wash their hands return to a bar where they grab bar snacks from a communal bowl. Makes you think twice about eating free "bar food," doesn't it?

The law mandates that employees must wash their hands after they use the restroom—let's hope they all do so. But deep down, we know that's not always the case. And as the episode "The Pie" (#79) illustrates, we do have reasons to be concerned about germs. (An overly irrational fear of germs leads to someone becoming a mysophobic.) Jerry's girlfriend Audrey refuses to try any of Jerry's apple pie at the coffee shop. She will not even provide an explanation. This dumbfounds Jerry. George later suggests to Jerry that maybe she is a diabetic. But Jerry discounts that because she carries Entenmanns doughnuts in her purse.

On their next date, Jerry and Audrey are dining together at her father's restaurant (Poppie's). He is still trying to figure out why she refused to try any of his apple pie on the previous date. Poppie comes over to their table and promises a very special dinner. In the next scene, both Jerry and Poppie are in the restaurant's bathroom. Jerry is washing his hands while Poppie flushes the toilet and exits the stall.

Poppie (while zipping up his pants) proclaims that Jerry is in for a real treat because he is preparing dinner personally. Poppie then exits the bathroom without washing his hands. Jerry notices this in disgust.

Jerry returns to his table but says nothing to Audrey about the bathroom incident. Jerry stares ahead at Poppie who is visible preparing Jerry and Audrey's meal. When the food arrives Jerry refuses to eat any of it and fails to offer an explanation. His mannerisms are the same as Audrey's when she refused to eat any of his pie at Monk's. Audrey is very upset with Jerry because he disrespected her and her father.

Near the end of "The Pie" episode, Jerry makes a return trip to Poppie's to see Audrey. Just then, an inspector from the Board of Health enters the restaurant and informs Audrey (who is working as a hostess) that he is looking for Poppie. Turns out there were "several complaints" against Poppie. Poppie leaves with the inspector and Audrey looks puzzled—what would the Board of Health want from Poppie? Jerry informs Audrey that "Poppie's a little sloppy." A sloppy chef is not good for the health of diners.

Health inspectors alone cannot fight the battle against germs. The medical profession can help treat the results of contact with germs, but they cannot eliminate germs from society. Most people try to block out the reality of germs in their house, workplace, and food. Others, however, find it difficult to function in a world filled with germs. (Billionaire Howard Hughes became so paranoid of germs that he locked himself in his hotel room for decades over an irrational fear of coming in contact with them.)

In the episode "The Apology" (#165), Elaine's coworker Peggy is a mysophobe. Despite the fact that Peggy and Elaine are the only two to share a bathroom, Peggy uses seat protector. Elaine believes that Peggy is disrespecting her by doing this. She eventually confronts Peggy; she wants to know why Peggy finds her so offensive. Peggy tells her it's because Elaine seems to be with a lot of men. Elaine insists that's not true. For the most part, she is just with Puddy, with an occasional guy here and there. Insulted by Peggy's insinuation that she sleeps around, Elaine rubs Peggy's keyboard on her butt, sticks her stapler under her arms, and coughs on the doorknob. Elaine spreads her germs all over Peggy's stuff. For a mysophobe like Peggy, this is too much to bear. The next day Peggy calls in sick. Elaine tries to discredit Peggy's claim to the sick role.

Elaine later discusses the whole Peggy issue with Puddy. She is looking for a sympathetic ear. Instead, she finds out that Puddy is a ten-year recovering mysophobe. Looking at Puddy's necklace, she asks about the symbol on it. Puddy tells her it's a germ. Puddy agrees to help Elaine by visiting Peggy. Puddy explains to Peggy that he is a recovering mysophobe and that once upon a time dating someone like Elaine would have made him sick, but he is okay with it now. Puddy hates Elaine's old slippers that she has worn since college. He views them as bacteria traps. Puddy believes that Peggy will be able to work with Elaine just as he is able to date her, without fear of getting her germs.

Smoking

Millions of people (including 25 percent of the US population) smoke on a daily basis. Consider these facts provided by the American Cancer Society (2004):

- More than 440,000 Americans die annually from tobacco use.
- About half of all Americans who continue to smoke will die because of their habit.
- Cigarette smoking accounts for a third of all cancer deaths.
- Cigarettes kill more Americans than alcohol, car accidents, suicide, AIDS, homicide, and illegal drugs combined.

Why should nonsmokers care if people smoke? There are two simple answers: (1) over forty thousand nonsmokers who are exposed to tobacco smoke die from cardiovascular diseases each year, and (2) the overall cost of health insurance has risen dramatically, due, in part, to the extreme medical costs related to smoking.

Smoking is a very sensitive issue. Smokers feel that they have the right to smoke and nonsmokers feel that they have a right to live and work in a smoke-free environment. Many nonsmokers will refuse to date someone who smokes. Their reasons vary but generally they don't want to kiss someone who tastes like an ashtray, they hate the smell of smoke on their clothes, smoke ruins the eating experience, and they wonder if they can trust the overall judgments of smokers considering the fact they have made such a poor decision to smoke in the first place. Oddly, young people think smoking makes them look cool—it certainly does not. And older people are addicted to smoking and realize it is nearly impossible to break a habit far more powerful than heroin addiction.

Elaine is a nonsmoker who refuses to date anyone who smokes. The smoking issue has caused her to end relationships with a number of people, including Keith Hernandez in "The Boyfriend (2)" (#35). Elaine and Keith were getting along fine, with plenty of flirting and kissing. Everything goes well until Keith takes out a cigarette. She did not know he smokes and this leads to the breakup.

In 1964 the US Surgeon General first warned the public that smoking causes lung cancer. Since that time, science has linked tobacco to a number of chronic diseases. Adults who choose to smoke have the legal right to do so. If they wish to pollute their lungs with smoke it is their decision. However, nonsmokers and children should not have to be exposed to the toxins emitted via tobacco smoke. Perhaps the saddest travesty is when a pregnant woman smokes. According to the American Cancer Society, smoking increases a pregnant woman's risk of miscarriage, early delivery, and stillbirth. Smokers' babies are also at increased risk of sudden infant death syndrome.[14]

In the episode "The Suicide" (#32), Elaine and George visit a psychic, Rula, who is pregnant. George wants some information on paranormal activity. While George and Rula are talking, Elaine fixates on Rula's smoking. She wonders how any woman could smoke while she was pregnant, especially with everything we know about prenatal care. Elaine tells Rula that her behavior is disgusting. Naturally, Rula kicks Elaine and George out of her apartment. Elaine is steamed that anyone can be so irresponsible as to smoke while pregnant. The child is defenseless.

Tobacco smokers are beginning to feel the effects of discrimination that marijuana smokers have experienced in this country. Many states have enacted smoking bans in public buildings, workplaces, restaurants, and bars. Predictably, smokers are upset by this intrusion into their personal habits. They are forced to smoke outside (in potentially inclement weather) and face a negative stigma seldom experienced by smokers in past generations.

Kramer confronts the smoking ban issue in the episode "The Abstinence" (#143). Kramer, George, and Jerry are at the coffee shop. While at their table, Kramer lights a cigar. He is told to put it out because you can't smoke inside New York restaurants. Kramer goes outside and smokes with a group of other disgruntled smokers. Kramer decides to do something to help out his fellow smokers, so he creates a "smoking lounge" out of his apartment.

The hallway in Kramer's building becomes filled with smoke from his apartment. Kramer goes over to Jerry's apartment to borrow some matches. Jerry wonders why it is so smoky in the hallway and why there are so many people at his place. Kramer tells him that he invited them up to his apartment to smoke, because someone had to. Jerry doesn't follow Kramer's logic.

> *Kramer*: "Well somebody had to. You know, just because a person's a smoker, that doesn't mean he's not a human being."
> *Jerry*: "It doesn't?"
> *Kramer*: "Well, you can confine them, you can punish them, you can cram them into the corner, but they're not going away, Jerry."
> *Jerry*: "All right."
> *Kramer*: "Yeah."

Time goes by, and Kramer's smoking lounge becomes quite popular. He has filter and nonfilter sections and special theme nights, like "pipe night." Kramer explains to Jerry that people really seem to be enjoying themselves; it's as if once they come over to his apartment, they are addicted. Before long, Kramer's teeth have become stained from the tobacco smoke. Jerry tells Kramer that his face looks like an old catcher's mitt. Kramer has experienced a lifetime of smoking in seventy-two hours. Kramer can't believe what has happened to him. Jerry asks him what he expected to happen.

> *Kramer*: "Emphysema, birth defects, cancer. But, not this. Jerry, my face is my livelihood. Everything I have I owe to this face."
> *Jerry*: "And your teeth, your teeth are all brown."
> *Kramer*: "Look away, I'm hideous."

Kramer was prepared for diseases caused by smoking, but he never thought about the other effects. Sociological research has shown that the role of nurture is far more important than the role of nature in dictating behavior. Furthermore, research on twins has shown that when one twin smokes (and/or tans) and the other one does not, the one exposed to smoke (and sun) will age more rapidly than the twin who does not engage in such harmful behaviors.

Kramer contacts his lawyer, Jackie Chiles, to sue the tobacco companies. Kramer does not feel that he should be responsible for his own behavior. Jackie, in typical defense lawyer fashion, believes that Kramer is a victim. He rationalizes his belief because the labels on the cigarettes fail to mention anything about damage to physical appearance. Once again people, it's smoke. It will *always* cause harm.

The Medical Profession

Nearly everyone will be sick at least once in their lifetimes. Sometimes, sickness is temporary (acute) and other times it is chronic (long-term, or life-long). People may suffer from minor aches and pains that are easily treated, or they may be forced to have surgery. At the top of the medical profession hierarchy are doctors. Doctors generally are held in high regard and many of them make a high salary. Because of this, there are people who dream of becoming a doctor and there are people who dream of marrying a doctor. Elaine is one of those people who has always dreamed of marrying a doctor.

In the episode "The Abstinence" (#143), Elaine is dating a doctor named Ben. In actuality, Ben still needs to pass his licensing exam—a test he has already failed three times. Dating a doctor is an important status symbol for Elaine. Many people dream of marrying a doctor as a means to improve their own socioeconomic status. Elaine loves telling her friends that she's dating a doctor. Elaine helps Ben study for his upcoming exam and realizes that he is not focused. They decide to abstain from sex so that Ben can concentrate on his studies. Ben does pass the exam and Elaine is ecstatic that she is now dating a doctor. Unfortunately for Elaine, Ben breaks up with her. He explains that part of the dream of becoming a doctor is to dump whatever girlfriend you have at the time to find someone better.

This is an interesting turn of events. Elaine dreamed of dating a doctor to improve her social standing through association only to find out that doctors dream of dating someone better, like a trophy wife, to improve their social status.

There are numerous episodes on *Seinfeld* that deal with doctors and medical procedures. In the opening monologue of "The Conversion" (#75), Jerry suggests that doctors may not be the most secure professionals; after all, they are the only people who feel the need to hang their diplomas on the wall as a means of proving to others they really do have a degree in their field. And that explains why they make their patients wait in two different waiting rooms, to gain a psychological edge. They often make the patients take their pants off, another sure sign of attempting to gain an edge.

Jerry brings up an interesting point. Why *do* doctors have their diplomas on the wall? College professors also put their diplomas on the wall of their offices. Obviously, in both cases, this is done so that patients and students (respectively) realize that they are dealing with a qualified professional. Interestingly, hair dressers also feel the need to put their diplomas on the wall. I guess that makes them as professional as doctors.

In the opening monologue of "The Note" (#18), Jerry describes how everyone likes to think of his doctor as the best. Clearly, as Jerry points out, not all doctors can be the best. Some of them have to graduate at the bottom of their class. Are they recommended by people who say things like, "You should see my doctor, he's the worst. Oh, yeah, he's the worst, he's the absolute worst there is."

Kramer has his own thoughts about doctors. He believes that proctologists are the most entertaining, and if you see a proctologist at a party hang out with him because he will have the funniest stories. In the episode "The Fusilli Jerry" (#107), Kramer goes to the Department of Motor Vehicles (DMV) to pick up his new car license plates. Because of a foul-up at the DMV, Kramer gets someone else's vanity plates that read "Assman." He tries to give them back to the DMV claiming that they are the wrong plates. The clerk informs Kramer that according to the state of New York, he *is* the Assman. Back at Jerry's apartment, Kramer discusses the situation with Jerry and George. They try to figure out whose plates they really are. George thinks they may belong to Wilt Chamberlain. Jerry thinks it could be someone who gets a lot of women. Or someone with a big ass. Kramer is sure it must be a proctologist, especially in light of their known great sense of humor. Every story they have is funny because no one wants to admit how they got something stuck up their ass. People always claim it was an accident. Kramer adds, "Every proctologist story ends in the same way: 'It was a million to one shot, Doc. Million to one.'"

Later in this episode, a bizarre incident occurs. Kramer has started a new hobby of making statue likenesses of his friends out of a variety of pasta. He matches the pasta to the individual personalities of his friends. Kramer made Jerry a little statue out of corkscrew fusilli shells because Jerry, as a comedian, is "silly." (Kramer tells George he will make one for him out of ravioli.) Frank Costanza (along with Kramer and George) is at Jerry's apartment and accidentally falls backward right on top of the "Fusilli Jerry." Everyone at Jerry's apartment gasps in horror, and they rush Frank to see a doctor (Cooperman).

In the waiting room at the proctologist's office, Kramer notices a photo on the wall of Dr. Cooperman on a boat called *Assman*. Kramer, Jerry, and George realize that Kramer's vanity plates belong to this proctologist. Meanwhile, Frank is with Dr. Cooperman in the examining room. He has to explain to the doctor how he got corkscrew pasta stuck up his rectum. Frank ends his discussion with the doctor by saying, "It was a million to one shot, Doc. Million to one."

There are times when doctors must perform medical surgeries. It is often said about surgeons that they have a "God complex" because they literally hold the lives of others in their hands. If a surgery goes wrong, the patient may die. A brilliant surgeon can save lives through a combination of precision skill and technological advancement.

There are times when a surgeon, despite all of his ability, will save the life of a patient even though he thought a patient was beyond hope. In times like these, people begin to look for explanations from other sources, such as divine intervention. An example of this type of occurrence can be found in "The Junior Mint" (#60).

In this episode, Elaine's former boyfriend Roy (an artist) is hospitalized and must have a delicate surgery (splenectomy) to save his life. Elaine, Kramer, and Jerry visit Roy in the hospital. The doctor (Dr. Siegel) stops by Roy's room to ask if he has any questions about the forthcoming operation. Kramer is concerned about the instruments (specifically the interabdominal retractors) to be used in the operation. He saw a special on *20/20* that warned about faulty retractors. Dr. Siegel assures Kramer (and everyone else in Roy's room) that he will not use that type of retractor for the operation. As a gesture (and a sign of a good "bed-side manner") the doctor invites Kramer, Jerry, and Elaine to watch the operation from a viewing gallery with a number of Dr. Siegel's students.

Kramer and Jerry decide to watch the operation. They have seats in the front row of the viewing gallery. Kramer begins to eat Junior Mints from a box he snuck into the operating area. He offers Jerry one but he declines. Kramer insists that he have one and Jerry keeps pushing it away. Suddenly, a mint becomes a projectile and gets launched right into the patient. The medical team hears a noise (like a *plop*), but they cannot find anything. When the operation is over, they seal Roy back together—with the Junior Mint still inside of him.

Immediately after the operation Roy takes a turn for the worse. Jerry feels guilty that the Junior Mint may have caused a problem that the doctors would be unaware of. George, in an attempt to profit from someone else's misery, decides to buy some artwork from Roy—assuming that if Roy dies, the value of his art will increase.

Back at the hospital, Roy is recovering. He gives credit to George for his recovery. Roy believes the fact that he sold some of his art served as an inspiration toward recovery. Just then, the doctor walks in and describes how he thinks there were other factors at play during the surgery. He believes something beyond science intervened; perhaps something from above. Dr. Siegel looks up, as if implying God intervened to help save Roy. The "miracle" in this case, if there was one, came from a secular source—a refreshing little peppermint covered in chocolate.

Mental Health

We have already learned that social processes affect physical health and the expectations associated with claiming the sick role. Social forces also have an obvious impact on mental health. Stress is an especially dangerous cause of poor mental health. A great number of people suffer from stress and if left untreated it may lead to more serious problems. Another very important social factor related to mental health is the actual labeling process of particular behaviors as evidence of mental illness. As with deviant behavior, mental disorders must be labeled as such.

In 2004 the results of the first comprehensive world study of mental health were released by the Harvard Medical School and the World Health Organization. The findings revealed that mental illness is a universal affliction. Treatment, on the other hand, is inconsistent from society to society and from social class to social class. As with physical health, the wealthier social class members tend to seek out and receive better care. The social class disparity related to mental health became very evident during the Reagan administration. In an attempt to cut taxes, many social programs were eliminated, including those designed to help the severely mentally ill. Many facilities were closed and the patients were simply "set free." Without treatment, they quickly became homeless people who sporadically committed serious crimes.

There are a number of social costs related to poor mental health and mental illness. For example, mental illness is responsible for as much job absenteeism as the physical health illnesses of cancer, heart attacks, and back problems combined.

Mental disorders, commonly defined as conditions that are psychological and that affect behavior, are generally treatable through proper medication. When some people with mental disorders stop taking their medication they represent a risk to society. Kramer and Jerry found out about this in their dealings with "crazy" Joe Davola.

Joe Davola is a friend of Kramer's. Davola gives Jerry the "creeps." In the episode "The Pitch (1)" (#43), Jerry has an awkward encounter with Davola at the NBC offices. Davola is dropping off a script for the NBC executives to look at. Struggling for something to say to Davola (in an attempt to decrease the tension), Jerry makes the mistake of mentioning Kramer's party on Sunday night. Davola did not know anything about the party and is upset with Kramer for not inviting him.

Later, Jerry tells Kramer that he inadvertently told Joe Davola about his party. Kramer had purposely not invited Joe Davola because he has been acting crazy lately. Kramer thinks he's a nut and tells Jerry that he is on medication.

We learn why Davola has been acting crazy when the scene shifts to a Paris hotel room where Elaine and her boyfriend, Dr. Reston, who is a psychiatrist, are on a romantic vacation. Reston, intuitively, pulls away from a kiss with Elaine. He thinks about his patient (Davola) back in New York and wonders whether he is taking medication. Elaine diverts Reston's attention away from Davola and back onto her.

Davola, of course, is off his medication. He is also falling apart, mentally. He is especially dangerous because he also knows karate. Davola sees Kramer on the street and suddenly whirls a karate kick to Kramer's head. Knocking Kramer to the ground, Davola says to Kramer, "That's what I think of your party." Only the bicycle helmet (the one he got in a trade with Newman) that Kramer was wearing saved him from a serious injury. The audience does not see the action just described, instead we learn of it via Kramer retelling the story to Jerry and George at the coffee shop. Kramer warns Jerry that Davola is after him next because he doesn't like Jerry.

The "crazy" Joe Davola saga would continue for a few more episodes. In the episode "The Wallet" (#45), Elaine and Dr. Reston return to New York. Dr. Reston is distracted from taking care of his patients right away because Elaine has broken up with him. But he wants her back. Meanwhile, Davola has made Jerry a "marked man." Kramer warns Jerry (in front of his parents who are visiting) that Davola is "after him." Helen Seinfeld can't imagine how anyone cannot like Jerry.

In the episode "The Opera" (#49), Davola's stalking of Jerry continues and expands to include Elaine. Davola reveals his hatred to Jerry by leaving a message on Jerry's answering machine. Davola blames Jerry for his own pilot being turned down by the execs at NBC. Thinking that Jerry was responsible for putting the kibosh on his deal, Davola vowed to put the kibosh on Jerry.

Elaine finally meets Joe Davola. She is outside Reston's office when he is on his way up to see him. Elaine and Davola hit it off and begin dating. She has no knowledge of the relationship between Davola and Jerry. She does a "pop in" visit at Joe's apartment only to find that Davola has created a "shrine" of photographs of her. He then makes a threatening move toward Elaine who has to spray him in the face with Cherry Bianca (she does not have any pepper spray).

In Davola's delusional state of mind, he confuses Elaine with the character Nedda from the opera *Pagliacci* (the opera that this episode centers on). Pagliacci is a clown whose wife is unfaithful to him. Just before Elaine sprays the Bianca in Davola's face, he asks her, "Do you think I'm a clown, Nedda?"

Before Elaine can find out what a nutcase Davola is, she invites him to the opera that she is attending with Jerry, George, Susan, and Kramer. She reneges on her offer to Davola, who decides to dress as a clown and attend anyway. On his way to the opera three thugs mock him (in the park). Davola quickly and efficiently kicks the crap out of the three of them and continues to the theater. When he sees Jerry and Elaine together he believes in his mind that she (as Nedda) is cheating on him. Jerry and Elaine rush into the theater to escape him. The episode ends, allowing Jerry and Elaine an opportunity to escape harm.

Finally, in the last episode of season four, "The Pilot (2)" (#64), the pilot for *Jerry* is taped before a live studio audience. Jerry begins with a short introduction to the studio audience about the concept of the show. Davola, who is steaming mad at Jerry, is seated in the upper balcony of the audience. Davola gets up from his seat and leaps toward the stage below where Jerry is talking to the audience and says, "sic semper tyrannis," which is Latin for "death to tyrants." John Booth yelled it out when he shot President Lincoln.

So ends the story of Joe Davola. The audience is left to ponder what happens next. From a sociological standpoint, the Davola saga underscores the seriousness of mental illness when patients go off their medicine. Doctors can prescribe medicine but patients must take it in order to achieve positive results.

Many people find it difficult to deal with the social and personal problems that confront them. Faced with seemingly insurmountable difficulties these individuals may experience a mental breakdown. Stress, an unhappy employment situation, and failed relationships are just a few causes of mental breakdowns.

On *Seinfeld* a few secondary characters have suffered from mental breakdowns. For example, in the episode "The Foundation" (#135), Elaine's boss, J. Peterman, has allowed the stress from his job to get to him. The pressure to continuously produce and market a product that is new and edgy has finally put Peterman over the edge. In his office, Elaine and her coworker Dugan are pitching ideas to him for the next catalog. He is bored with everyone's presentations and begins to mentally drift away. He gets up from his chair and abruptly leaves the meeting. His employees are concerned and surprised by his behavior. In a later scene, he calls Elaine at her office. He informs her that he is burnt out. His mind is fried. He can no longer run the catalog and places Elaine in charge. Unfortunately, Elaine does not possess all the skills necessary to successfully put out a catalog but she does the best she can.

As with many people suddenly thrust into a position of power, Elaine begins to abuse her position. She purchases many personal items and charges them to the company account. When the accountant (Robert Ipswitch) calls Elaine on her misappropriation of funds, she asks whether or not she can fire him. The accountant informs her that she does not have that power, and that she must answer to the board of directors concerning her purchases. Ipswitch informs Elaine that he is going to recommend to the board that she be fired. Only the approval of Peterman himself will save her. So, Elaine goes to Burma to find him.

In a later scene, Elaine is visiting Peterman in his hut somewhere in the Burmese jungle. A boy cuts a piece of fruit in the background and Peterman yells at him in another language. Elaine thinks Peterman can speak Burmese, but he informs her it was just gibberish. He asks Elaine whether she had any trouble finding him. Elaine responds, "No, you're the only white poet warlord in the neighborhood." Peterman is spaced out; he thinks Elaine is an assassin. She tries to talk him back to reality and reminds him that she works for his catalog. She seeks his signature to sign off on her expense report.

Elaine also shows Peterman the catalog that she put out while he's been in Burma. She put her ill-advised Urban Sombrero on the cover. Peterman responds, "The horror, the horror" (a reference to Joseph Conrad's novel *The Heart of Darkness*). Well, apparently the Urban Sombrero "scared straight" Peterman enough to stimulate his self-recovery and before long his recuperation would lead him back to his company and back into a new and invigorating person.

Serenity Now

In "The Serenity Now" (#159) George's father, Frank, is suffering mental anguish from the stress that is compromising his physical health. The Costanzas are driving in a car. Frank complains about his lack of leg room in the back seat. He loses his temper over Estelle's inability to adjust the seat for his comfort. Frank shouts, "Serenity now! Serenity now!" George wonders why he said that. Frank tells George that the doctor gave him a relaxation cassette. The patient is supposed to say "Serenity now" whenever his blood pressure gets too high. George doesn't think he is supposed to yell. Frank responds, "The man on the tape wasn't specific."

In this episode, Frank has started his own business selling computers from a makeshift office in the garage of his family home. He has hired Lloyd Braun, a childhood friend of George's (and a former mental patient), to help him sell computers. George is also trying to sell computers for his father and soon a competition develops between George and Lloyd. As the boss and owner, Frank is encouraging a sales contest. Both George and Lloyd "claim" sales that neither has made in an attempt to win the competition and gain the favor of both Frank and Estelle. Frank has also offered a Water Pik to the winner.

Estelle (out of sight, and yelling from inside the house): "You're not gonna give away that Water Pik."

Frank: "You wanna bet? Serenity now, serenity now!" (Frank exits the garage and goes inside the house.)

Lloyd: "You know, you should tell your dad that 'serenity now' thing doesn't work. It just bottles up the anger, and eventually you blow."

George: "What do you know? You were in the nut house."

Lloyd: "What do you think put me there?"

George: "I heard they found a family in your freezer."

Lloyd: "Serenity now. Insanity later."

Meanwhile, in this same episode, Kramer is having mental difficulties of his own—and yes; it might be argued that he always had mentally difficulties! He has adopted Frank's technique of repeating "serenity now." Kids in the apartment building are irritating Kramer by doing such things as throwing eggs at his door, and he responds calmly by saying, "Serenity now. Serenity now." He set up a little "country-style" environment outside his door. He has attached Frank's broken screen door, added some potted plants and flowers, and a lawn chair.

George, who was pretending to sell computers, had to "hide" them someplace. Jerry was having his own problems, so George left the computers in Kramer's apartment. Well, just as Lloyd predicted, when you bottle things in, eventually you're going to blow. When Jerry steps on Kramer's last remaining living flower and says he's sorry, Kramer calmly reassures Jerry that everything is okay. Kramer excuses himself and goes inside his apartment. Suddenly, Kramer screams loudly, "Serenity noooooooww!" The audience can hear a lot of crashing and banging and Kramer still yelling, "Serenity now!" Kramer has bottled in so many emotions that he unleashes his anger in a violent rage. He also destroys all of George's computers. But at least Kramer feels better now. He needed to get rid of his pent-up frustrations. The "serenity now" technique clearly did not work for Kramer.

There are many important things in life. Good mental and physical health rank at the top. Everything must be put in proper perspective. If you stress over every little thing, your mental health will be compromised. And generally, mental stress will lead to physical ailments. This chapter ends appropriately, with a brief dialogue between George and his girlfriend Debby in the episode "The Scofflaw" (#99).

> *George* (very frustrated): "Oh, look at this. There's no place to park around here. I don't even know why they sell cars in Manhattan."
> *Debby*: "Don't complain—at least you have your health."

Chapter 13

Population, Aging, and Death

"Kramer, You Can't Live Down Here [Florida].
This Is Where People Come to Die."—Jerry

In 1798 Thomas Malthus published *An Essay on the Principles of Population,* in which he presented a pessimistic view of human society. Malthus warned, two centuries ago, that the world's population was growing too quickly in proportion to the amount of food available. Malthus believed that nature, in an attempt to keep human population in check, would provide relief in the form of the "Four Horsemen": war, famine, pestilence, and disease.

Herbert Spencer, although not as pessimistic as Malthus, believed that overpopulation and the search for scarce resources would inevitably lead to the "survival of the fittest." (Note: Darwin did not coin the term *survival of the fittest,* as many people mistakenly believe; he coined the term *natural selection.*) Spencer first used *survival of the fittest* in *Principles of Biology* (1864). In this publication, Spencer argued that both nature and social forces lead to the selection process that determines who survives and who perishes.

In *Contemporary Social Theory: Investigation and Application* (2005), I wrote a chapter on future society where I presented an updated version of the survival of the fittest concept and the Four Horsemen in the form of the "Five Horrorists." I explain that the Five Horrorists are the new destroyers of life, and warn that if the human population continues to explode in growth and if humanity continues in its failure to protect the environment, humanity as we know it will be altered forever.

249

The study of population, aging, and death has long been a concern of sociology, and for good reason. After all, for humans, as with all living creatures, what is more important than life? And life, inevitably, concludes with death.

Population

The study of human populations is known as demography. Demographers conduct studies on birth rates (fertility), death rates (mortality), and migration patterns. Statistical data gathered primarily from the US Census Bureau provides social policy makers and academics with a great deal of useful information. For example, the United States gains one person every thirteen seconds. This statistic is determined by the demographic realities that (in the United States) a birth occurs every eight seconds, a death every twelve seconds, and an immigrant enters the country every twenty-nine seconds.

Today, anyone forty years old or older has been alive long enough to have seen the world's population double. The current world population is six billion. Trend analysis indicates that the world's population will likely increase an additional three billion by 2050. (Note: Predictions regarding future populations are influenced by many factors including the spread of global infectious disease, mass destruction caused by warfare and terrorism, and environmental changes.) A safe prediction is that the continual growth in human population will put great demands on the limited number of scarce natural resources, especially water.

Now that I have painted a potentially gloomy future for humanity, aren't we all glad that *Seinfeld* exists so that we can at least find some humor in the very serious topic areas of population, aging, and death?

One of the variables involved with population is migration. As a general rule, migration patterns within the United States over the past few decades have involved people moving from the Northeast and Midwest to the South and Southwest. People leave these regions to escape the cold winters, to find employment, and to retire. In the 1980s and 1990s, nearly all the states in the Northeast and Midwest experienced net outmigration (more people left these states than moved to them). There were a number of references in *Seinfeld* that described the migratory process of people moving from New York to Florida—a fairly common practice, especially for the elderly.

For example, in the opening monologue of "The Pony Remark" (#7) episode, Jerry describes the migration of New Yorkers to Florida as a type of social obligation and expectation of people once they reach their sixties. They should retire their snow shovels and move to the sunshine and golf carts of leisure living in Florida.

George envies Jerry because his parents moved to Florida. In the episode "The Showerhead" (#126), Elaine and George are at Jerry's apartment as the topic of parents living in Florida is discussed. Elaine asks George why his parents never moved there. Reflecting on this question, George begins to realize that maybe they should. They are retired, economically secure, and have few friends in New York.

George leaves Jerry's apartment with a brochure of Del Boca Vista, a retirement complex that Jerry's parents had left on his table when they were visiting. George is on a mission now. He attempts to convince his parents to move to Florida. The scene shifts to the Costanza house in Queens, on a cold wintry day. George emphasizes how cold the New York winters are and tells his parents that the temperature in Florida that day is seventy-nine degrees. George mentions that he "read someplace the life expectancy in Florida is eighty-one and in Queens, seventy-three." George drops the Del Boca Vista brochure on the coffee table. His mother glances at it. George describes all the wonderful attractions that Florida offers (such as swimming with dolphins, which Estelle does not find interesting).

No matter how hard George tries to convince his parents of the advantages of living in Florida (the warmth, increased life expectancy, and leisure opportunities) he fails. Only when the Costanzas run into the Seinfelds and Morty suggests to Frank that there's nothing available in the Del Boca Vista development (because Morty and Helen can't stand Frank and Estelle) does Frank show any interest in moving there. Later, back at Frank and Estelle's house, George hears the news that he's been dying to hear. His parents have decided to move to Florida. However, instead of moving for the typical reasons, the Costanzas are moving to Florida out of spite for the Seinfelds.

To my knowledge, the US Census does not track the number of people who move because of spite, and yet, here we have it. George's happiness will be short-lived as Frank and Estelle do not go through with the move. The only explanation offered is provided by Jerry, at the end of the episode, when he tells his mother that the Costanzas changed their mind and decided not to move because they couldn't bear being away from George.

The Costanzas do move to Florida in the episode "The Money" (#146). This time, George has mixed feelings about them moving. He finally realizes that his parents must be worth some money. He may be right. According to a 2004 report by the National Institute on Aging, today's elderly are healthier, wealthier, and better educated (and fatter) than previous generations. All indicators show that the vast majority of older Americans are doing quite well in overall well-being and health. The median net worth of older white households in 2002 was at $205,000. The statistics paint a gloomier picture for older black households as their net worth is estimated at $41,000.

According to George's calculations, he stands to inherit $300,000. Jerry points out, however, that he may have to wait some time to inherit it. So, George decides to ask his parents a number of questions about the family health record. After this discussion, Frank and Estelle realize that they don't have a lot of time left to live. As a result, and much to George's chagrin, they decide to start "living it up." George prefers that if his parents are going to spend his potential inheritance, they should at least do it in Florida. Otherwise, he wants them to stay in New York but not spend their savings.

Frank and Estelle move to Del Boca Vista in Florida. This is the same complex that Seinfelds live in. It is also the complex where Jack Klompus lives. As mentioned in chapter 10, Jerry had once bought a Cadillac for his parents. They sold it to Jack because the car was too much to handle. While his parents were visiting him in New York, Jerry decided to fly down to Florida and buy the car from Jack and give it back to his father. Jack wanted one last day to drive the car and he ends up driving the Cadillac into a swamp. Now Jerry has to fly back to Florida to deal with Jack a second time. After all this, Jerry is cash-strapped and can not afford a hotel to spend the night before his return flight to New York the next day. Jack won't let him stay at his place because Jerry insulted him. Jerry decides to sleep in the Cadillac.

Frank, walking along a street in Del Boca Vista notices someone (Jerry) sleeping on the back seat with his face covered. Frank is disgusted by this and gives a "What is this world coming to" kind of look and gesture. A couple of days later, Frank remains preoccupied with the car and continually peers out the window of his living room condo. Estelle is growing tired of his preoccupation. Frank believes that homeless people make their homes in people's cars and that they urinate inside of them. Finally Frank cracks and yells to Estelle that they are moving back to Queens.

Going against migration trends, George's parents return to New York. But only after they had spent much of the money that George hopes to inherit. Perhaps George should have attempted a compromise with his parents, that is, suggesting that they move to Florida during the winter season. This way, George could be free from them for many months of the year. Florida's seasonal residents, known as "Snowbirds," number nearly one million. In 2004 the University of Florida duplicated its famous 1997 study "The Florida Elusive Snowbird."[15] The Florida snowbird is likely to be a New Yorker over age fifty-five who is generally healthier and wealthier than retirees who call Florida home year-round.[16] January is the peak month for Snowbirds.

Aging

Demographic analysis reveals that Americans are getting older. According to census statistical analysis, by the year 2050, nearly 21 percent of Americans will be age sixty-five or older, compared with 12 percent now. Furthermore, advancements in health and healthcare have led to a burgeoning older population. By 2050, it is estimated that 5 percent of the country will be eighty-five or older, compared with 1.5 percent now. The aging population will necessitate that numerous social institutions be transformed. Social security is the most obvious one. Many people who once hoped to retire at age sixty-five and live off social security now realize that they must continue to work in order to survive. Delayed retirement among the elderly will result in fewer job opportunities for the young.

Because of Western society's focus on youth, the elderly often fall victim to ageism—discrimination and prejudice on the basis of age. The workplace is one area where older Americans find it increasingly difficult to compete with younger ones.

Throughout human history, it has been assumed that individuals and their families took care of themselves and the elderly, a survival of the fittest ideal. Germany first established an old-age pension in the 1930s. They arbitrarily picked sixty-five as the age designated as "old" and defined a system to help those in need. This was more or less an empty gesture as few people were expected to ever reach the age of sixty-five.

As a result of the Social Security Act of 1935, the United States adopted the age of sixty-five from the German plan as their criteria to help the elderly. In comparison, based on current life expectancy, the age for social security should be in the mid- to late-seventies. (If this plan were adopted, social security funds would not be in jeopardy as they allegedly are now.) In 2005 the average life expectancy for all Americans was 77.6 years. Females born in 2000 can expect to live 80.1 years and males 74.8 years.

A subfield of sociology, gerontology (the study of aging), has become very important to society. Statistics clearly show that Americans are aging and living longer than ever before. A large number of people will be responsible to help assist the elderly. Many social institutions, especially quality nursing homes and elderly-care providers, will become invaluable to aging America. Some elderly people need a great deal of attention (e.g., medical supervision, provision of meals, transportation to medical facilities), others just need some companionship. To address this later concern, a number of volunteer groups have been organized.

In the episode "The Old Man" (#58), Elaine announces to George and Jerry that she has just signed up to do volunteer work with senior citizens. She is quite proud of herself and suggests to Jerry and George that they should also volunteer. Elaine explains that volunteers go over to a designated elderly person's home to try to comfort them. Volunteers may also take little walks with their assignee, or go to a coffee shop, anything to make them feel better. George decides he would like to help out and agrees to sign up as a volunteer. Initially, Jerry is not interested.

Volunteer work is not for everyone and only those who truly want to help others should even be involved with programs such as those designed to work with the elderly. Well, Jerry does decide to join Elaine and George and signs up with the Senior Citizen's Volunteer Agency. Kramer, by the way, refuses to volunteer. He is under the impression that volunteer agencies are "fronts" for some sort of money laundering scheme. As odd as Kramer's opinion is, there are people out there who share Kramer's misguided logic.

In typically hilarious *Seinfeld* fashion, the three volunteers have a number of problems. Elaine is paired with an elderly woman (Mrs. Oliver) who has a huge goiter. She later complains to Jerry and George that the agency should have "warned" her about Mrs. Oliver (because the goiter was so large, Elaine was not prepared for their first meeting).

George is assigned to Ben Cantwell who is eighty-five years old, and Jerry is assigned to eighty-seven-year-old Sidney Fields. George asks Jerry whether or not he thinks they will reach such an old age. In a sarcastic tone, Jerry responds, "*We*? No." Implying, of course, that George will not make it to that age, while Jerry will.

George and Mr. Cantwell are having soup at Monk's. George asks him about his health, considering his elderly age. Ben tells George that he feels great for eighty-five. George points out to him that he is way beyond the average life expectancy for an American male. When he informs George that he is not worried about dying, George is stunned. George is already worried about his impending death and Ben's cavalier attitude toward his own mortality baffles his mind. Mr. Cantwell has clearly found peace within himself. He tries to explain to George that at this point in his life he is actually grateful for every moment that he has remaining. George responds in a manner very inappropriate for anyone, but especially as a volunteer to help the elderly: "Grateful? How can you be grateful when you're so close to the end? When you know that any second—poof! Bamm-O! It can be over. I mean you're not stupid, you can read the handwriting on the wall. It's a matter of simple arithmetic, for God's sake." But he tells George that he does not care. This blows George's mind all the more. How can he not care?! George is actually angry at him.

Not surprisingly, Mr. Cantwell gets up and walks away. George asks where he's going and he just says, "Life's too short to waste on you." It seems that he has found true happiness, he knows that life is a gift, and every moment is to be cherished. George can only dwell on the negative.

Jerry does not do much better with his guy, Mr. Fields. When Jerry shows up at his apartment, a housekeeper answers the door. (Housekeeping is another area that assists the elderly.) She points Jerry toward Mr. Fields. Jerry tries to introduce himself to him by saying he is from the agency. Mr. Fields, a little out of it, thinks Jerry is from the CIA (as in *the* Agency). Jerry tries to explain his role as volunteer. Mr. Fields is quite paranoid. He thinks that Jerry is the housekeeper's boyfriend who has let him in the apartment to rob him. He believes that his housekeeper is practicing voodoo in an attempt to turn him into a zombie so she can rob him blind. He tries to kick Jerry out of his apartment. Jerry tries to reassure him that everything is okay and safe, but Mr. Fields is convinced that he is about to be murdered.

Jerry tries his best, but Mr. Fields is in no mood to deal with strangers in his apartment. Every other gesture that Jerry makes is shot down by him. Jerry notices a bunch of his old albums and asks him about them. He says they are junk and he is going to throw them away. He refuses to give them to his family. Jerry asks if his friends (Kramer and Newman) can have them. He agrees.

Later, Jerry, Newman, Kramer, and George all arrive at Mr. Fields's place. He is obviously intimidated by all these people in his apartment. He's an ornery old dude and begins to fight with Kramer. He bites Kramer on the arm. As Kramer shakes his arm free, Mr. Fields's dentures fly in the air. No one can find them, but they all assume the dentures landed in the kitchen. George turns on what he believes to be a light switch so that he can see better. As it turns out, the switch George turns on is the garbage disposal and the dentures, which landed in the sink, are being ground up. During the confusion of finding a cab to take Mr. Fields to the dentist, Jerry and the gang manage to lose him. They look for him, but he is lost.

In a later scene, an agency rep is in Jerry's apartment. She is scolding Jerry about how irresponsible he is. She reminds Jerry that the agency's sole purpose is to care for senior citizens. Furthermore, she claims that he "single-handedly destroyed [their] reputation."

The episode ends with Mr. Fields and Mr. Cantwell in the coffee shop discussing "bits of nothing" in a scene reminiscent of the many conversations that Jerry and George have shared over the years.

An interesting portrayal of the elderly is presented in "The Bookstore" (#173) episode. While at a bookstore (Brentano's), Jerry notices Uncle Leo stealing a book. He is amazed by this. Jerry feels that he must confront Leo on this matter and, consequently, he asks Leo to meet with him at the coffee shop. After they greet one another, Jerry asks his uncle if he's doing all right for money. Leo assures him that he is fine. Jerry tells him that he saw him steal a book at Brentano's the day before. Leo amazes Jerry with his lack of remorse. Leo tries to explain to Jerry that business owners don't mind because they know all elderly people steal. Leo informs Jerry that if he is caught stealing he just starts to cry and act senile. He pleads for forgiveness because he is an old man and confused. Leo even admits to saying things like, "I thought I paid for it. What's my name? Will you take me home?"

It is true that society is far more forgiving toward the elderly when they commit a crime, especially if they appear pathetic and/or are poor, weak, or senile. However, when able-bodied and mentally capable elderly persons are caught committing a crime, they should generally be prosecuted.

Later, Jerry finds out that his parents also steal. Jerry calls his parents who are living in Florida. Jerry's father, Morty, tells his son that "it's not stealing if it's something you need." Jerry cannot understand this logic. His mother adds that no one pays for everything. Jerry is really hurt to hear that his mother steals. She admits to stealing batteries, because they wear out so quickly. She is rationalizing her behavior. Jerry hangs up the phone in disbelief. All the elderly people he knows are stealing. And, they are justifying it as acceptable behavior. I am not aware of any sociological studies to substantiate that elderly people accept shoplifting as normal behavior.

As described earlier, many New Yorkers retire in Florida. They generally do this when they are in their mid- to late-sixties. Some people don't know what to do with themselves after they have retired. Most people, however, look forward to retirement. This is especially true if they have financial security and good health. And let's face it, most people work because they *have* to and if given a choice (which implies financial security) they would rather pursue leisure activities than labor for a wage.

In the episode "The Wizard" (#171), Kramer informs Jerry and George that his coffee table book has been optioned for a movie. Jerry and George wonder how it is possible for a coffee table book to be converted into a movie. But Kramer is not worried how it is being done; he is only concerned that it *is* being done. And it is being done for a hefty price. Kramer is paid so much money that he decides to retire in Florida. Interestingly, Kramer moves into a condo across from Jerry's parents. He makes himself at home with the Seinfelds in Florida, much as he did with Jerry in New York.

Shortly after (it is hard to determine but most likely only a couple of days) Jerry visits his parents for his father's birthday. Kramer enters the Seinfelds' condo. As he walks by Jerry, on his way to the refrigerator, Kramer says hello.

> *Jerry*: "Kramer, what are you doing here?"
> *Kramer*: "I told you, I was retiring. I moved in next door."
> *Helen*: "Mr. Kornstein died, and it's a beautiful apartment."
> *Kramer*: "Yeah, your, uh, folks said it was for rent, so I jumped on it."
> *Jerry*: "Kramer, you can't live down here. This is where people come to die." (getting nasty looks from his parents) "Not you. Older people."

Kramer adjusts to retirement life very easily, and he should be able to, considering he has hardly worked a day in his life. But after an unsuccessful run for condo president of Del Boca Vista, Phase Three, Kramer decides to move back to New York City.

The aging cycle begins at birth. As soon as a baby enters the world it is inevitable that death will follow, but hopefully not until after she has enjoyed a long and happy life. Jerry pretty much sums up the "typical" life cycle of people in his opening monologue in "The Fire" (#84) episode. Jerry describes how first birthdays and last birthdays (assuming you reach old age) are quite similar because you are not really aware of what is going on, you just kind of sit there and watch all the activities. People are all around you and someone else has determined they are your friends. Then someone enters with a cake and candles afire on top of it. What a strange ritual. And the guest of honor is barely conscious of the meaning of the whole occasion.

Death

There are two facts of life, and we can't control either one of them: when (and to whom) we are born and when we die (suicide being an exception to this rule). Assumingly, we would all like to live as long as possible, especially if we have our health, a purpose or function in life, and financial security. Religious people take comfort in the idea that there is some sort of afterlife; it seems to lessen the inevitable conclusion of an earthly life. Other people believe that since we are made up of energy, and energy can never be destroyed, we become a part of the cosmic system. No matter how we look at it, the life we lead now eventually will come to an end. Perhaps the true answer is revealed after we die.

Sociologists have studied the ceremonial rites and practices of different cultures for centuries. The sociology of death and dying is a staple course in sociology departments across the United States. Among the more interesting studies conducted by scholars in this area (certainly one the most cited in popular culture) is Elisabeth Kubler-Ross's concept of the "five stages of death."[17] The five stages

1. Denial—I am not dying, there must be a mistake.
2. Anger—Why me, why not someone else?

3. Negotiation—Bargain with God (or the devil), fate, or the disease itself.
4. Depression—Why should I go on?
5. Acceptance—Putting affairs in order, making arrangements.

Of course, not everyone goes through these stages, especially in the case of sudden or accidental death.

As suggested by the episode "The Old Man" (#58) (described earlier in this chapter), some people are ready for death (Mr. Cantwell) and others are not (George). It would seem fairly logical that our own death should rank as our greatest fear. But as Jerry points out in the opening monologue of "The Pilot" (#63), statistics reveal that we have an even greater fear: public speaking. As Jerry explains, *"Death* is number two! Now this means to the average person, if you have to go to a funeral, you're better off in the casket than doing the eulogy."

There are numerous causes of death. Death may occur as a result of complications related to old age, an accident, working in dangerous occupations, suicide, or purposely perpetrated by another (e.g., gang rival, jealous lover, war). *Seinfeld* addresses a variety of topic areas that (may) result in death.

Suicide and Comas

The topic of suicide was discussed in great length by French sociologist Emile Durkheim. In 1895 he published his appropriately named book, *Suicide*. Durkheim showed that although suicide is (generally) a highly individualistic act, it can be understood sociologically. As a sociologist, Durkheim was not concerned with why any individual committed suicide, but rather, he was interested in explaining differences in suicide rates. He identified four different types of suicide: egoistic, altruistic, anomic, and fatalistic. Durkheim linked each of the types of suicide to the degree of integration into, or regulation by, society. Integration refers to the degree to which the collective sentiments are shared. Altruistic suicide is associated with a high degree of integration and egoistic suicide with a low degree of integration. Regulation refers to the degree of external constraints on people. Fatalistic suicide is associated with high regulation and anomic suicide with low regulation.

For example, there exists a "suicide season." Statistics dating back to 1856 reveal that the peak months for suicide are July (15 percent of all suicides), August (15 percent) and September (17 percent). Only 1 percent of all suicides occur in October. There are geographic locations that people like to go to commit suicide. San Francisco's Golden Gate Bridge is the nation's most popular place to end it all. Niagara Falls is the second most popular place. Interestingly, 73 percent of the victims of suicide in Niagara Falls are local residents.

Suicide can be studied sociologically for other reasons as well. There are suicide pacts made between couples and groups of people. In addition, 70 percent of suicide victims tell someone of their plan to commit suicide but that information is generally not acted upon. An even larger percentage leaves a note behind to explain their actions—thus revealing the social nature of their suicide.

The topic of suicide is very relevant today as fifteen hundred Americans attempt suicide daily; eighty will succeed. More women attempt suicide, but men are almost five times as likely to succeed. Experts attribute this gender difference to women attempting suicide as a cry for help, whereas men just want to end their lives.

Physician-assisted suicide is another major social and political topic of interest to sociologists. The compassion-minded Dr. Jack Kevorkian became famous in the 1990s for his involvement with physician-assisted suicide. Approached by numerous patients who were so ill and suffered so much pain that they no longer wished to live, Kevorkian argued that people have a "right to die." In July 1997, the US Supreme Court found that there was no constitutional "right to die." Dr. Kevorkian created a suicide-assistance machine to help people die painlessly and with dignity. Over thirty states have enacted statutes prohibiting assisted suicide. In October 1997, Oregon legalized it. Dr. Kevorkian is currently serving a ten- to twenty-five-year sentence for second-degree murder after giving a lethal injection to a patient suffering from Lou Gehrig's disease.

Suicide is a very sensitive subject area, and when someone attempts to interject humor into such a delicate topic, extreme caution should be exercised. In the *Seinfeld* episode "The Suicide" (#32), Jerry walks a thin line in his opening monologue about suicide when he ponders why the suicidal person who tries to commit suicide and for some reason does not die stops trying? His life is not any better; in fact it is worse because he found out one more thing he is not good at. Jerry speculates that is why suicidal people don't succeed in life to begin with, because they give up too easily.

What Jerry is glossing over in his discussion of suicide is the fact that most people who attempt suicide don't really want to succeed. They are trying to send a message to someone. The attempted suicide may actually represent the "hitting rock bottom" point that some people need in order to turn their lives around. The person who attempts suicide is also sending a message that other important people in their lives have failed them. Attempting suicide, however, should be one of (if not *the*) last option people exercise to make their point regarding their own personal unhappiness.

In "The Suicide," Jerry's neighbor Martin tries to kill himself with pills. Martin's girlfriend Gina knocks on Jerry's door for help. Jerry and Gina go to the hospital and look over Martin, who is now comatose. One of the many downsides of a "failed" suicide attempt is the fact that the person may survive the suicide but endure physical damage (e.g., a comatose state leading to brain damage).

Jerry happens to have a thing for Gina and flirts with her in the hallway prior to Martin's attempted suicide. In Martin's hospital room Gina admits to Jerry that she has feelings for him. Jerry admits to caring for Gina as well but believes it is unethical to get involved with her considering Martin is in a coma. Gina tells Jerry that she wishes Martin was dead. She even mentions "pulling the plug" on his life-support machines. Gina tries to kiss Jerry right in front of the comatose Martin. Jerry is understandably hesitant. Gina teases him to kiss her. She questions Jerry's manhood for being afraid to kiss her in front of an unconscious man. Jerry tries to explain to Gina that he respects a man in a coma.

The scene shifts to Jerry's apartment. Jerry is talking with Kramer about Martin's coma. He wonders how long you have to wait before dating the girlfriend of a comatose man. Kramer tells Jerry not to wait and that Mediterranean women like Gina enjoy forbidden love. Kramer also teases Jerry for not being man enough to kiss Gina in front of a comatose Martin. Jerry believes that there must be some sort of "coma etiquette" that dictates when it's okay. Kramer says there is no coma etiquette and suggests that everything a comatose person owns is up for grabs after twenty-four hours. Jerry doesn't think that sounds right; surely people must be given more time to recover before all their property is open for the taking. Civil law, of course, protects the property rights of comatose people, at least until a point where family members may have to take over the responsibilities and obligations of the comatose person.

Martin remains in the coma. Jerry and Gina start to date.

Newman, who is Jerry's archenemy, also happens to be good friends with Martin. Newman has threatened Jerry that if Martin wakes up from his coma, he is going to tell Martin that Jerry is dating his girl-friend. Sure enough, one day while Newman, Jerry, and Gina are in Martin's room, he wakes up from his coma. Newman immediately spills the beans. Martin, who is much bigger and tougher than Jerry, reaches up from his bed and starts choking him. At the end of the episode we learn that Gina and Martin have made up and got an apartment together in the Village.

The topic of comas is reintroduced in "The Comeback" (#147) episode. Kramer begins watching the movie *The Other Side of Dark-ness* and freaks out about the possibility of being in a coma. He has good reason to be concerned about comas. Modern medical tech-nology has found a way to prolong life via machines such as respira-tors and feeding tubes. Today, there are about ten thousand patients who lie irreversibly comatose in hospital beds across the United States, kept alive only by machines. Many people feel that this tech-nology simply extends the period of time that loved ones experience the agony of watching the hopelessly ill die. Kramer is so moved by the movie he is watching, that he walks over to Jerry's apartment and hands him a piece of paper granting Jerry power of attorney in case Kramer falls into a coma. Jerry points out that this piece of paper does not constitute a legally binding document.

What Kramer has attempted to do is to create a living will. Living wills are legal documents (acknowledged in all fifty states) that pro-vide advanced instructions about the manner in which individuals want their doctors to treat them in case of terminal illness. In effect, living wills allow patients to die "with dignity" by refusing life-sus-taining treatments. (Note: Living wills are much different than doctor-assisted suicides.)

Jerry is not comfortable being potentially responsible for making a decision that results in Kramer dying. Elaine, however, enthusiasti-cally agrees to be Kramer's executor. Kramer chooses Elaine because she is "a calculating, cold-hearted businesswoman. And when there's dirty work to be done, [she] doesn't mind stomping on a few throats." Elaine and Kramer visit a lawyer (Mr. Shellbach). They discuss a number of scenarios in which Elaine would have to decide whether or not to "pull the plug." Elaine coldly pushes on. She will clearly have no trouble pulling the plug. The forms are signed. Kramer has an eerie feeling about outlining the conditions of his own death.

Equally problematic is the fact that Kramer has not watched *The Other Side of Darkness* through to the end. He is shocked to find that the woman comes out of the coma. (Note: How could he be shocked by this, when his friend and former neighbor Martin came out of a coma?!) Kramer has changed his mind now about the living will; he is not so eager to have the plug pulled now that he finally realizes that people can and do survive comas. The comatose woman in the movie awakes "rested and refreshed."

Dangerous Occupations

When people think of the most dangerous occupations they tend to think law enforcement, firefighters, taxicab drivers, and convenience store clerks. None of these professions are in the top ten. As a point of reference, the Bureau of Labor Statistics reports that the average death rate for all jobs is 4.8 (per 100,000). These statistics refer specifically to deaths on the job, covering it all from accountants dying of heart attacks at their desks to police officers gunned down by bank robbers.

According to 2002 statistics provided by the Bureau of Labor Statistics (a division of the US Department of Labor) America's top ten most dangerous jobs are listed below, followed by the number of deaths per 100,000 workers:

1. Logging—118
2. Fishing—71
3. Commercial pilot—70 (most come from general aviation, like crop dusters)
4. Structural metal—58
5. Driver-sales workers—37
6. Roofing—37
7. Electric power installation—33
8. Farming—28
9. Construction—28 (mostly laborers)
10. Trucking—25

The top three most dangerous professions listed above have consistently ranked in the top for years.

None of the *Seinfeld* characters were involved in these dangerous professions. We certainly don't hear of many comedians dying on the job, so Jerry Seinfeld picked a safe profession for his career. One of the few episodes to specifically address dangerous occupations is "The Maid" (#175); and no, being a maid is not the dangerous profession they discuss. Instead, it is the phone-installation profession that merits a description here. In this episode, Elaine is having problems with her phone. The scene begins with the phone man working inside her apartment. She is holding a candle stick in a potentially menacing manner. For some odd reason, Elaine is thinking to herself how easy it would be to kill the phone man because no one would ever find out. He informs her that her new phone number includes the 646 area code. She wants *the* New York City area code, 212. Upset over this, Elaine mentions to him that she could've killed him and no one would've known. He turns the tables by pointing out to Elaine that he could've killed her and no one would've known.

The scary thing is they are both right. Any time anyone enters your home, you risk being harmed, just as they risk the potential of being harmed. Later in this episode, an old lady dies in Elaine's building. She immediately asks the phone company if she can have her old number because it has the 212 area code. A different phone guy shows up to do the installation. Elaine asks for the other guy. The new phone man informs her that an odd thing happened: the first phone man went out on a job and never came back. Nobody has heard from him since.

Attempted Murder

In some cases, people experience death as the direct result of others who have purposely perpetrated a crime. A person who finds her lover in bed with another may commit a crime of passion. Rival gang members routinely execute one another.

In the episode "The Friars Club" (#128), Kramer is involved with a woman named Connie who only wants to meet him privately in his apartment. They do not go out in public on their dates. This fact alone should've tipped Kramer off that something is amiss. Then again, something always seems to be amiss with Kramer. In this episode, Kramer is experimenting with an evolutionary form of sleeping that he learned about from Leonardo da Vinci. Kramer explains to Jerry that da Vinci only slept twenty minutes every three hours, which (according to Kramer) equates to an extra two and half days awake per week. Kramer is excited that he will accomplish so much more with this new sleep regimen.

Kramer's catnap approach to life messes with his biological need for more sleep. He suffers from sleep deprivation and begins to pass out during very inappropriate times. One such occasion occurs while he is making out with Connie on his couch. Kramer is lying on top of her when he suddenly becomes unresponsive. Connie panics. She assumes Kramer is dead. She doesn't know what to do. He is just dead weight on top of her.

Most people, of course, would call 911 for help—that is, unless they have something to hide. In this case, Connie has something to hide—she is married to a mob guy and she can't be caught cheating on him. She calls her friend Tommy to get the dead guy off her.

Later, as Jerry walks up to his door, Kramer's door opens and two guys emerge carrying a large body-shaped object wrapped in a rug (or some fabric). They carry it away down the hall. Jerry does not think too much of it because Kramer is always up to something. The two guys drive Kramer, who is still wrapped inside the rug, down a lonely stretch of road on the banks of the Hudson River and dump him into the river. Kramer wakes up while he is in the water and struggles to reach the surface before he really dies. When he gets there a ferry boat is bearing down on him. He swims away to safety.

Arriving at Jerry's apartment, Kramer is still confused. He believes that Connie drugged him because she must be jealous. He thinks she is a murderer and decides to call the cops. In reality she is a cheat. But, the cops follow up on Kramer's complaint and appear outside her door with Kramer and an arrest warrant. She is shocked to see Kramer alive. The police arrest her. She asks if she can call her lawyer. Her lawyer happens to be Jackie Chiles. When Jackie finds out that she is accused of attempted murder on Kramer, he adamantly refuses to have anything to do with him. Jackie hangs up the phone, happy to escape another encounter with Cosmo Kramer. The episode ends.

Accidental Death

A large number of accidental deaths occur daily. Some are bizarre (e.g., a construction worker accidentally drops a hammer from high atop a building and it hits a pedestrian below and crushes his skull), others are more commonplace (e.g., auto accidents and pool drownings) but just as tragic.

The saddest tragedy to occur on *Seinfeld* is the accidental death of Susan, George's fiancée. Her death occurs in the episode "The Invitations" (#134). George, if you remember, is not looking forward to his impending marriage; he is merely going through the motions. The only stand George takes is the purchase of the cheapest invitations available. In fact, the invitations that George selects from Melody Stationeries are discontinued and would have to be shipped from the warehouse in New Jersey. Susan does not like George's choice. The clerk also informs Susan and George that the invitations are discontinued because the glue on the envelopes is not very adhesive. George tells Susan they can buy some glue. She is disappointed but allows him to have his way.

The scene shifts to Jerry's apartment and George is discussing his options of getting out of the marriage. He thinks about writing a "Dear Susan" letter where he apologizes for leading her on. He even wishes that she would take a plane someplace and hopes for a crash that kills her. Jerry reminds George that the odds of someone dying in a plane crash are like "a million to one." George replies, "It's something. It's hope." George is certainly wishing some bad karma on Susan.

While George is contemplating his life as a married man, Susan is addressing the invitations and licking the envelopes. Suddenly she collapses. When George returns home he finds her out cold. George gets her to the hospital and calls Jerry. Elaine, Kramer, and Jerry meet George at the hospital. The doctor informs him that Susan has died. The doctor also claims that the cause of death was exposure to a certain toxic adhesive commonly found in very low-priced envelopes. George shows little emotion. He tells the doctor that they were expecting over two hundred guests.

The doctor leaves (a little confused by the lack of emotion from George) and George joins his friends to tell them the news. They are all in shock. But, then again, they also realize that George is not unhappy about the news.

There is certainly plenty of blame to go around in this accident. George could have purchased more expensive envelopes. He could have also called off the engagement. The stationery store should be held responsible for selling toxic envelopes. And Susan, well, she should have used a moisture pad or scotch tape to seal so many envelopes. But, this is why they call deaths like Susan's "accidents."

Ceremonies of Mourning

Death sets in motion a number of social (and generally religious) ceremonies. As a sign of respect to the dead and the surviving family members, a mourning process begins and is followed by a number of burial rituals. Mourning is a social process that reflects each mourner's relationship to the deceased. The closer one was to the deceased, the greater the level of mourning. Strangers would not be mourned (and remember, a death occurs every twelve seconds in the United States, so no one person could possibly mourn every death).

Mourners pay their tribute to the dead in a variety of ways. Typically a mourning debt is paid through the purchase of floral arrangements, visiting the funeral home, assisting in preparation of postfuneral meals for the immediate family, and general offers of assistance. Once again, the closer the mourner is to the deceased and the deceased's family, the greater the mourning obligation. Grieving the deceased at their final "resting place" is a major social expectation during the mourning period. Grief is a universal feature of human behavior.

In "The Foundation" (#135), the first episode to follow Susan's death, Jerry, George, and the Rosses are at the cemetery, standing in front of Susan's tombstone. The Rosses expect George to demonstrate a great deal of grief. They make small talk about such things as the magnificent gravestone. The Rosses turn to George and tell him they will leave him alone long enough to say a few words (or prayers) to Susan at her gravesite. Not having much of anything to say to Susan, dead or alive, George stands alone at Susan's gravesite searching his mind for something to say or do. He ends up talking to her about the Yankees.

Meanwhile, Jerry is standing near the car with the Rosses. Mr. Ross offers Jerry some sort of alcoholic beverage. He turns it down. Jerry, trying to offer the proper eulogy, suggests to the Rosses that Susan's death "takes place in the shadow of new life. She's not really dead if we find a way to remember her." He took those words of wisdom from *Star Trek II*. His words would later inspire the Rosses to set up a foundation in honor of the memory of their daughter.

Back at Jerry's apartment, George suggests to Jerry that he has mourned long enough—three months. And not just any three months, three summer months. As George reasons, anyone can mourn in the winter. Apparently, grieving in the summer has more value than grieving in the winter.

While mourning someone's death, mourners tend to take stock of their lives. This self-reflection is a part of the life-death cycle. The social ritual of mourning, then, serves two primary purposes. First, it provides the proper social outlet to acknowledge the passing of a loved one. Second, it serves as a reminder of how precious life is.

This second function of mourning is articulated in "The Pony Remark" (#7). In this episode, George, Jerry, and Elaine are at the coffee shop discussing the passing of Jerry's Aunt Manya. They take stock of their own lives and vow not to waste any more precious time. But then they contemplate, what exactly is a "waste of time"? Does talking with friends at a coffee shop constitute a waste of time? Aren't we allowed to hang out and relax with our friends? Or should we always be doing something "productive?"

The Last Big Move

Death represents many different things for people. Religious people believe that death is just one more step in the spiritual life cycle. Whatever death *means* to people (clinical, biological, or social), it is surrounded by a complex web of rituals that serve to establish relationships between the living and the deceased.

Jerry views death as "the last big move of your life." Jerry provides his sociological view of the life cycle in the monologue of the episode "The Boyfriend (2)" (#35). Whenever someone moves, they need boxes to put their stuff in. Finding the right box for moving is critical and all-consuming. When someone is about to move they become obsessed with finding boxes. Even if you are at a funeral you look at the casket and wonder if it came in a box because that would be one great moving box. Jerry equates death to the last big move of your life: "The hearse is like the van. The pall bearers are your close friends, the only ones you could ask to help you with a big move like that. And the casket is that great perfect box you've been waiting for your whole life. The only problem is, once you find it, you're in it."

Here's hoping life is filled with many moves before the final one arrives.

Chapter 14

Sports

"Hey, You Gotta Let Them Know You're Out There —This Is the Play-Offs."—Puddy

Many people admire sports stars, and they would love to spend time with their favorite heroes discussing big games. In the episode "The Boyfriend (2)" (#35), Elaine lives Jerry's fantasy (and that of any fan of the New York Mets) by discussing game 6 of the 1986 World Series (won by the Mets) with Keith Hernandez. Jerry idolizes Hernandez. He is also jealous of Elaine's time spent with Keith, especially as she retells her evening with him.

> *Elaine*: "Uh, who else? Mookie. Mookie was there. Do you know him?"
> *Jerry*: "I don't *know* him. I know who he is."
> *Elaine*: "Hum, he's such a great guy. You should meet him. You know he's the one who got that hit—"
> *Jerry*: "I know. He got the hit in game 6. So, so then what happened?"

Jerry is like a little kid who worships a ball player and wishes to be just like one. As an adult, Jerry would be happy just to hang out with a famous ball player, especially one that he admires so much. This is fairly common of most sports fans. Sports fans invest so much emotionally (not to mention monetarily and physically) into their devotion of sports that they often become consumed by them.

Sport Sociology

I have taught a number of sociology-of-sport classes. Sport is a fascinating topic. Most sports fans think they know everything about sports, and their opinions are always the correct ones. And yet, when you ask someone to define sport they usually get a blank look on their face. Go ahead, think of a definition that fits all the parameters of sport. This definition must allow for such diverse activities as golf, football, and skateboarding to fall under one umbrella term. Classifying sports as indoors or outdoors, professional or amateur is a little easier, but still inadequate.

Jay Coakley, considered one of the leading sport sociologists, and author of *Sport in Society*, has provided the field of sport sociology with a definition that is commonly accepted and used by all sport sociologists. He defines sport as "institutionalized competitive activities that involve rigorous exertion or the use of relatively complex physical skills by participants motivated by personal enjoyment and external rewards."[18]

Sports have always implied the idea of physical activities. Therefore, chess is not considered a sport, and chess players are not athletes. Chess is more cognitive than it is physical. The mandate of physicality, as a criterion, introduces the question, "How physical must the activity be?" In other words, are billiards and pool physical enough to qualify as sports? Is golf a sport? Mark Twain once wrote that "golf is a good walk ruined." The physical skills aspect usually allows for golf being labeled a sport. However, that does not mean that all golfers are athletes.

The idea that sports are institutionalized reflects the sociological reality of sport as a social institution characterized by a number of specific processes, behavioral expectations, formal organization, and a regulatory body designed to enforce the rules of the game.

Sports are played for a combination of intrinsic and extrinsic rewards. Intrinsic rewards include such things as increased self-esteem as the result of meeting a goal, better health, and general feelings of satisfaction for accomplishing a challenge (e.g., running a marathon). Extrinsic rewards come in the form of money, medals, championships, and praise and accolades from others.

The Role of Sports in Society

Sports are as much a part of American society as are the other social institutions such as family, education, and religion. Sport is such a pervasive activity in contemporary America that to ignore it is to overlook a social phenomenon that extends into multiple social arenas, from education, economics, art, the mass media, and community, to international diplomatic relations.

It has been said that sport is a microcosm of society. That is, sport reflects the mores, values, and general culture of a society. In American culture, winning and success are highly valued, and sport often reflects this cherished win-at-all-costs mentality. This prevailing attitude often leads to elitism, sexism, nationalism, extreme competitiveness, abuse of drugs, illegal gambling, and a number of other deviant behaviors. On the other hand, the true spirit of sport often reveals itself as well. The notions of cooperation and loyalty are also revered values of American society, and that is, perhaps, the primary reason that Americans love sports as much as they do.

Loyalty is a major aspect of sport. Perhaps no other institution, except for religion, receives such a high level of loyalty than sport. The emotional attachment of some fans to their team verges on religious fanaticism. Sport, as with religion, involves commitment and passion. Among fans, some are far more passionate about their teams than others. In other words, some fans are highly identified with their favorite sport teams and others have a moderate or low level of identification with a sports team. Many fans, especially the highly identified ones, believe that they play (at least) some small part in the outcome of the game through their support and cheering of the team.

Seinfeld provides us with a perfect example of fanaticism and deep devotion and loyalty to team by its fans in "The Face Painter" (#109). In this episode, David Puddy, Elaine's boyfriend, is shown as a die-hard New Jersey Devils fan. (Note: when this episode first aired on May 11, 1995, the Devils had historically been a bad hockey team. However, they won their first NHL championship weeks after this episode aired. Realizing that this episode was taped in advance of the play-offs, it is quite interesting that the Devils would win the championship that particular year. Is this a reflection of the power of *Seinfeld*? The Yankees started winning championships again after George got a job with the Yankees. Coincidence?)

Elaine is in Puddy's living room, waiting for him to finish getting dressed for the Devils–Rangers play-off game at Madison Square Garden. They are supposed to meet Jerry and Kramer. Puddy enters the living room with his face painted in green, red, and black and Devils logos, and he is wearing a Devils' team jersey. Elaine is in shock. She did not know that he is a "face painter." Puddy informs her that he paints his face to support his team, "Hey, you gotta let them know you're out there—this is the play-offs."

Puddy answers a knock on the door. It is Kramer and Jerry who are a little taken aback by Puddy's appearance. Kramer understands Puddy's fanaticism. Puddy is outwardly showing his loyalty by wearing specific clothing and painting his face. Devout religious people also show their strong allegiance to their religion by wearing specific clothing (e.g., Orthodox Jews who wear long robes and religious hats, Islamic women who wear scarves to cover their faces) and external face paintings (e.g., Catholics who wear ashes on their foreheads on Ash Wednesday). Puddy represents the type of fan that all sports teams wish to have cheering them on.

The scene shifts to Madison Square Garden. The four of them have Alec Berg's season seats right behind the glass in the front row (for those of you not familiar with hockey, these are great seats because they are very close to the rink and you almost feel as though you are in the game). Kramer, Elaine, and Jerry are sitting in their seats in stunned disbelief by Puddy's rowdy, yet supportive, behavior. Puddy is standing and yelling at the Rangers' star player Mark Messier. He is disturbing all the other fans seated behind him. Puddy believes he is messing with the Rangers players' heads by his yelling and taunting. At this very moment, the Devils score a goal and Puddy stands up and, banging on the glass, shouts, "GO DEVILS!!"

The Devils win the game and Puddy is beyond excited. He can hardly contain himself; and he certainly feels as though he helped to contribute to the team's victory because of loyalty and commitment to the team. His self-esteem is also very high as a result of his team's performance—a common trait for the highly identified fan. Conversely, the highly identified fan will suffer an emotional letdown if the team loses. In extreme cases, the highly identified fan will go into a state of depression when his team loses.

Puddy is also experiencing what sport sociologists refer to as BIRG. BIRG stands for basking in reflected glory, a term first used by Cialdini and associates.[19] BIRGing involves identifying oneself with successful others. In sports, that would include such behaviors as wearing team apparel following a victory, reading news accounts about the victory, watching as many highlights as possible of the victory, and so on. On the other hand, Kramer, Jerry, and Elaine (although certainly not highly identified fans) are CORFing. CORF stands for cutting off reflective failure. In other words, people distance themselves from those who have failed.

Daniel Wann and Nyla R. Branscombe theorized that the extent to which allegiance to a group or team a person has will modify the effects of BIRGing and CORFing. They suspected that individuals high in identification would demonstrate a stronger tendency to BIRG in their team's success when compared to persons low in identification. The reverse was anticipated for CORFing; persons high in identification should CORF less than those low in identification.[20]

Elaine is clearly a moderate fan at best. She cannot comprehend why Puddy would paint his face. A couple of days after the game Elaine asks Jerry why a seemingly normal person would do that. Jerry replies (imitating Puddy's voice), "Gotta support the team." Elaine has such a problem with this that she threatens to break up with him. (Sports fans everywhere are thinking to themselves right now, "Dump her, Puddy!" And, non-sports fans are saying to Elaine, "You go, girl!") But Puddy offers to stop painting his face if Elaine does not break up with him. She is pleased.

Elaine has made a naive mistake. She thinks that she can change a highly identified sports fan. Speaking as a highly identified sports fan, I can guarantee you, no highly identified sports fan gives up sports for a relationship. It is the relationship that must compromise because sports fanatics will never give up their dedication to their favorite sports (and teams).

Jerry and Kramer have lost the opportunity to use Alec Berg's season tickets for the second game at the Garden (see chapter 2). Berg does, however, have a friend with two extra tickets in the "nosebleed" section. Berg informs Jerry that there is one catch attached to the free tickets (this catch is not revealed until later).

The scene shifts to Elaine's apartment where she is making out with Puddy on her couch. She unbuttons his shirt and notices something odd. Puddy has painted the letter "D" on his chest. He explains to Elaine that he is going to tonight's game with five other guys and they are going to take their shirts off and spell out "DEVILS." Elaine asks about his promise not to paint. Puddy said that he agreed to no more face painting, but body paint was different.

Elaine is disappointed that she could not change Puddy's habits. Puddy is undeterred in his dedication and commitment to supporting his favorite team. Near the end of the episode, the scene shifts back to Madison Square Garden where a shirtless Puddy is cheering for the Devils. The Devils score a goal and Puddy stands up screaming and yelling. His five friends join him in spelling out the Devils. As each fan stands they shout out their letters. Jerry is the "E" and Kramer is the "V"—the condition to their accepting the tickets from Berg.

Sport Participation

Sport represents a vital social institution in nearly all societies of the world. Sporting events often become the focal point within communities. Millions of people are consumed with sport and leisure activities and pursuits. Sport has a way of uniting people (and dividing people) within communities (and societies). Many communities host events such as 5K or 10K charity races. This is a wonderful opportunity for people to gather together, centered on a healthy, physical endeavor. On the other hand, some members of the community will complain because they are temporarily inconvenienced by the traffic restraints of a small number of street closings.

For many sport fans, watching a ball game simply represents a chance to unwind from the stress of daily life. If the preferred team wins then it was time well spent. Watching a sporting event with friends provides an opportunity for bonding. Thus, one of the primary roles of sport is that it serves as a diversion from everyday events. And for that reason, many sport sociologists have amended Karl Marx's statement (see chapter 11) that "religion is the opiate of the masses" to "sport is the opiate of the masses."

Let's face it, for a large number of people, sports are more fun than most other activities that they participate in (of course, there are a few exceptions). However, participating in sports is actually productive and provides opportunities to exercise. Exercise, in turn, improves one's health. With that in mind, many people join health and fitness centers. Most people who join health clubs do so for intrinsic purposes: they want to improve their health, they want to increase their self-esteem, they want to look better, and, sometimes, they want to meet other people who act and look healthy.

Not everyone's experience with sports and physical fitness is positive. Some youths burn out from sports by the time they are in high school. This usually happens when they were pushed into sports by parents who wish to live vicariously through their children's sporting accomplishments. Some youths are turned off from sports because they were not good at them. Anyone can play sports, it is a matter of personal dedication, support from primary group members, and good coaches and physical education instructors.

It is hard to imagine why people would want to be a school physical education teacher unless they really want to help youths. They are responsible for stimulating youths into participating in healthy activities. Phys Ed instructors and coaches are also responsible for protecting youths who are picked on by other kids in gym class and on sports teams.

Despite George's love for sports, he did not receive the proper nurturing into a healthy lifestyle in his gym classes. In fact, his high school gym teacher, Mr. Heyman, was another agent of socialization that failed George. (Remember it was suggested in chapter 10 that George's parents did a poor job raising him.) We learn of George's nightmarish experience with his gym teacher in the episode "The Library" (#22).

In this episode, Jerry is at the New York City Library to pay a fine for a book (*Tropic of Cancer*) that he took out in 1971. Kramer has tagged along with Jerry, and George is about to join them. When George arrives at the front desk he anxiously tugs at Jerry's jacket to get his attention. George thinks that the homeless guy on the library steps screaming obscenities and doing some calisthenics is their old gym teacher from high school. He was covered in filth but still has his whistle. Kramer asks about Heyman and Jerry tells him a story of how George got Heyman fired because of an incident.

The "incident" is not revealed until the friends are back at Jerry's apartment. George first tells the group how the gym teacher purposely mispronounced his name. Instead of saying, "Costanza," Heyman would say, "Can't stand ya! Can't stand ya!" Heyman even made George smell his own dirty gym socks. But the worst thing of all was the abuse that George had to endure. The gym teacher used to lead George's classmates in giving George a wedgie. George told the school principal about the incident, and Heyman was fired. Elaine had not heard of wedgies before. Jerry explains that there is such a thing as "atomic wedgies" as well. An atomic wedgie is accomplished when the waistband is pulled all the way on top of the head of the victim.

Later in the episode, George confronts the homeless man to find out if he really is George's old tormentor from high school (this scene is retold by George to Elaine and Jerry; the audience does not see it). And after some prompting (George says to the homeless man, "Can't stand ya! Can't stand ya!") George finds out the hard way that the homeless man is, indeed, Heyman. Heyman looks up at George and as George tries to leave the library steps Heyman gives George a wedgie—an atomic wedgie. As part of another sidebar, it was Heyman who stole the *Tropic of Cancer* that Jerry had to pay the fine on. Jerry had lent the book to George back in high school on the day of the "incident." And while George went and complained about the wedgie, Heyman took the book, which was right on the steps of the library.

Traditional Sports

Sport participation instills a number of valuable life lessons for participants of all ages, but especially for youths. Many life lessons can be learned on the playing field including the development of team work, the value of dedication and commitment to a task at hand, hard work equating to success, and the transmission of culture (values and norms).

The socialization process is easily illustrated within the sports world. George H. Mead and Jean Piaget are the foremost authorities who have recognized the social value of play and game participation. Mead used baseball to explain how the child in the "play stage" learns to take the role of the other, and in the "game stage" learns to integrate his actions into a network of organized activities. They learn the role of the others. Collectively, the roles of all the members of society are referred to as the generalized other by Mead. The generalized other is represented as community.[21]

Throughout the *Seinfeld* series a great deal of attention is given to a number of specific sports. Jerry is certainly the best athlete of the group, although they all play sports as adults. Attention is now shifted toward a number of specific sports that the regular characters participate in.

Running

Who wouldn't want to be able to run "faster than a speeding bullet" like Superman? Jerry would certainly love to be Superman. In the vast majority of the *Seinfeld* episodes there is some reference to or reminder of Jerry's admiration of Superman. And if Jerry wants to be like Superman, he should date a woman named Lois. Well, all of these elements come into play in the episode "The Race" (#96). Jerry is at his new girlfriend's office. Her name is Lois. He loves saying her name.

Lois introduces her boss, Duncan Meyers, to Jerry as he passes by her office. Duncan and Jerry went to high school together. Duncan does not like Jerry because of an incident in high school. Later in the day Jerry admits to Elaine something that only George knows about—Jerry cheated in a (running) race in ninth grade. He jumped the gun, and only George noticed. Jerry won the race by a landslide (as if he were Superman). Jerry gained such a reputation as a fast runner that a myth began to grow about his speed. But Duncan always suspected something was amiss and he has hated Jerry ever since. Jerry always refused a rematch with Duncan, and it has festered with him since high school.

Now that Jerry has reemerged in Duncan's life, he seeks revenge. Duncan puts pressure on Lois to make Jerry run in a rematch. He even threatens to fire her if Jerry does not admit to Lois that he cheated in the high school race. Feeling pressure from Lois as well, Jerry reluctantly agrees to the rematch.

The day of the race arrives and Jerry is very nervous. Duncan warns Lois that she is about to find out that Jerry is a liar. Lois demands a pay raise if Jerry wins the race. Duncan offers to give her both a raise and a paid vacation to Hawaii if Jerry beats him. The scene is set. Jerry and Duncan are lined up next to each other at the starting line (they have blocked off part of a street). Mr. Bevilacqua, one of Jerry and Duncan's old gym teachers, shows up for the race to control the start of it. He reviews the commands. When the gun fires the runners are to start the race. Mr. Bevilacqua raises his gun. Nearby, Kramer enters his car. As Mr. Bevilacqua shouts out, "Ready —on your mark—" Kramer's car backfires. Jerry takes off running. Duncan hesitates because the starter's pistol has not gone off. The crowd cheers. They think the gun went off. Duncan starts running but Jerry is so far ahead he wins easily. The crowd goes crazy. Lois asks Jerry to join her on the Hawaiian vacation. Jerry tells Lois he has to think about it and then winks at the camera like in the *Superman* movie. Duncan argues with Mr. Bevilacqua but to no avail. Jerry's mythical status as an extremely fast runner lives on.

The New York Marathon is the subject of two *Seinfeld* episodes. In "The Apartment" (#10), Elaine's friend, Roxanne, has an apartment right above First Avenue, which has a perfect view of the race. Elaine was told to invite friends along for a marathon party at Roxanne's place. Jerry and George accept Elaine's invitation. Roxanne tells Jerry how much she loves the marathon. Her only regret is that she does not have a view of the finish line. Jerry does not possess the same "spirit" of the marathon as Roxanne. He quips, "What's to see? A woman from Norway, a guy from Kenya, and twenty thousand losers."

Roxanne is not happy with Jerry's comment; she makes a face at him and walks away. She later yells out encouragement to the runners telling them that they are all winners. Certainly from one perspective, anyone who completes a marathon is a winner.

Of course, in competition one winner is always declared. In the Olympics the winner is awarded a gold medal—a symbol of highest achievement. In the opening monologue of "The Hot Tub" (#115), Jerry expresses his sympathy for the losers in the Olympics, especially the second-place finisher. Jerry wonders how anyone goes on with the rest of their lives knowing that all the hard work and training they endured led to a second-place finish. So close, and yet, so far.

As difficult as it must be to settle for second place in the Olympics, imagine an athlete's horror if they miss the race because he overslept. In the episode "The Hot Tub," Elaine plays host to such an athlete, Jean-Paul. Jean-Paul is in New York to run in the marathon. Elaine met Jean-Paul when she worked at Pendant Publishing while editing a book on running. Jean-Paul is a Tobaggan from Trinidad. He overslept at the last Olympics and missed the marathon. Obviously, he was devastated. The New York Marathon is his big comeback, and Elaine is in charge of getting him to the race on time. Jerry does not think that Elaine can handle the responsibility.

After a series of mishaps, Jerry takes responsibility for Jean-Paul from Elaine. He is worried about her clock and her overall ability to get him to the race on time. A series of hilarious mishaps also occur with Jerry that leads to Jean-Paul oversleeping again! But, Jerry gets him to the race just as it starts. The story has a happy ending as Jean-Paul wins.

In the episode "The Sponge" (#119), Kramer is participating in a charity walk to benefit the fight against AIDS. Kramer does not want to wear the AIDS ribbon during the walk-a-thon. He believes that some people just wear the ribbon to ease their own conscience, whereas he "walks the walk." The day of the charity event Kramer is told by the organizer working the sign-in desk that he must wear the ribbon. Kramer calls the woman a "ribbon bully." As Kramer begins his walk, he is harassed by the rest of the walkers for not wearing his ribbon. Kramer insists that in America, people don't have to wear anything they don't want to wear. Kramer is angrily confronted by two walkers—the same two guys that mugged him of Elaine's armoire in "The Soup Nazi" episode—who encourage others to join in on beating up Kramer for not wearing the ribbon. Kramer is the last one to cross the finish line. He literally crawls on the street but does not receive any sympathy from George and Jerry because they think Kramer finished last because of his all night poker game that ended mere hours before the start of the walk-a-thon. Adding salt to the wound, George asks Kramer why he is not wearing an AIDS ribbon.

Softball and Baseball

Jerry loves sports. He especially likes to play softball. In the episode "The Pony Remark" (#7), Jerry returns to his apartment after a softball game. His parents are visiting from Florida. We learn just how important softball is to Jerry when he explains the importance of a big play he made in his softball game. Jerry threw out a runner from left field who was trying to reach third base on a tag-up. Because of that play his team has advanced to the championship game. Jerry tells his parents it was the "single greatest moment of my life." Jerry's mother cannot believe that his greatest moment was a game. Jerry admits that actually his greatest achievement was a former girlfriend, Sharon Besser.

Well, after all, no matter how much Jerry loves sports, his top priority has always been women. But this game did qualify his team for the championship game of his league and he was really looking forward to it. Unfortunately (as described in chapter 13), Jerry's Aunt Manya dies in this episode and the funeral is scheduled for the same day and time as the big game. Jerry has a dilemma. Should he uphold his family responsibility to attend the funeral, or does he play in the biggest game of his life? Jerry discusses this matter with his mother who just got off the phone discussing the funeral arrangements. Helen tells Jerry that the funeral is going to be held on Wednesday, the same day of the championship game. Jerry, looking for a way out, tries to explain to his mother that he barely knew Manya. Helen tells Jerry that he is not obligated to attend the funeral and should go play in his game.

Jerry, however, decides to attend the funeral. He believes it is the right thing to do. He is really happy that he did the right thing when it starts to rain during the funeral, which means that the championship game would be postponed. Unfortunately for Jerry, the "karma gods" do not shine upon him as he has the worse game of his life during the rescheduled championship game. George and Elaine suggest to Jerry that maybe the "spirit world" had something to do with his poor play. Meaning, maybe Manya put a hex on Jerry for inadvertently causing her death by his "pony remark."

The sport of baseball is discussed frequently in *Seinfeld*; mostly in conjunction with George's position of assistant to the traveling secretary for the New York Yankees. In the episode "The Chaperone" (#87), George is responsible for changing the Yankees uniform from polyester to cotton. His theory is that the players would be cooler and consequently would not sweat so much during hot summer games. As a result, their performances will increase, resulting in more victories. The players love the change of uniforms and compliment George for his role in the switch. George's plan backfires because the uniforms shrink in the wash making it difficult for the players to run. Yankee captain Don Mattingly even splits his pants.

In the episode "The Abstinence" (#34), George must refrain from having sex with his girlfriend because she has mononucleosis. Faced with the reality that he has a girlfriend, but no chance of having sex, George puts his mind to pursuits other than wanting ways of "getting some." He gradually becomes more intelligent—because he is no longer focusing on sex. He learns to speak Portuguese and solves mathematical problems. Soon, his focus turns to the mechanics, or science, of baseball. George attempts to explain the science of hitting a ball to two Yankee standouts, Derek Jeter and Bernie Williams during batting practice at Yankee Stadium.

> *George*: "Guys, hitting is not about muscle. It's simple physics.
> Calculate the velocity, 'V,' in relation to the trajectory, 'T,'
> in which 'G,' gravity, of course remains a constant."

(George demonstrates and promptly hits a homerun.)
"It's not complicated."

Jeter: "Now, who are you again?"

George: "George Costanza, assistant to the traveling secretary."

Williams: "Are you the guy who put us in that Ramada in Milwaukee?"

George: "Do you wanna talk about hotels, or do you wanna win some ball games?"

Jeter: "We won the World Series."

George (gives a look that indicates he is less than impressed): "In six games."

By the end of this episode, George has sex (not with his girlfriend, but with a Portuguese waitress), and reverts to his "normal" intellectual self.

Baseball seating etiquette is discussed in "The Letter" (#38). In the opening monologue, Jerry asks if anyone has ever tried to sneak better seats at a ballgame, only to be thrown out by the rightful ticket-holder. Jerry says it is okay as a kid, because kids are used to getting chased out of the way. But as an adult, it is kind of embarrassing and therefore adults go into a big act and pretend that it is some big misunderstanding. Adults will look at their tickets and wonder "How can this be?" when all the while they know that their seats are not as good.

In one of the skits of "The Letter," Elaine, George, and Kramer are the beneficiaries of Yankee owner box seats via Jerry's girlfriend, Nina. (Nina's father, Leonard West, is the accountant for the Yankees.) Elaine, who grew up outside Baltimore, is wearing an Orioles cap to the game. Mr. West asks the trio if they like the seats. He then makes a rather odd request of Elaine; he wants her to remove her cap. Elaine, assuming West is just teasing her because the Orioles are not playing well, says, "Yeah, I better." As it turns out, West is serious and insists that Elaine remove her cap. West thinks that since he gave the trio the seats it is a bad reflection on him that someone is wearing apparel of the opposing team in the Yankee owner box seats. Elaine, justifiably so, angrily responds that in America, she has the right to wear a cap at a ballgame if she wants. West motions for a couple of ushers to remove Elaine from the game. A minor scuffle ensues and Elaine's hat lands on top of the dugout. As Elaine is being escorted out of the stadium Kramer retrieves her cap. He is promptly hit in the head with a foul ball, knocking him out.

A great number of people believe that athletes get away with certain deviant and illegal behavior simply because of their status as athletes. In the episode "The Boyfriend (2)" (#35), Elaine is dating former baseball great Keith Hernandez. At the end of their first date, Keith and Elaine are sitting in his car. This scene is reminiscent of the awkwardness that most couples have at the end of the first date. Should there be a kiss? Who initiates the kiss? What type, and how long of a kiss? Keith and Elaine make small talk all the while we hear what they are thinking.

> *Keith*: "Maybe we should get together." (In his mind: "Go ahead. Kiss her. I'm a baseball player, dammit.")
> *Elaine* (in her mind): "What's he waiting for? I thought he was a cool guy."
> *Keith* (in his mind): "Come on, I won the MVP in '79. I can do whatever I want to."
> *Elaine* (in her mind): "This is getting awkward."
> *Keith*: "Well, good night."
> *Elaine*: "Good night."

(Keith leans over and starts kissing Elaine—a very long passionate kiss.)

> *Elaine* (in her mind and highly impressed with the kiss): "Who does this guy think he is?"
> *Keith* (in his mind and pleased with his own performance): "I'm Keith Hernandez."

This scene reflects the common beliefs that ball players are "cool" and they feel that they can get away with things because they are ball players.

Of interest to sport sociologists is the phenomenon of adults who participate in fantasy baseball camps. Fantasy baseball camps are designed to provide adults an opportunity to play ball with some of their favorite old-time baseball players. Most camps last a couple of weeks. The participants go through a mock training period and then play ball with ex-baseball players. The fantasy participants pay quite a bit of money to escape their normal lives and live out a fantasy.

In the episode "The Visa" (#55), Kramer is at a baseball fantasy camp. The very idea of this puzzles George because he thinks Kramer's whole life is a fantasy camp (Kramer does nothing, falls into money, eats for free off his neighbor, and has sex with a number of beautiful women) and that people should pay to live his life.

Interestingly, there are now Internet-based "fantasy leagues" for most of the major team sports where participants "draft" real players and form their own teams. In other words, participants are acting like general managers/owners. The real-life statistics of the players "drafted" are used to determine winners and losers in the fantasy leagues. In that manner, fantasy teams can win and lose based on real-life players. Internet fantasy leagues have great sociological significance. For starters, why would people waste their time in a fantasy world? Shouldn't they be working or doing something productive? And imagine how poorly one must feel if they are losers in their fantasy worlds. I know that in my fantasy world (admit it, we all have one) I always end up a winner—and I wind up with Christina Applegate! Why crush the fantasy world by losing in fantasy sports? And because it is a fantasy world, the "winner" has not actually won anything outside the context of the fantasy world. Although it is true that fantasy sport league winners may be rewarded with real-life monetary rewards. Still, the victory is hollow nonetheless because it was gained in a make-believe world.

Basketball

In the episode "The Boyfriend (1)" (#34), George, Kramer, and Jerry have just finished playing basketball and are now in the locker room. George is complaining because they never threw the ball to him. George wants to know why they don't pass him the ball. Kramer and Jerry look at each other, as people do that share information on another person. Jerry hesitates but Kramer proceeds to provide the answer why no one throws him the ball; George is a "chucker." This comes as news to George—he did not know why that after all these years of playing hoops together no one ever told him this.

A chucker is someone who takes a shot at the basket as soon as he or she is thrown the ball. Generally, chuckers are not good ball players, because if they made the shots they took, they wouldn't be a chucker, they'd be a scorer. Even Keith Hernandez calls George a chucker in the locker room (this is the first scene where Keith Hernandez appears in this two-part episode) after George makes a very insensitive comment about the increased probability of a plane crash involving ball players. George reasons that with all the teams and all the travel involved by professional sports teams, you'd think eventually a plane would go down, killing an entire team.

Tennis

In the episode "The Lip Reader" (#70), the sport of tennis is the focus of attention. In the opening monologue, Jerry, more or less, mocks the sport and especially the scoring system:

> Professional tennis. To me, I don't understand all the shushing. Why are they always shushing? Shhh, shhh. Don't the players know that we're there? Should we duck down behind the seats so they don't see us watching them? Tennis is basically just ping-pong and the players are standing on the table. That's all it is. And that goofy scoring, you win one point and all of a sudden you're up by 15. Two points, 30-love. 30-love. Sounds like an English call girl. "That'll be 30, love. And could you be a little quieter next time, please? Shhh."

In this episode, Jerry does find one thing that he really likes about tennis: the lineswoman at a tennis match that he and George are attending. Jerry is infatuated with her. At the end of the match, Jerry tries to get her attention while she picks up her gear, but she just ignores him. Jerry, getting upset, mockingly asks whether she is deaf. He feels that she is disrespecting him by ignoring him. Eventually, the lineswoman turns and notices Jerry talking to her. Reading his lips, Laura informs Jerry that she *is* deaf. Jerry apologizes to her, and they start to date.

Kramer, meanwhile, informs Jerry that it is a dream of his to be a ball boy and asks Jerry if he would say something to Laura about helping him get a tryout as a ball boy. Jerry refuses initially because, after all, Kramer is not a boy, but a grown adult. Nonetheless, Kramer wants to be a ball boy. With Laura's help, Kramer secures a tryout and wins a spot. The "ball man" experiment fails miserably. During a tennis match Kramer runs after a loose ball and runs into one of the players, Monica Seles, knocking her down to the ground in pain. (In real life, when this episode first aired in 1993, Seles was just beginning her tennis comeback after an on-the-court stabbing by a fan of rival Steffi Graf. The woman playing Seles in "The Lip Reader" episode fell to the ground in a similar manner as the Seles stabbing.)

Jerry plays tennis in "The Comeback" (#147). In this episode, Jerry enters the pro shop of the New York Health and Racquet Club carrying his gear and looking to purchase tennis balls. Milos, the counter person, mocks Jerry's tennis racquet. Jerry is a little taken aback by having his racquet insulted, but he allows Milos to talk him into buying a new racquet. Jerry reasons that if a pro shop owner recommends a particular racquet it must be good. Jerry changes his mind later, however, when he observes Milos playing tennis. Milos is terrible, and that is a generous review of his tennis skills. Jerry now feels like he got ripped off. He took the word of a professional, but the professional is incompetent. Jerry wants his money back and threatens to reveal his secret. To keep Jerry quiet, Milos offers him a one-year free membership.

Jerry is happy about this seemingly positive change of events. Milos leaves the counter area of the pro shop to talk to someone. He returns and apologetically says that he is sorry, but management has refused his attempt to give Jerry a free one-year membership extension. Milos offers Jerry a refund, but Jerry is more concerned by the fact that he feels as though he "was taken in by the worst tennis player" he ever saw. In a storyline twist more appropriate for the chapter on deviance, Milos "offers" Jerry his wife for an evening of sex to keep him quiet. Milos sends his wife to Jerry's apartment, but she breaks down and cannot go through with it.

In the episode "The Switch" (#97), we find out that both Elaine and Newman are really good tennis players. In this episode Jerry jokes with his girlfriend, "Next time, let's play ping pong. It's easier to jump over the net." This joke parallels the monologue from "The Lip Reader" when Jerry says that tennis is just people playing ping pong while standing on the table.

Golf

Golf, like tennis, is another one of those peculiar sports where the players demand silence from the audience. Fans of football, baseball, basketball, and so on are greatly amused by this etiquette demand. Imagine expecting a crowd in a basketball game not to scream and yell at an opposing team's player as he or she attempts a free throw. Golf should borrow basketball's twenty-four-second clock as a time limit for golfers to line up a shot. But golf has enough problems with the rules that it has; and golfers are very strict about enforcing them. Kramer provides a perfect illustration of the importance of rules in golf in the episode "The Big Salad" (#88). Kramer, carrying his golf clubs, enters Jerry's apartment. Elaine is also there.

Kramer complains that his playing partner, Steve Gendason, a former baseball player, cheated while they played golf. Kramer met Gendason years earlier and they have played a lot together ever since. But today, on the fifteenth hole, as he was about to hit his second shot, Gendason picks up his ball and cleans it. Elaine does not understand the problem. Kramer emphatically points out that the rules clearly state that you cannot clean the ball unless it's on the green. Kramer is a stickler for golf etiquette and rules, so he penalized Steve a stroke. Steve was very upset and almost gets into a fight with Kramer over the penalty. Elaine still does not understand the significance. But Kramer insists that a rule is a rule and without rules, there's chaos.

As any enthusiast would, Kramer takes his golf seriously. In fact, there was a time when Kramer was getting so good at golf, he thought about turning professional. In the episode "The Caddy" (#122), Kramer is receiving invaluable input from Stan, the caddy. Even though the golf courses are not open for the season yet, Stan has been sneaking Kramer onto one through the caddie's entrance. Stan's advice has transformed Kramer's game. Stan is so impressed with Kramer's game that he thinks Kramer might make it big on the senior tour. Golfing on the senior tour is now Kramer's dream.

Kramer's golf game is fantastic. Stan the caddy is giving him dead-on accurate advice on everything from clothing advice (how to dress appropriately for various weather conditions) to working with him on his swing. Kramer's dream is shattered when he injures himself in a car accident. The accident occurs while Kramer is driving his car (Jerry is his passenger) and becomes distracted by a woman wearing only a bra for a top (Elaine's friend, Sue Ellen Mishke).

Surfing

One of the most neglected subcultural groups that have undergone extensive sociological research is surfers. Many years ago, as a graduate student in Los Angeles, I wrote a paper on surfers and their subculture. Surfers have a very distinctive style of their own. They have their own clothing fashions, mannerisms, norms, customs that govern the waves, and a unique language. So, let's get stoked (excited) about duck-diving (while paddling out, the technique of submerging the surfboard under oncoming waves) on filthy (flawless) waves, and hope there aren't too many Barneys (clueless surfers), grommets (young surfers) or kooks (inexperienced surfers) in the lineup (the area where surfers linger for waves).

The regular characters do not surf; Elaine and Kramer swam the Hudson River, and they all went to the Hamptons, but none of them ever surfed. However, in the episode "The Hamptons" (#85), Jerry does reference surfing in a rather humorous manner in the opening monologue:

> Look at the work people do to get to the ocean. They'll fight the traffic and the heat and the parking and the hot sand. Trying to get through the waves and the ironic thing is the ocean doesn't even want us in there. That's what surfing is. Surfing is the ocean throwing us out of itself, you see? We keep trying to paddle in, the ocean's saying, "No you don't." The ocean is like a nightclub and the waves are bouncers tossing us out. The undertow's like a really mean bouncer. Instead of throwing you out, they take you back in and rough you up a little bit. "Oh, you wanna come in? How about coming in like twenty-five miles?"

Alternatives to Traditional Sports

Many youths are not into traditional sports. They are either intimidated by the competitive nature of organized sports, they are not talented enough to compete, they lack the sort of training and preparation necessary to play, or they simply do not find them interesting. There's also a sad reality that many youths that participate in organized youth sports beginning at a young age get burned out by the time they reach high school.

Although traditional sports, which are usually team-oriented (especially for youths), have historically dominated American culture, the past decade has witnessed a tremendous increase in the development of individualistic, nontraditional sports. Individual sports and recreation such as windsurfing, jogging, and aerobics represent an extension of the consumer culture that expresses individualism in sport participation and consumption. Many youths today participate in skateboarding, an individual sport that can be played with others (just as the previously mentioned sports may be played with others).

With the growth of power and influence of such cable sports networks as ESPN, the public is bombarded with a seemingly neverending barrage of sporting events. And yet, with all the traditional sports that exist in society, both nationally and internationally, ESPN has been instrumental in spearheading the growth of nontraditional sports in the form of X-Games. X-Games refer to extreme sports like rock climbing, bungee jumping, snowboarding, and so on, all of which are designed primarily as individualistic sports.

It is important to note that a number of nontraditional team sports have also developed in recent years. Indoor soccer, indoor lacrosse, and arena football are just a few examples of alternatives to traditional sports.

Seinfeld does not pay a lot of attention to nontraditional sports, but there is one episode of special note—"The Stall" (#76). In the opening monologue of this episode, Jerry discusses skydiving. He questions why anyone bothers with the helmet asking, "Can you *almost* make it?" He suggests that people might just as well wear a party hat because if you're jumping out of a plane at twenty thousand feet and the chute does not open, "The helmet is now wearing you for protection."

In this same episode, Elaine is dating an extreme guy named Tony. Tony is a thrillseeker. Traditional sports do not stimulate Tony; he needs real, life-threatening danger. For example, while on a date with Elaine at the movies, Tony asks Elaine if she thinks he would hurt himself jumping off the balcony of the theater. Jerry refers to Tony as a mimbo—a male bimbo. George is mesmerized by Tony's tales of hijinks and thrilling encounters. Kramer teases George that he has a crush on Tony.

George will do anything to be Tony's sidekick and agrees to go rock climbing with him. (George had suggested to Tony that they go bowling, because that was "wild stuff.") George is upset when Kramer tags along for the rock climbing. George wanted to be alone with Tony, like best buds, not in the manner in which Jerry and Kramer are teasing him. George can barely get by on firm ground; linked by ropes on the side of a huge rock is just asking for trouble. The predictable occurs, George messes up (he fails to tie and knot the rope to protect Tony during his climb) and Tony falls an indeterminate number of feet. He lands hard on a rock and is immediately rushed to the hospital. Tony survives. However, George is heartbroken when he tries to apologize to Tony and Tony says to him, "Step off, George." ("Step off" is Tony's "cool" term that George admired so much.) George looks like a kid who just lost his best friend.

A final thought on sports and leisure. Individuals are best advised to eat right and exercise regularly. Eating healthy and staying fit should be a lifelong pursuit taken in proper perspective. Working out for short periods of time, say, as a result of a New Year's Eve resolution, and dieting sporadically are not the best ways to stay healthy. People should work out for the benefit of their overall health, not as if they are preparing for a tryout with the Cleveland Browns.

Jerry shares his views about working out in a monologue in the episode "The Boyfriend (1)" (#34). Jerry notes that people are not getting in shape for anything specific. Instead, "we get in shape to work out."

Chapter 15

The Finale

"Yada, Yada, Yada."—George

There's an old saying that all good things must come to an end. For the legions of *Seinfeld* fans this reality took place on May 14, 1998, when the last original episode aired on television. The series finale was watched by 76.3 million viewers that evening—the third-highest figure for a series finale in the history of television. Only *M*A*S*H** (with 105.4 million viewers in 1983) and *Cheers* (80.4 million in 1993) attracted larger audiences.

The *Seinfeld* series conclusion was actually a two-part retrospective of the nine-year run of the show. Initially, most *Seinfeld* fans were disappointed with the ending, as it did not provide anything "new." On the other hand, the audience was given the chance to reacquaint itself with nearly all the characters that ever made an appearance on the show. It was quite the going-away bash, all things considered.

The main plot line of the two-part finale was previously discussed (see chapter 8), but in brief, the four main characters are arrested for violating the Good Samaritan Law of Latham, Massachusetts. The presiding judge at the Fourth District County Court of Latham, Massachusetts, was Arthur Vandelay. The significance of this name (Art Vandelay) goes beyond the fact that it was first used in "The Stakeout" (#2) by George and Jerry in reference to a fictitious friend who was an importer/exporter; it revealed the fact that perhaps the show had run its course.

Jerry Seinfeld and the other decision makers on the show must have realized this as well, for once again, *Seinfeld* mastered presenting the obvious in a humorous manner. I say this because, not only was the use of Judge Art Vandelay a reference to the series premiere episode ("The Stakeout"), the ending dialogue between the four characters—just before their incarceration—is a reference to the show's pilot episode, "The Seinfeld Chronicles." In "The Finale (2)" (#180) Jerry, George, Kramer, and Elaine are contemplating their impending one-year imprisonment. As usual, they are making small talk about everyday life events.

> *Jerry*: "See now, to me, that button is in the worst possible spot."
> *George*: "Really?"
> *Jerry*: "Oh yeah. The second button is the key button. It literally makes or breaks the shirt. Look at it, it's too high, it's in no-man's land."
> *George*: "Haven't we had this conversation before?"
> *Jerry*: "You think?"
> *George*: "I think we have."
> *Jerry*: "Yeah, maybe we have."

Jerry and George have, in fact, had that conversation before. In "The Seinfeld Chronicles" (#1), Jerry and George are at Pete's luncheonette sitting at a table.

> *Jerry*: "Seems to me, that button is in the worst possible spot. The second button literally makes or breaks the shirt, look at it: It's too high! It's in no-man's land, you know, like you live with your mother."
> *George* (a little upset): "Are you through?"
> *Jerry*: "You do, of course, try on when you buy?"
> *George*: "Yes, it was purple, I liked it, I don't actually recall considering the buttons."

George and Jerry have come full circle. They have indeed left off (in "The Finale [2]") where they had started (in "The Seinfeld Chronicles"). For the real-life Jerry Seinfeld it was time to move on.

There are a number of parallels between *Seinfeld* and sociology that are reflected in "The Finale" episodes. Sociologists also tend to repeat themselves. A number of studies are conducted on the same subject area over a period of time and by a variety of sociologists.

However, as with *Seinfeld*, there inevitably comes a point when it becomes necessary for sociologists to move on to the next subject area (or the next chapter of life). The return of the guest stars to the series finale of *Seinfeld* was very clever and symbolic of the fact that all of our lives are a product of the social interactions that we have had with others over a lifetime. In the case of the four main characters, a great number of people felt that they were negatively impacted. Every one of us can take stock of our own lives and ascertain whether or not we have had a positive or negative impact on the lives of the people we have come in contact with.

For the millions and millions of *Seinfeld* fans, our lives have become a little bit better and a little less stressful because of the comedic genius of Jerry Seinfeld and cocreator Larry David. And yet, there seems to be a void. Fans of *Seinfeld* seem to need more. We were teased by the manner in which the show ended, for the one-year sentence levied by Judge Vandelay presented a ray of hope that maybe, just maybe, Jerry Seinfeld, cast and crew, would opt to come back after a one-year hiatus. We all hoped for that "Yada, Yada, Yada" principle to kick in.

The "Yada, Yada, Yada" principle is introduced in the episode "The Yada, Yada" (#153). George's girlfriend Marcy has a very succinct way of talking. She begins a story, throws in a yada, yada, yada as a means of skipping over the details, and then proceeds to the end of the story. The dialogue between Jerry, George, and Marcy (while having lunch at Monk's coffee shop) illustrates the usage of the yada, yada, yada.

> *Marcy*: "You know, a friend of mine thought she got Legionnaire's disease in the hot tub."
> *George*: "Really? What happened?"
> *Marcy*: "Oh, yada, yada, yada, just some bad egg salad. I'll be right back." (She gets up and heads toward the restroom.)
> *Jerry*: "I noticed she's big on the phrase 'Yada, yada.'"
> *George*: "Is 'yada, yada' bad?"
> *Jerry*: "No, 'Yada, yada' is good. She's very succinct."
> *George*: "She is succinct."
> *Jerry*: "Yeah, it's like you're dating the *USA Today*."

This succinct approach to life has its advantages and disadvantages. The major plus of the yada, yada, yada approach to storytelling is the fact that usually, we don't want to hear a long, drawn-out story filled with every little detail. For example, when someone has a baby the mother may want to provide "24-7" details when, clearly, the yada, yada, yada approach is more than adequate. "The baby woke up, did something cute, yada, yada, yada, we were all tired by the end of the day"—that seems to be enough information!

George sees many advantages of the yada, yada. For example, when Marcy asks George if he is close to his parents he clearly does not want to get into a long discussion about them, so he simply replies, "Well, they gave birth to me, and yada, yada, yada." In another conversation between Marcy and George, Marcy asks about Susan. George replies, "Well, we were engaged to be married, uh, we bought the wedding invitations, and, uh, yada, yada, yada, I'm still single."

However, there are times when someone uses the "yada, yada, yada" approach and you really wish that you knew the whole story. (That is, unless you prefer living in a world of denial.) For example, Marcy says to George, "Speaking of ex's, my old boyfriend came over late last night, and, yada, yada, yada. Anyway, I'm really tired today." George has no idea what the yada, yada, yada represents, but he thinks the worst, of course. He assumes that she yada, yada, yada'd sex.

The yada, yada, yada is what sociology is all about: the details. Sociologists examine the everyday world and the everyday life events, from the mundane (e.g., conversations between members of a group) to the complicated (e.g., examination of socio-political-economic social systems). Some of the material covered by sociologists is a little boring because some aspects of life are boring. On the other hand, a great deal of the material covered by sociologists is fascinating and exciting because life, if you choose to live it to its fullest, can be very stimulating and invigorating. The fact that sociology finds the topic of *Seinfeld* a worthwhile subject area should endear it (at least a little) to the millions of *Seinfeld* fans around the world.

Seinology is also an attempt to show the relevancy of *Seinfeld* to the field of sociology. As the preceding chapters demonstrate, nearly any topic discussed by *Seinfeld* is of sociological interest. It would be pointless to review all sociological principles illustrated in the show here because that would be repetitive, and this is not a summary chapter. However, it should be clear that *Seinfeld* has greatly influenced American culture. In 2004, the "puffy shirt" worn by Jerry Seinfeld went on display at the Smithsonian Institution, alongside Kermit the Frog, Archie Bunker's chair, and Dorothy's magic slippers from *The Wizard of Oz*.

The puffy shirt was an odd choice to memorialize *Seinfeld* at the Smithsonian, but then again, considering that *Seinfeld* is best known for its dialogue and story lines, there are few tangible relics suitable for enshrinement.

Yada, yada, yada refers to the gap of a story. When *Seinfeld* went off the air, fans were left with a big gap in their lives. We still watch reruns of *Seinfeld* religiously on television and look for other materials to fill the *Seinfeld* void. *Seinology: The Sociology of Seinfeld* is an attempt to help fill the void between original episodes of *Seinfeld* and Jerry Seinfeld's next project. Furthermore, the sociological analysis presented in *Seinology* clearly reveals that *Seinfeld* is much more than an entertaining show about nothing. It is a show about everything.

Notes

1. "Together Again? Get Out!" *TV Guide*, November 21–27, 2004, p. 36.

2. John Farley, *Sociology*, 4th ed. (Upper Saddle River, NJ: Prentice Hall, 1998), p. 64.

3. Richard T. Schaefer, *Sociology: A Brief Introduction* (Boston: McGraw Hill, 2004), p. 58.

4. Diana Kendall, *Sociology in Our Times*, 4th ed. (Belmont, CA: Wadsworth, 2004), p. 50.

5. John J. Macionis, *Society: The Basics*, 7th ed. (Upper Saddle River, NJ: Prentice Hall, 2004) p. 61.

6. Schaefer, *Sociology*, p. 73.

7. Tim Delaney, *Classical Social Theory: Investigation and Application* (Upper Saddle River, NJ: Prentice Hall, 2004).

8. George Herbert Mead, *Mind, Self, and Society*, ed. Charles W. Morris (Chicago: University of Chicago Press, 1934).

9. Erving Goffman, *Presentation of Self in Everyday Life* (Garden City, NY: Anchor, 1959).

10. Farley, *Sociology*.

11. Delaney, *Classical Social Theory*, p. 158.

12. Ibid.

13. Alfred R. Lindersmith, Anselm L. Strauss, and Norman K. Denzin, *Social Psychology*, 7th ed. (Englewood Cliffs, NJ: Prentice Hall, 1991).

14. American Cancer Society, "Take a Deep Breath, Resolve to be a Quitter," *(Syracuse) Post-Standard*, November 19, 2004, p. A-12.

15. Janet Galvez, *The Florida Elusive Snowbird* (Gainesville: University of Florida Publications Services, 1997).

16. "Aging Report: Older Americans Healthier, Richer—and Fatter,"*(Syracuse) Post-Standard*, November 19, 2004, p. A-12.

17. Elisabeth Kubler-Ross, *On Death and Dying* (New York: Macmillan, 1969).

18. Jay Coakley, *Sport in Society*, 7th ed. (Boston: McGraw Hill, 2001), p. 20.

19. Robert Cialdini, Richard J. Borden, Arril Thorne, Marcus R. Walker, Stephen Freeman, and Lloyd R. Sloan, "Basking in Reflected Glory: Three (Football) Field Studies," *Journal of Personality and Social Psychology* 34 (1976): 366–75.

20. Daniel Wann and Nyla R. Branscombe, "Sports Fans: Measuring Degree of Identification with Their Team," *International Journal of Sport Psychology* 24 (1993): 1–17.

21. Mead, *Mind, Self, and Society*; and Jean Piaget, *The Language and Thought of the Child* (New York: Harcourt Brace, 1926).

Bibliography

"Aging Report: Older Americans Healthier, Richer—and Fatter." *(Syracuse) Post-Standard*, November 19, 2004, p. A-12.

American Cancer Society. "Take a Deep Breath, Resolve to be a Quitter." *(Syracuse) Post-Standard*, November 19, 2004, p. A-12.

Cialdini, Robert, Richard J. Borden, Arril Thorne, Marcus R. Walker, Stephen Freeman, and Lloyd R. Sloan. "Basking in Reflected Glory: Three (Football) Field Studies." *Journal of Personality and Social Psychology* 34 (1976): 366–75.

Coakley, Jay. *Sport in Society*. 7th edition. Boston: McGraw Hill, 2001.

Delaney, Tim. *Classical Social Theory: Investigation and Application*. Upper Saddle River, NJ: Prentice Hall, 2004.

———. *Community, Sport and Leisure*. 2nd edition. Auburn, NY: Legend Books, 2001.

———. *Contemporary Social Theory: Investigation and Application*. Upper Saddle River, NJ: Prentice Hall, 2005.

Edwards, Owen. "The Shirt Off His Back." *Smithsonian* (March 2005): 20–22.

Farley, John. *Sociology*. 4th edition. Upper Saddle River, NJ: Prentice Hall, 1998.

Glaser, B., and A. L. Strauss. *Time for Dying*. Chicago: Aldine, 1967.

Goffman, Erving. *Presentation of Self in Everyday Life*. Garden City, NY: Anchor, 1959.

Henslin, James M. *Essentials of Sociology*. 5th edition. Boston: Allyn & Bacon, 2004.

Kendall, Diana. *Sociology in Our Times*. 4th edition. Belmont, CA: Wadsworth, 2004.

Lindersmith, Alfred R., Anselm L. Strauss, and Norman K. Denzin. *Social Psychology*. 7th edition. Englewood Cliffs, NJ: Prentice Hall, 1991.

Macionis, John J. *Society: The Basics*. 7th edition. Upper Saddle River, NJ: Prentice Hall, 2004.

Mead, George Herbert. *Mind, Self & Society*. Edited with an introduction by Charles W. Morris. Chicago: University of Chicago Press, 1934.

Parsons, Talcott. *The Social System*. Glencoe, IL: Free Press, 1951.

Piaget, Jean. *The Language and Thought of the Child*. New York: Harcourt Brace, 1926.

Salkin, Allen. "Fooey to the World: Festivus Is Come." *New York Times*, December 19, 2004, p. 1.

Schaefer, Richard T. *Sociology: A Brief Introduction*. Boston: McGraw Hill, 2004.

"Seinfeld's Puffy Shirt Joins Icons at Smithsonian." *(Syracuse) Post-Standard*, November 20, 2004, p. A-2.

"Together Again? Get Out!" *TV Guide*, November 21–27, 2004, pp. 34–48.

Wann, Daniel, and Nyla R. Branscombe. "Sports Fans: Measuring Degree of Identification with Their Team." *International Journal of Sport Psychology* 24 (1993): 1–17.

Index of
Cited Episodes

Episode	Original Air Date	Episode Title	Appears in Chapter(s)
1	July 5, 1989	Good News, Bad News	3, 14
2	May 31, 1990	The Stakeout	3, 5, 15
3	June 7, 1990	The Robbery	2, 5, 7, 8
4	June 14, 1990	Male Unbonding	2, 3, 6
5	June 21, 1990	The Stock Tip	2, 3
6	January 23, 1991	The Ex-Girlfriend	6
7	January 30, 1991	The Pony Remark	10, 13, 14
8	February 6, 1991	The Jacket	10
10	April 4, 1991	The Apartment	1, 4, 14
11	April 11, 1991	The Statue	5
12	April 18, 1991	The Revenge	5
13	April 25, 1991	The Heart Attack	12
14	May 2, 1991	The Deal	2
15	May 16, 1991	The Baby Shower	2, 6, 10
16	May 23, 1991	The Chinese Restaurant	2
18	September 18, 1991	The Note	12
19	September 25, 1991	The Truth	2
22	October 16, 1991	The Library	2, 4, 5, 14
25	November 13, 1991	The Tape	2, 6
26	November 20, 1991	The Nose Job	1
27	November 27, 1991	The Stranded	7, 12
28	December 4, 1991	The Alternate Side	3, 8
30	January 8, 1992	The Subway	8, 10
32	January 29, 1992	The Suicide	1, 12, 13
33	February 5, 1992	The Fix-up	3
34	February 12, 1992	The Boyfriend (1)	4, 7, 14